HANDBOOK IN RESEARCH AND EVALUATION

A Collection of Principles, Methods, and
Strategies Useful in the Planning,
Design, and Evaluation of Studies in
Education and the Behavioral Sciences

SECOND EDITION

Stephen Isaac
Department of Evaluation Services
San Diego Unified School District
San Diego, California

and

William B. Michael
University of Southern California
Los Angeles, California

EdITS publishers
San Diego, California 92107

Cover Design: Terri Thompson

SECOND EDITION

LIBRARY OF CONGRESS CATALOG CARD NUMBER 81-82949

ISBN 0-912736-25-9

MANUFACTURED IN THE UNITED STATES OF AMERICA

FOREWORD TO THE FIRST EDITION

NEED FOR A RESEARCH AND EVALUATION HANDBOOK

The importance of research and evaluation in the behavioral sciences has gained in momentum in recent years. The demand for both presses hard upon the resources of time and knowledge available to the researcher in the fast-moving stream of activity. The range of possibilities and changes in methodologies often confuse, rather than clarify, the decision maker's task. The plentiful supply of books on research design and statistics meets one need but creates another—their sophisticated, in-depth treatment demands time and attention to detail when often the researcher simply wants an overview, a summary of alternatives, an exhibit of models, or a listing of strengths and weaknesses. This book was prepared especially to meet these latter needs and should prove useful to a wide range of people:

- The busy project director
- The "occasional" researcher
- The proposal writer
- The evaluator

- The reviewer and consumer of research
- The undergraduate student in beginning courses
- The graduate student preparing for theses, dissertations, and examinations
- A general reference for a research staff or project team

FOREWORD TO THE SECOND EDITION

The first edition of the Handbook in Research and Evaluation appeared in 1971. At that time the established body of knowledge from which the bulk of material could be drawn was in the field of *research. Evaluation,* program evaluation in particular, was just beginning to surface as an endeavor in its own right. This second edition sets out to strike an improved balance between what are now two overlapping disciplines. Though many of the tools and techniques are shared, their respective purposes and methodologies differ sufficiently to warrant separate treatment.

WHY RESEARCH AND EVALUATION IN EDUCATION IS TIMELY AND IMPORTANT

1. In educational assessment and decision-making, it is the only way to make rational choices between alternative practices, to validate educational improvements, and to build a stable foundation of effective practices as a safeguard against faddish but inferior innovations.
2. Policies of private and government agencies currently make approval of research grants contingent upon evidence of good planning and sound evaluation procedures.
3. The influence of behavioristic viewpoints on education which emphasize observable behaviors and objective evaluation.
4. The impact of computer technology and the systems approach which necessitate quantifiable input information, mathematically and logically defined concepts and relationships, and a systems operation based on terminal objectives.
5. The overall power and facility of computers to order, store, and process information rapidly and economically, analyzing large volumes of data with complex statistical programs.
6. The advent of cost effectiveness accounting procedures to evaluate educational programs using behaviorally defined objectives and tangible evaluation criteria which, often, are scores on standardized tests.
7. The recent upswing of interest by industry to develop new educational materials, equipment, and programs with built-in features for feedback and evaluation.
8. The availability of people, techniques, and funds to meet the challenge of research and evaluation needs in the applied educational setting.

evaluation needs in the applied educational setting.

9. The persistence of negative or inconclusive findings in the literature of educational research which raise serious questions about the validity of many current programs, both established and innovative, and the viewpoints underlying them.

WHO SHOULD DO RESEARCH AND EVALUATION

Research and evaluation is most relevant when it builds upon and involves the people directly affected. Too often research in education is done by outsiders for their own purposes using the schools as a source of data: departments of universities or colleges, graduate students doing projects, theses, or dissertations, and publishers or industrial firms field testing new publications, products, and programs. While this may eventually benefit education, the local school's needs are often neglected. The classroom teacher and the guidance consultant, along with the director or administrator, should have the opportunity to identify problems, set goals, formulate plans, gather data, analyze outcomes, and reach conclusions.

HOW THE HANDBOOK WILL HELP IN RESEARCH AND EVALUATION

Few people in education have opportunities to apply whatever training they received in research and evaluation. Furthermore, most of the textbooks on this subject are detailed and technical, making their occasional use impractical. A helpful aid should be a handbook summarizing basic information drawn from several key sources. It should be useful in several ways:

1. As a pool of guidelines, methods, and technqiues selected from various references on research design, measurement, and statistics and ordinarily not available in a single document.
2. As a refresher to the individual who has not kept current on methods and techniques in this area.
3. As a checking and comparing aid for the researcher to insure that he has taken into account the important considerations, correctly weighed the advantages and limitations among alternatives, and has placed himself in the strongest position to reach useful and defensible conclusions.

WHAT THE HANDBOOK DOES NOT DO: A CALCULATED RISK

The Handbook presents only highlights, outlines, and essentials to achieve emphasis, clarity, and brevity. The risk involved in gaining these advantages is *oversimplification*. Each user is expected to supplement this document with more complete information from the standard texts or qualified consultants in this field, once he has his bearings.

BACKGROUND AND ACKNOWLEDGEMENTS

The need for such a handbook initially occurred to the first author while working on an R&D team in industry, but it was not until his return to education that serious work began. Essential to the quality and scope of the original handbook was the invaluable assistance of the first author's teacher and friend, Bill Michael. The present volume is a significant revision and extension of the first edition. It is worth noting that the first edition itself became a reality only after the appearance of two preliminary versions with limited circulation. Particular appreciation remains due to Mr. J. Richard Harsh of the Educational Testing Service, Los Angeles office, and Mrs. Isabel H. Beck and staff members of the Southwest Regional Laboratory (SWRL) who carefully reviewed the early manuscripts, making many valuable suggestions.

Finally, the first edition, on which this second one builds, became a reality in 1971 through the support of the Superintendent and Governing Board of the Department of Education, San Diego County — a debt of gratitude that time and this revision must not overlook.

TABLE OF CONTENTS

CHAPTER ONE - PLANNING EVALUATION STUDIES

Planning evaluation studies 1
Research and evaluation − two disciplines. 2
Program evaluation in a nutshell 4
Models for program evaluation 6
Educational accountability and the CIPP model 10
Metfessel-Michael paradigm for evaluation of school programs 15
Needs assessment 19

CHAPTER TWO - PLANNING RESEARCH STUDIES

Formulation of the problem. 32
Steps in preparing a research investigation. 32
Ten steps in planning good research 33
Advantages of a pilot study 34
Common mistakes made by graduate students 35
Planning for computer analysis and data processing 40

CHAPTER THREE - GUIDE TO RESEARCH DESIGNS, METHODS, AND STRATEGIES

Nine basic methods of research 42
Basic steps in the planning and conduct of good research 44
Historical research 44
Descriptive research. 46
Developmental research 47
Case and field study research 48
Correlational research 49
Causal-comparative research. 50
True experimental research 52
Quasi-experimental research. 54
Action research 55
Differences among formal educational research, action research, and the causal approach to
   problem solving in education 56
Overview: internal and external validity in an experimental design. 59
Internal validity. 60
External validity 62
A "poor" research design: the "one-shot case study" 63
Design 1 − One-group pretest-posttest design 64
Design 2 − Randomized control-group pretest-posttest design 65
Design 3 − Randomized Soloman four-group design 68
Design 4 − Randomized control-group posttest only design. 69
Design 5 − Nonrandomized control-group pretest-posttest design 69
Design 6 − Counterbalanced design. 71
Design 7 − One-group time-series design 72
Design 8 − Control-group time-series design. 73
A comparison of the eight experimental designs 74
Factors jeopardizing the validity of experimental designs 76
The 2 x 2 factorial design 77
Extended factorial designs. 78
Additional concerns, strategies, and pitfalls in the design of research. 79
Control − a key concept in experimental design 80
Confounding and cancellation of effects: two pitfalls of interaction 81
Generalizability of research findings 82
Some common sources of error 85
Making meaningful comparisons 88
Reactive versus nonreactive measures. 90
Measurement: single versus multiple outcomes − triangulation 92
Statistical regression effects 93
Short-term and long-term studies 94
Five points about research design 95
Large samples versus small samples 96
Individual differences. 97
Matching as a control technique: some disadvantages 99

CHAPTER FOUR - INSTRUMENTATION AND MEASUREMENT

A form for evaluating tests. 102
Chart comparing various test scores. 103
Interpreting test scores 104
Comparing norm-referenced and criterion-referenced tests 108
The Rasch Scaling Model. 112
The Delphi Technique 114
Item analysis. 116
Validity 119
Reliability 123
Survey design and techniques for school related use 128
Mailed questionnaires. 133
The research interview 138
Attitude scaling 142
The semantic differential. 144
Kinds of tests and measurements commonly used 149
The role of measurement in program evaluation: some perspectives 149
Multiple criterion measures for evaluation of school programs 151

CHAPTER FIVE - STATISTICAL TECHNIQUES AND THE ANALYSIS OF DATA

Overview of statistical methods 158
Measures of central tendency and variability 159
Frequency distribution. 160
Scatter diagrams, scattergrams, scatter plots. 162
The analysis of crossbreaks 163
Computing Guide 1 — Determining percentile equivalents graphically 164
Computing Guide 2 — Determining the mean and standard deviation for ungrouped data. . . 166
Computing Guide 3 — Determining the mean and standard deviation for grouped data 167
Appropriate correlational techniques for different forms of variables 168
Computing Guide 4 — The product-moment correlation coefficient (Pearson r) 170
Computing Guide 5 — Rank-difference correlation (Spearman rho) 172
Computing Guide 6 — The point-biserial correlation coefficient for data where one variable
  is continuously distributed 173
Computing Guide 7 — Use of the Spearman-Brown formula to estimate reliability after a
  test is lengthened or shortened 174
Computing Guide 8 — The z-test, or critical ratio, to determine a significant difference be-
  tween two sample means but not necessarily equal variances 174
Computing Guide 9 — The t-test to determine a significant difference between two sample
  means 176
Chi square 177
Computing Guide 10 — Chi square for a 2 x 2 table 178
Computing Guide 11 — Median test for a difference between two medians 179
Computing Guide 12 — Chi square for categories exceeding a 2 x 2 table 180
Analysis of Variance & Covariance 182
Hypothesis testing and statistical significance 184
The search for promising practices: avoiding the Type II error 188
Sampling. 189
Ways of interpreting correlation coefficients 194
The problem of hits and misses in predictive validity 198
Multivariate statistical procedures. 200

CHAPTER SIX - STATING COGNITIVE AND AFFECTIVE OBJECTIVES

Writing behavioral objectives 207
Summary of the taxonomy of educational objectives — cognitive & affective domains 210
Some limitations in assessing objectives in the affective domain 216

CHAPTER SEVEN - CRITERIA AND GUIDELINES FOR PLANNING, PRE-PARING, WRITING, AND EVALUATING THE RESEARCH PROPOSAL, REPORT, THESIS, OR ARTICLE

Form for evaluating an article. 220
A research proposal: a checklist of items for possible inclusion 221
Criteria for evaluation of a research report, article, or thesis. 223
Research methodology — a dissenting view 226
APPENDIX OF STATISTICAL TABLES 227
INDICES, Author and Subject 232

The purpose of evaluation is to improve, not to prove.

Daniel L. Stufflebeam

CHAPTER ONE

PLANNING EVALUATION STUDIES

PLANNING EVALUATION STUDIES

Research and evaluation studies stand or fall according to how well they measure up to established scientific standards of excellence. Pitfalls, sources of contamination, and invalidating factors by many names abound to challenge the findings and interpretations reported in any given study.

The most effective insurance against unwitting errors is sound and thorough planning which foresees problems and makes acceptable allowances where unavoidable difficulties exist. A critic is always impressed by a study anticipating its own limitations and choosing the most appropriate and powerful solution to a given problem.

After a distinction is made between research and evaluation studies on the next page of this chapter, attention is given to the topic of evaluation as a form of educational inquiry. Much of the material to be found in subsequent chapters has relevance to the completion of evaluation studies just as it does to that of research investigations. In particular, a great deal of the information about instrumentation and measurement in Chapter Four and many of the criteria and guidelines set forth for planning, preparing, writing, and evaluating research proposals, reports, theses, dissertations, and articles in Chapter Seven are just as relevant to evaluation studies as to the more traditional endeavors in basic and applied research. In short, the interrelationships among the seven chapters are substantial indeed and largely mutually reinforcing.

RESEARCH AND EVALUATION – TWO DISCIPLINES

Historically, research in the behavioral sciences goes back to the emergence of psychology as a scientific discipline in the 1800's. As psychology matured, it evolved a collection of methodologies and techniques borrowed from the physical and biological sciences, including principles of scientific inquiry, measurement, and data analysis—the latter incorporating statistical models many of which were developed for agricultural applications. Anthropology, sociology, education, and other behavior-oriented fields added further adaptations to research methodology in these new areas.

Research, having its origin in science, is oriented toward the development of theories and its most familiar paradigm is the experimental method, in which hypotheses are logically derived from theory and put to a test under controlled conditions. Evaluation, on the other hand, has come the way of technology rather than science. Its accent is not on theory building but on product delivery or mission accomplishment. Its essence is to provide feedback leading to a successful outcome defined in practical, concrete terms. Such a process has functioned informally since the beginning of time, although its more formal version coincided with the advent of the computer to give rise in the 1950's to the "man-machine systems" movement, and currently, to the "systems approach." Its general steps are: (1) setting objectives; (2) designing the means to achieve these objectives; and (3) constructing a feedback mechanism to determine progress toward, and attainment of, the objectives. Its basic paradigm, in computer language, is:

input ⟶ processing ⟶ output

Paradoxically, this is a sequence that actually is designed in reverse order. First, it is determined what the system must accomplish (output); second, all the intermediate steps to accomplish this outcome must be programmed (processing); and, lastly, all the necessary ingredients to be fed into the system must be determined (input).

In distinguishing evaluation from research, Stufflebeam has said, "The purpose of evaluation is to improve, not to prove."

The statement *to improve* suggests that a judgment must be made regarding what constitutes worth or *value*. In other words, the term evaluation typically is associated with how effective or ineffective, how adequate or inadequate, how good or bad, how valuable or invaluable, and how appropriate or inappropriate a given action, process, or product is in terms of the perceptions of the individual who makes use of information provided by an evaluator.

The figure on the next page furnishes a distinction between research and evaluation with respect to each of ten criteria. The similarities and differences noted should help clarify variations and emphases accompanying these two forms of inquiry. Incidental mention should probably be made of the fact that a third component of educational inquiry entitled *development* (as in the preparation of curricular materials, program learning exercises, and certain forms of so-called software in educational technology) is not a central topic of consideration in this volume.

TWO TYPES OF DISCIPLINED INQUIRY

CHARACTERISTIC:	Research	Evaluation
Purpose	New Knowledge, Truth	Mission Achievement, Product Delivery
Outcome	Generalizable Conclusions	Specific Decisions
Value	Explanatory and Predictive Power	Determining Worth and Social Utility
Impetus	Curiosity and Ignorance	Needs and Goals
Conceptual Basis	Cause and Effect Relationships	Means-Ends Processes
Key Event	Hypothesis Testing	Assessing Attainment of an Objective
Classic Paradigms	1. Experimental Method	1. Systems Approach

	Research	Evaluation
	2. Correlational Method r_{xy}	2. Objectives Approach

CHARACTERISTIC:	Research	Evaluation
Discipline	Control and Manipulation of Variance	Program Planning and Management
Criteria	Internal and External Validity	Isomorphism (fit between the expected and the obtained) and Credibility
Functional Types	Pure and Applied True Experimental Quasi-experimental	Formative - Summative Process - Product

*Originally presented by Stephen Isaac at the first annual conference of the California Society for Educational Program Auditors & Evaluators, San Diego, May, 1975. The authors are indebted to discussions by Blaine R. Worthen & James R. Sanders in *Educational Evaluation: Theory and Practice,* Charles A. Jones Publishing Co., Worthington, Ohio, 1973; and Daniel I. Stufflebeam, et. al., *Educational Evaluation and Decision Making,* F. E. Peacock Publishers, Inc., Itasca, Illinois, 1971.

PROGRAM EVALUATION IN A NUTSHELL

Though program evaluation is often a complex process involving many components and considerations, at its heart lies a simple three step sequence:

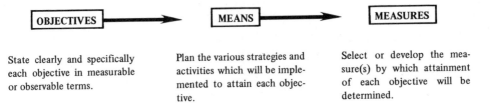

OBJECTIVES	MEANS	MEASURES
State clearly and specifically each objective in measurable or observable terms.	Plan the various strategies and activities which will be implemented to attain each objective.	Select or develop the measure(s) by which attainment of each objective will be determined.

Simply stated, decide what objectives are to be accomplished; determine how they will be accomplished; then find out whether, in fact, they were accomplished.

In actuality, program evaluation most often manifests in one of two guises: (1) *accountability,* analogous to the bank auditor checking the books to determine whether or not there is an acceptable balance across the original expectations, final accomplishments, and associated cost-effectiveness considerations; and (2) *feedback,* analogous to the athletic coach skillfully shaping and refining the performance of an individual or team toward continuing improvement.

A Salient Point

Although great care should be taken to insure that the objectives are substantive and worthwhile, that the means of achieving the objectives are among the most promising and effective available, and that the measures themselves are sound and valid, once the program design is complete, one fact acquires paramount significance. The measures on which the successful attainment will be based have now become the operational definition of the objectives. Regardless of the wording of the objectives, a particular measuring instrument only will give back what was built in to it — that, and nothing more. Program materials, activities, or content that lie outside the sensitivity of the instrument, however meritorious or valued in the eyes of the program staff, are likely to contribute nothing to the *measured success* of the program. This circumstance does not mean the program should slavishly focus on what the instruments measure or that it should abandon activities unrelated to them. It does mean that the staff should clearly recognize what has a direct bearing on the outcome measures and what does not and that an optimum effort should address those things which contribute to this measurement.

A corollary to this observation is to select or to develop measures that have the best possible fit with the program objectives to minimize any lack of correspondence between them. In the area of educational achievement this goal is the principal rationale behind the criterion-referenced testing movement, in contrast to the widespread use of norm-referenced tests which tend to have only a modest overlap with instructional content.

As program evaluation increases in complexity, additional components are added to the three basic steps. One widely used model is the following:*

NEEDS ASSESSMENT

A need has been defined as the discrepancy between *what is* and *what ought to be*. Once identified, needs are placed in order of priority. They are the basis for setting program goals.

PROGRAM PLANNING

From program goals, specific, measurable objectives are derived and a plan containing the means to attain these objectives — the program procedures, strategies, and activities — is formulated.

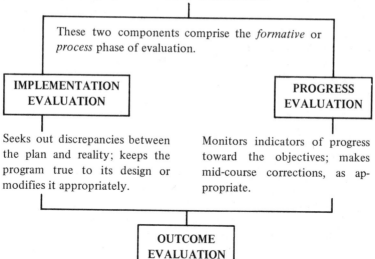

These two components comprise the *formative* or *process* phase of evaluation.

IMPLEMENTATION EVALUATION

PROGRESS EVALUATION

Seeks out discrepancies between the plan and reality; keeps the program true to its design or modifies it appropriately.

Monitors indicators of progress toward the objectives; makes mid-course corrections, as appropriate.

OUTCOME EVALUATION

This step is the *summative* or *product* phase of the evaluation; it determines whether or not the objectives have been attained. This phase often includes an analysis of program strengths and weaknesses, with recommendations for future modifications, if appropriate.

---

*Based on a monograph by Marvin C. Alkin, *A Theory of Evaluation,* Center for the Study of Evaluation, UCLA Graduate School of Education, Los Angeles, California, August, 1971; subsequently adapted for workshop presentations by CTB McGraw-Hill, Monterey, California. Notations added.

MODELS FOR PROGRAM EVALUATION

In the pages to follow tables and figures are set forth that highlight various models of program evaluation. Specifically, in the table entitled "Some Models of Program Evaluation" on page 7, six different approaches to evaluation are examined from the standpoint of what they emphasize. References are furnished for the reader to consult if more information is desired regarding the orientation to evaluation identified. The detailed table on pages 8 and 9 affords a descriptive summary of several models that have been intended to serve as frameworks for planning evaluation studies. With respect to each of twelve characteristics, brief statements are made for each of eight different models. This table provides a basis for examining similarities and differences among a number of the better known models for program evaluation.

In the pages following this comprehensive table, three models are considered in detail. Perhaps the best known one—and certainly the one that has received the greatest amount of attention—is the model formulated by Stufflebeam and his associates. Several pages are devoted to both the presentation of a narrative and the inclusion of diagrams to illustrate the major features of this important model, which is called the context-input-process-product (CIPP) evaluation model. Following this important formulation is a brief presentation of the eight-step Metfessel-Michael paradigm that allows the specification of a series of steps to be pursued in carrying out an evaluation of the outcomes or products of educational programs relative to specified objectives. Next, a teaching-learning-evaluation model that represents an expansion by the second author of this volume of work done by other psychologists is summarized in diagrammatic form for ease of interpretation.

THE CIPP MODEL

Intended to provide a basis for making decisions within a systems analysis of planned change, the CIPP model constitutes the culmination of almost four years of work by the Phi Delta Kappa National Study Committee of Evaluation under the chairmanship of Daniel Stufflebeam with the assistance of six coworkers—Walter J. Foley, William J. Gephart, Egon G. Guba, Robert L. Hammond, Howard A. Merriman, and Malcolm M. Provus. This model is consistent with the definition of educational program evaluation proposed by the Committee as being "the process of delineating, obtaining, and providing useful information for judging decision alternatives." This definition, in effect, incorporates three basic points. First, evaluation is a continuous, systematic process. Second, this process includes three pivotal steps: (1) stating questions requiring answers and specifying information to be obtained, (2) acquiring relevant data, and (3) providing the resulting information as it becomes available to potential decision makers who can consider and interpret it in relation to its impact upon decision alternatives that can modify or improve existing educational programs. Third, evaluation supports the process of decision making by allowing the selection of an alternative and by following up on the consequences of a decision.

In the CIPP model evaluation serves four types of decisions: (1) *planning decisions,* which influence selection of goals and objectives, (2) *structuring decisions,* which ascertain optimal strategies and procedural designs for achieving the objectives that have been derived from planning decisions, (3) *implementing decisions,* which afford the means for carrying out and improving upon the execution of already selected designs, methods, or strategies; and (4) *recycling decisions,* which determine whether to continue, change, or terminate an activity or even the program itself. To serve these four types of decisions are four respective kinds of

Some Models of Program Evaluation

Model	Emphasis	Selected References
Goal-Oriented Evaluation	Evaluation should assess student progress and the effectiveness of educational innovations.	Bloom, B. S., Hastings, J. T., & Madaus, G. F. *Handbook on formative and summative evaluation of student learning.* New York: McGraw-Hill, 1971. Provus, M. *Discrepancy evaluation for educational program improvement and assessment.* Berkeley, CA: McCutchan, 1971.
Decision-Oriented Evaluation	Evaluation should facilitate intelligent judgments by decision-makers.	Stufflebeam, D. L., Foley, W. J., Gephart, W. J., Guba, E. G., Hammond, R. L., Merriman, H. O., and Provus, M. M. *Educational evaluation and decision-making.* Itasca, IL: F. E. Peacock, 1971.
Transactional Evaluation	Evaluation should depict program processes and the value perspectives of key people.	Rippey, R. M. (Ed.). *Studies in transactional evaluation.* Berkeley, CA: McCutchan, 1973. Stake, R. E., et al. *Evaluating the arts in education: A responsive approach.* Columbus, OH: Charles E. Merrill, 1975.
Evaluation Research	Evaluation should focus on explaining educational effects and devising instructional strategies.	Campbell, D. Reforms as experiments. *American Psychologist,* 1969, *24,* 409-429. Cooley, W. W., & Lohnes, P. R. *Evaluation research in education.* New York: Irvington Publishers, 1976.
Goal-Free Evaluation	Evaluation should assess program effects based on criteria apart from the program's own conceptual framework.	Scriven, M. Prose and cons about goal-free evaluation. In W. J. Popham (Ed.), *Evaluation in education: Current applications.* Berkeley, CA: McCutchan 1974.
Adversary Evaluation	Evaluation should present the best case for each of two competing alternative interpretations of the program's value with both sides having access to the same information about the program.	Levine, M. Scientific method and the adversary model: Some preliminary suggestions. *Evaluation Comment,* 1973, *4*(2), 1-3. Owens, T. R. Educational evaluation by adversary proceedings. In E. R. House (Ed.), *School evaluation: The politics and process.* Berkeley, CA: McCutchan, 1973.

Source: Morris, Lynn L., and Fitz-Gibbon, Carol T., *Evaluator's Handbook,* Beverly Hills, California: Sage Publications, 1978, page 7. Adapted and produced with permission.

A DESCRIPTIVE SUMMARY OF

FRAMEWORKS FOR PLANNING EVALUATION STUDIES

Chart adapted and reprinted with permission of the authors and publisher, from Worthen, B. R. and Sanders, J. R. Educational Evaluation: Theory and Practice, Chapter 3. Worthington, Ohio: Charles A. Jones, 1973. Original version appeared in SRIS Quarterly, Spring, 1972, Vol. 5, No. 1; Phi Delta Kappan, Inc., Bloomington, Ind., pp 10 - 13.

	HAMMOND	PROVUS	SCRIVEN	STAKE
DEFINITION	Assessing effectiveness of current & innovative programs at the local level by comparing behavioral data with objectives.	Comparing performance against standards.	Gathering & combining performance data with weighted set of goal scales.	Describing and judging an educational program.
PURPOSE	To find out whether innovation is effective in achieving expressed objectives.	To determine whether to improve, maintain, or terminate a program.	To establish & justify merit or worth. Evaluation plays many roles.	To describe and judge educational programs based on a formal inquiry process.
KEY EMPHASIS	Local program development.	Identifying discrepancies between standard and performance using team approach.	Justification of data gathering instruments, weightings & selection of goals. Eval. model: combining data on different performance scales into a single rating.	Collection of descriptive & judgmental data from various audiences.
ROLE OF EVALUATOR	Consultants who should provide expertise in data collection. He is also a trainer of local evaluators (program personnel).	A team member who aids program improvement & counsels administration. He should be independent of the program unit.	Responsible for judging the merit of an educational practice for producers (formative) & consumers (summative).	Specialist concerned with collecting, processing & interpreting descriptive & judgmental data.
RELATIONSHIP TO OBJECTIVES	Evaluation focuses on the definition & measurement of behavioral objectives.	Agreement of evaluation team & program staff on standards. Comparison of performance against standards to see whether a discrepancy exists.	Look at goals & judge their worth. Determine whether they are being met.	Examination of goal specifications and priorities. Identification of areas of failures & successes. It is up to the evaluator to assist in writing behavioral objectives.
RELATIONSHIP TO DECISION-MAKING	Evaluation is the source on which to base decisions about instructional, institutional & behavioral dimensions.	Evaluation staff collects information essential to program improvement & notes discrepancies between performance & standards. Every question involves a criterion (C), new information (I), & a decision (D). Eval. provides the new information.	Evaluation reports (with judgments explicitly stated for producers or consumers) used in decision-making.	Descriptive & judgmental data result in reports (including recommendations) to various audiences. Judgments may be based on either absolute or relative standards.
TYPES OF EVALUATION	(1) Instructional dimension (2) Institutional dimension and (3) Behavioral dimension used for describing programs.	(1) Design (2) Installation (3) Process (4) Product (5) Cost.	(1) Formative—summative (2) Comparative—noncomparative (3) Intrinsic—payoff (4) Mediated.	(1) Formal vs. informal.
CONSTRUCTS PROPOSED	(1) The application of evaluation design to existing program, (2) decisions about adequacy of current program in relationship to the objectives, (3) feedback from (2) leads to innovation, (4) application of evaluation to innovation itself and (5) notion that feedback could continue.	(1) Discrepancy concept (2) Feedback & revision of objectives and/or program.	(1) Distinction between goals (claims) & roles (functions), (2) Several types of evaluation.	(1) Data matrices: description (intents & observation) & judgment, (2) Processing descriptive data: contingency among antecedents, transactions, outcomes; congruence between intents & observations, (3) Bases for forming absolute & relative judgments.
CRITERIA FOR JUDGING EVALUATION	(1) Related to behavioral objectives, (2) an on-going process, (3) provides feedback on goal achievement for program modification, (4) uses local personnel, and is part of local educational program.	(1) Team involvement, (2) assume one-to-one correspondence between design & solution, (3) compare performance against standards as a tool for improvement & assessment, (4) periodic feedback.	(1) Should be predicated on goals, (2) must indicate worth, (3) should be construct validity, (4) should be a wholistic program evaluation.	(1) Should be panoramic, not microscopic, (2) should include descriptive & judgmental data, (3) should provide immediate relative answers for decision making, (4) should be formal (e.g. objective, scientific, reliable).
IMPLICATIONS FOR DESIGN	(1) Use of multi-variate structure-focus on interactions of dimensions, (2) generate empirical research, (3) necessity for inclusion of local personnel.	(1) Provide continuous evaluation (feedback loops), (2) provide relevant & timely information for making decisions, (3) provide cost-benefit analysis, (4) involvement of evaluation in program development.	(1) Look at many factors, (2) be involved in value judgments, (3) require use of scientific investigations, (4) evaluate from within (formative) or from without (summative).	Very general structure. Matrices should be included in design.
CONTRIBUTIONS	(1) Makes use of local personnel who can carry on evaluation process once initiated, (2) considers interaction of several dimensions & variables, (3) provides feedback on program development & revisions; stresses self-evaluation, (4) requires specification of behavioral objectives.	(1) Provides continuous communication between program & evaluation staff thru feedback loops, (2) allows for program improvement as well as assessment either at early stages or end, (3) acknowledges alternative procedures in adjusting objectives & in changing treatment, (4) forces explicit statement of standards.	(1) Discriminates between formative (on-going) & summative (end) evaluation, (2) focus on direct assessment of worth: focus on value, (3) applicable in diverse contexts, (4) analysis of means & ends, (5) delineation of types of evaluation, (6) evaluation of objectives.	(1) Provides a systematic method for arranging descriptive & judgmental data, thus emphasizing inter- & intra-relations between them, (2) considers both absolute & relative judgment, (3) requires explicit standards, (4) generalizability of the model.
LIMITATIONS	(1) Difficulty of quantifying data involving several dimensions & variables, (2) may be complex & time-consuming to set up, (3) possible fixation of evaluation on the "cube," (4) neglects judgmental dimension, (5) motivation problem in local personnel.	(1) Demands a lengthy time commitment; may be expensive to carry thru, (2) Inadequate methodology for establishing standards, (3) requires large, expert well-articulated staff, (4) designed for complete evaluation; partial evaluation not considered.	(1) Equating performance on differing criteria & assessing relative weights to criteria creates methodological problems, (2) no methodology for assessing validity of judgments, (3) several ambiguous overlapping concepts.	(1) Inadequate methodology for obtaining information & assigning weights, (2) cells of design matrix overlap; distinctions not clear; no methodology of leading to internal strife within program; value conflicts possible.

	STUFFLEBEAM	METFESSEL-MICHAEL	ALKIN	PERSONAL JUDGEMENT (e.g. Accreditation)	TYLER
DEFINITION	Defining, obtaining & using information for decision-making.	Tylerian; comparing measured performance with behavioral standards.	The process of ascertaining the decision areas of concern, selecting appropriate information & collecting & analyzing information.	Focusing attention on processes of education using professional judgment. Development of standards for educational programs.	Comparing student performance with behaviorally stated objectives.
PURPOSE	To provide relevant information to decision-makers.	To formulate recommendations that furnish a basis for further implementation, for modifications & for revisions in broad goals & specific objectives.	To report summary data useful to decision makers in selecting among alternatives.	To identify deficiencies in the education of teachers & students relevant to content & procedures; self-improvement.	To determine the extent to which purposes of a learning activity are actually being realized.
KEY EVALUATOR EMPHASIS	Evaluation reports used for decision-making.	Specification of objectives & using multiple criterion measures to assess outcomes, involvement of many different audiences.	Evaluation reports used for decision making.	Personal judgment used in evaluating processes of education; self-study.	Specification of objectives & measuring learning outcomes of pupils.
ROLE OF EVALUATOR	Specialist who provides evaluation information to decision makers.	Measurement specialist who involves lay individuals, schoolmen and students in developing a set of recommendations.	Specialist who provides evaluation information to decision-makers.	Professional colleagues who make recommendations—a professional judge.	Curriculum specialists who evaluates as part of curriculum development and assessment.
RELATIONSHIP TO OBJECTIVES	Terminal stage in context eval. is setting objectives; input eval. produces ways to reach objectives; product eval. determines whether objectives are reached.	Evaluation entails measurement of congruency of outcome behaviors with objectives.	Range & specificity of program objectives determined in systems assessment; program planning produces ways to reach objectives; program improvement provides data on the extent to which objectives are being reached; program certification determines whether objectives are reached.	Self-study judgments are based on sets of predetermined criteria.	Actual pupil performance data will provide information for the decision-maker to use to identify strengths and weaknesses of a course of curriculum.
RELATIONSHIP TO DECISION MAKING	Evaluation provides information for use in decision-making.	Suggestions are made concerning revisions in objectives or program strategies. Feedback is given to all individuals involved in the school program.	Evaluation provides information for use in decision-making.	When deficiencies are found, program revisions are required, thus correcting sub-standard conditions; corrective process built in.	Evaluation implies attainment of behavioral objectives stated at the beginning of the course.
TYPES OF EVALUATION	(1) Context (2) Input (3) Process (4) Product.	Eight-stage evaluation process.	(1) Systems assessment, (2) Program planning, (3) Program implementation, (4) Program improvement, (5) Program certification.	(1) Self-study (2) Visitation (3) Annual reports (4) Evaluation panels.	Pre-post measurement of performance.
PROPOSED CONSTRUCTS	(1) Context-evaluation for planning decisions, (2) input-evaluation for programming decisions, (3) process-evaluation for implementing decisions, (4) product-evaluation for recycling decisions.	Multiple criterion measurement.	Evaluation of educational systems vs evaluation of instructional programs; five areas of evaluation.	Use of content specialists as judges.	(1) Statements of objectives in behavioral terms, (2) teaching objectives are pupil-oriented, (3) objectives must consider: pupil's entry behavior, analysis of our culture, school philosophy, learning theories, new developments in teaching, etc.
CRITERIA FOR JUDGING DESIGN	(1) Internal validity, (2) external validity, (3) reliability, (4) objectivity, (5) relevance, (6) importance, (7) scope, (8) credibility, (9) timeliness, (10) pervasiveness, (11) efficiency.	Involvement of diverse audiences, specification of objectives required, use of valid, reliable and objective measures, use of multiple criterion measures.	Information provided to decision-maker should be effective & not confusing or misleading. Appropriate evaluation procedures should not be used for different techniques.	(1) Reflects interests of program administrators, (2) Standard criteria often used.	(1) Behavioral objectives clearly stated, (2) objectives should contain references not only to course content but also to mental processes applied.
IMPLICATIONS FOR DESIGN	(1) Experimental design not applicable, (2) use of systems approach for evaluation studies, (3) directed by administrator.	Eight stage evaluation process; involve various audiences, specify objectives, make periodic observations using multiple criteria on measures; make recommendations to various audiences.	Evaluation domain determined by decision maker; the objects of evaluation vary along a continuum from discrete, definable objects to complex systems.	(1) Involvement of professional community, (2) quick feedback.	(1) Need to interpret & use results of assessment, (2) develop designs to assess student progress.
CONTRIBUTIONS	(1) Provides a service function by supplying data to administrators & decision-makers charged with conduct of program, (2) is sensitive to feedback, (3) allows for evaluation to take place at any stage of the program, (4) wholistic.	Involvement of various audiences, forces specifications of objectives, continuous feedback at multiple periodic observations, appendix of multiple criterion measures, reporting to various audiences, based on measurement technology, easy to apply.	(1) Provides a service function to administrators & decision-makers, (2) Allows for evaluation to take place at any stage of the program, (3) Wholistic.	(1) Is easy to implement; team can observe & make judgment, (2) has little lag time between observations made, data collected & feedback, (3) breadth of variables noted is large, (4) leads to self-study habit and self-improvement.	(1) Is easy to assess whether behavioral objectives are being achieved, (2) is easy for practitioners to design evaluative studies, (3) checks degree of congruency between performance & objectives; focus on clear definition of objectives.
LIMITATIONS	(1) Avoidance of value concerns, (2) decision-making process is unclear; methodology undefined, (3) may be costly & complex is used entirely, (4) not all activities are clearly evaluative.	Focus on available instrumentation, testing can become excessive, focus only on outcome behaviors (little process or antecedent concern), lack of methodology for establishing standards or evaluating objectives.	(1) Role of values in evaluation unclear, (2) Description of decision-making process incomplete, (3) May be costly & complex, (4) Not all activities are clearly evaluative.	(1) Objectivity & empirical basis are questionable, (2) attention to process of education not balanced by attention to consequences, (3) replicability is questionable.	(1) Tendency to oversimplify program & focus on terminal rather than on-going & pre-program information, (2) tendency to focus directly & narrowly on objectives, with little attention to worth of the objectives.

evaluation. *Context* evaluation yields information regarding needs (the extent to which discrepancies exist between what is and what is desired relative to certain value expectations, areas of concern, difficulties, and opportunities) in order that goals and objectives may be formulated. *Input* evaluation furnishes information about strong points and weak points of alternative strategies and designs for the realization of specified objectives. *Process* evaluation provides information for monitoring a chosen procedure or strategy as it is being implemented so that its strong points can be preserved and its weak points eliminated. *Product* evaluation affords information to ascertain to what extent the objectives are being achieved and to determine whether the strategies, procedures, or methods being implemented to attain these objectives should be terminated, modified, or continued in their present form.

Central to most evaluations is an ongoing simultaneous interplay between product and process evaluation in which the feedback derived from the level or quality of products achieved can be employed in process evaluation to improve future products by overcoming deficiencies and by making refinements in ongoing activities based on implementing decisions. Moreover, feedback can also be used in input evaluation to redesign strategies so as to achieve more nearly suitable products. Thus, the CIPP model allows four questions to be answered: (1) Which objectives should be obtained? (2) Which strategies or procedures should be tried? (3) How adequately are these strategies or procedures working? and (4) How effectively are the goals and objectives being accomplished?

Supplementary information concerning the CIPP model is set forth in the figure on page 11 and an elaboration of the dynamic activities within the CIPP model is given in the figure on page 12. An additional insight about the model may be noted in the figure on page 11 in terms of these facts: (1) the planning and recycling decisions are aimed toward the realization of *ends* (goals or objectives), (2) structuring and implementing decisions are directed toward the *means* of reaching these ends, (3) planning decisions and structuring decisions portray *intentions,* and (4) implementing and recycling decisions relate to *actualities.* Examination of the figure on page 12 reveals how each of the four kinds of evaluations interacts in a dynamic manner to serve each of four types of decisions. The use of lines and arrows to designate feedback functions shows the continual interplay between an immediately supportive or servicing type of evaluation and a given type of decision as well as the feedback activities that take place from decisions of any kind or from evaluation of any type to another kind of decision and its respective type of evaluation. In short, information can be communicated from any stage of the decision making activity to an earlier stage so that modifications can be introduced in the type of evaluation performed and in the resulting decisions arrived at from these modified evaluations. Finally, it might be mentioned that the model has application not only to a large program setting, but also to the ongoing activities within a classroom environment. (Additional information regarding the CIPP model is summarized in the table on page 13.

EDUCATIONAL ACCOUNTABILITY AND THE CIPP MODEL

Educational accountability represents the designation or assignment of responsibility to personnel in the educational environment for the realization or lack of realization of educational outcomes that are expected by members of the educational community—not only teachers and administrators, but also parents, taxpayers, and other concerned citizens. The CIPP model affords one framework within which accountability can be defined in terms of a past orientation or retroactive view in which records of prior actions, realized achievements, and visible products are examined in relation to educational decisions previously initiated. This retrospective perception of the CIPP model in the context of accountability is in contrast to one of proactive or future orientation of decision-making activities in evaluation.

Information set forth in the figure at the top of page 15 helps to clarify the distinction between decision-making activities for various types of evaluation and the corresponding ones associated with accountability. Additional insights regarding data requirements for accountability relative to certain key questions are explicated for each of four evaluation types in the figure at the bottom of page 15.

Four types of decisions in relation to four types of evaluation:
A typology in a given educational system or framework.

	Intentions *Phase 1*	Actualities *Phase 4*
Ends (consequential goals or objectives)	Intended ends (objectives) *Planning decisions*—choice of alternative change-oriented objectives (existing, modified, or new improvement-oriented objectives) in an educational system represented by a project or program. served by *Context evaluation*—provides information to develop systematic rationale for objectives largely through analysis of unrealized needs and unused opportunities and through diagnosis of those difficulties preventing needs being met and contributing to discrepancies between intentions and actualities	Actual ends (attainments) *Recycling decisions*—choice of alternative interpretations of how well objectives have been attained in relation to context, input, and process information and the judging of alternatives to continue, terminate, develop, or modify activities intended to solve problems posed by an educational system served by *Product evaluation*—provides information from which reactions and judgments of program or project attainments (products) can be made regarding extent to which objectives (change efforts) have been met either at the end or at any temporal point in a project cycle
	Phase 2	*Phase 3*
Means (instrumental objectives)	Intended means (procedural designs) *Structuring decisions*—choice of alternative designs, strategies, and procedures arising from planning decisions served by *Input evaluation*—provides information for identifying and assessing relevance and capabilities of designs, strategies, and procedures in light of human and material resources for achieving those objectives arising from planning decisions	Actual means (procedures in use) *Implementing decisions*—choice of alternative courses of action involved in operationalizing, carrying out, controlling, and refining a previously chosen project design or strategy of known specifications served by *Process evaluation*—provides information (feedback) for monitoring by personnel responsible in implementing previously chosen procedures—information that allows (1) detection of existing or potential defects. (2) data generation for programmed decisions, and (3) record keeping of activities as they occur

(From J. A. R. Wilson, M. C. Robeck, and W. B. Michael, *Psychological foundations of learning and teaching*, 2nd ed., New York: McGraw-Hill, 1974, p. 446; reproduced with permission).

Dynamic Action in CIPP Evaluation Model

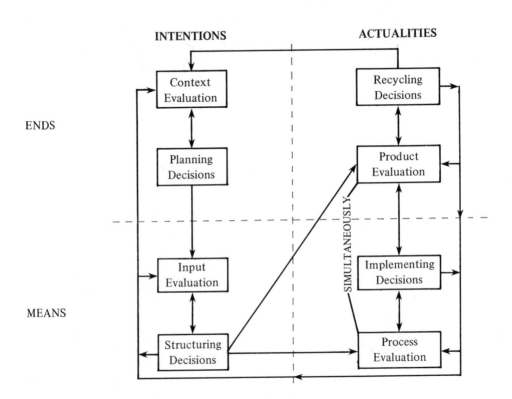

(From J. A. R. Wilson, M. C. Robeck, and W. B. Michael, *Psychological foundations of learning and teaching,* 2nd ed., New York: McGraw-Hill, 1974, p. 447; reproduced with permission).

The Objectives and Methods of Four Types of Evaluation In Relation to Decision Making in the Change Process

	Four Types of Evaluation			
	CONTEXT EVALUATION	**INPUT EVALUATION**	**PROCESS EVALUATION**	**PRODUCT EVALUATION**
Objectives	To define the *operating context*, to identify and assess *needs* and *opportunities* in the context, and to diagnose *problems* underlying the needs and opportunities.	To identify and assess *system capabilities*, available *input strategies*, and designs for implementing the strategies.	To identify or predict, in process, *defects* in the procedural design or its implementation, to provide information for the preprogrammed decisions, and to maintain a record of *procedural events* and *activities*.	To relate *outcome information* to objectives and to context, input, and process information.
Methods	By describing the context; by comparing actual and intended inputs and outputs; by comparing probable and possible system performance; and by analyzing possible causes of discrepancies between actualities and intentions.	By describing and analyzing available human and material resources, solution strategies, and procedural designs for relevance, feasibility and economy in the course of action to be taken.	By monitoring the activity's potential procedural barriers and remaining alert to unanticipated ones, by obtaining specified information for programmed decisions, and describing the actual process.	By defining operationally and measuring criteria associated with the objectives, by comparing these measurements with predetermined standards or comparative bases, and by interpreting the outcomes in terms of recorded context, input and process information.
Relation to Decision-Making in the Change Process	For deciding upon the *setting* to be served, the *goals* associated with meeting needs or using opportunities, and the *objectives* associated with solving problems, i.e., for *planning* needed changes.	For selecting sources of *support*, solution *strategies*, and procedural designs, i.e., for *structuring* change activities.	For *implementing and refining the program design and procedure*, i.e., for effecting process control.	For deciding to *continue, terminate, modify,* or *refocus* a change activity, and for linking the activity to other major phases of the change process, i.e., for recycling change activities.

(From B. R. Worthen and James R. Sanders, *Educational evaluation: Theory and practice*. Worthington, Ohio: Charles A. Jones, 1973, p. 139; reproduced with permission).

The Relevance of the CIPP Model to Decision Making and Accountability

| | EVALUATION TYPES | | | |
	CONTEXT	INPUT	PROCESS	PRODUCT
DECISION MAKING U S E S **ACCOUNTABILITY**	Objectives	Solution strategy Procedural design	Implementation	Termination, continuation, modification, or installation
	Record of objectives and bases for their choice	Record of chosen strategy and design and reasons for their choice	Record of the actual process	Record of attainments and recycling decisions

Data Requirements For Accountability That Can Be Met By The CIPP Evaluation Model

| Data Requirements for Accountability | EVALUATION TYPES | | | |
	Context	Input	Process	Product
What objectives were chosen?	√			
Why?	√			
Were they adopted?			√	√
Were they achieved?				√
What designs were chosen?		√		
Why?	√	√		
Were they implemented?			√	
What were their effects?				√

(From D. L. Stufflebeam, The relevance of the CIPP evaluation model for educational accountability, *Journal of Research and Development in Education*, 1971, 5, 19-25; reproduced with permission).

THE METFESSEL-MICHAEL PARADIGM INVOLVING MULTIPLE CRITERION MEASURES FOR THE EVALUATION OF THE EFFECTIVENESS OF SCHOOL PROGRAMS[1]

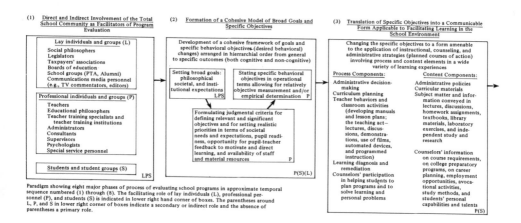

(1) Direct and Indirect Involvement of the Total School Community as Facilitators of Program Evaluation

Lay individuals and groups (L)
Social philosophers
Legislators
Taxpayers' associations
Boards of education
School groups (PTA, Alumni)
Communications media personnel
(e.g., TV commentators, editors)

Professional individuals and groups (P)
Teachers
Educational philosophers
Teacher training specialists and teacher training institutions
Administrators
Consultants
Supervisors
Psychologists
Special service personnel

Students and student groups (S)
LPS

(2) Formation of a Cohesive Model of Broad Goals and Specific Objectives

Development of a cohesive framework of goals and specific behavioral objectives (desired behavioral) changes) arranged in hierarchial order from general to specific outcomes (both cognitive and non-cognitive)

Setting broad goals: philosophical societal, and institutional expectations
LPS

Stating specific behavioral objectives in operational terms allowing for relatively objective measurement and/or empirical determination P

Formulating judgmental criteria for defining relevant and significant objectives and for setting realistic priorities in terms of societal needs and expectations, pupil readiness, opportunity for pupil-teacher feedback to motivate and direct learning, and availability of staff and material resources
P

P(S)(L)

(3) Translation of Specific Objectives into a Communicable Form Applicable to Facilitating Learning in the School Environment

Changing the specific objectives to a form amenable to the application of instructional, counseling, and administrative strategies (planned courses of action) involving process and content elements in a wide variety of learning experiences

Process Components:
Administrative decision-making
Curriculum planning
Teacher behaviors and classroom activities (developing manuals and lesson plans; the teaching act—lectures, discussions, demonstrations, use of films, automated devices, and programmed instruction)
Learning diagnosis and remediation
Counselors' participation in helping students to plan programs and to solve learning and personal problems

Content Components:
Administrative policies
Curricular materials
Subject matter and information conveyed in lectures, discussions, homework assignments, textbooks, library materials, laboratory exercises, and independent study and research

Counselors' information on course requirements, on college preparatory programs, on career planning, employment opportunities, avocational activities, study methods, and students' personal capabilities and talents
P(S)

Paradigm showing eight major phases of process of evaluating school programs in approximate temporal sequence numbered (1) through (8). The facilitating role of lay individuals (L), professional personnel (P), and students (S) is indicated in lower right hand corner of boxes. The parentheses around L, P, and S in lower right corner of boxes indicate a secondary or indirect role and the absence of parentheses a primary role.

Eight major steps in the evaluation process:

1. Involve both directly and indirectly members of the total school community as participants, or facilitators, in the evaluation of programs—lay individuals and lay groups, professional personnel of the schools and their organizations, and students and student-body groups.

2. Construct a cohesive paradigm of broad goals and specific objectives (desired behavioral changes) arranged in a hierarchical order from general to specific outcomes (both cognitive and noncognitive) in a form, for example, that might resemble one or both of the taxonomies set forth by Bloom *et al.* (1956) and Krathwohl *et al.* (1964). Substeps involved in this second phase include (a) setting broad goals that embrace the philosophical, societal, and institutional expectations of the culture; (b) stating specific objectives in operational terms permitting relatively objective measurement whenever possible and/or empirical determination of current status or of changes in behaviors associated with these objectives; and (c) developing judgmental criteria that permit the definition of relevant and significant outcomes as well as the establishment of realistic priorities in terms of societal needs, of pupil readiness, of opportunities for pupil-teacher feedback necessary in motivating and directing learning, and of the availability of staff and material resources.

3. Translate the specific behavioral objectives into a form that is both communicable and applicable to facilitating learning in the school's environment.

4. Develop the instrumentation necessary for furnishing criterion measures from which inferences can be formulated concerning program effectiveness in terms of the objectives set forth.

1. Metfessel, Newton S., and Michael, William B., "A Paradigm Involving Multiple Criterion Measures for the Evaluation of the Effectiveness of School Programs," *Educational and Psychological Measurement*, 1967, 27, 931–943.

Eight major phases of process of evaluating school programs in approximate temporal sequence numbered (1) through (8). The facilitating role of lay individuals (L), professional personnel (P), and students (S) is indicated in lower right hand corner of boxes. The parentheses around L, P, and S in lower right corner of boxes indicate a secondary or indirect role and the absence of parentheses a primary role.

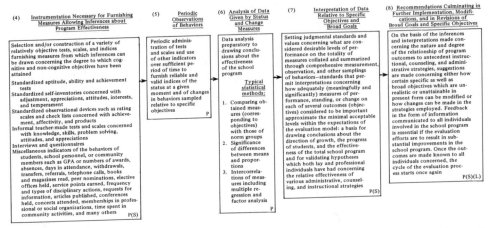

5. Carry out periodic observations through use of the tests, scales, and other indices of behavioral change that are considered valid with respect to the objectives sampled.

6. Analyze data furnished by the status and change measures through use of appropriate statistical methods.

7. Interpret the data in terms of certain judgmental standards and values concerning what are considered desirable levels of performance on the totality of collated measures—the drawing of conclusions which furnish information about the direction of growth, the progress of students, and the effectiveness of the total program.

8. Formulate recommendations that furnish a basis for further implementation, for modifications, and for revisions in the broad goals and specific objectives so that improvements can be realized—recommendations which for their effectiveness depend upon adequate feedback of information to all individuals involved in the school program and upon repeated cycles of the evaluation process.

A few cautions: It should also be emphasized that judgmental decisions are involved throughout all phases of the evaluation process, as the participants at each stage may be expected to make adjustments in their activities in terms of the amount and kinds of feedback received. The alert evaluator needs also to be aware that measures may yield indications of false gains or false losses that are correlated with (1) experiences in the school environment as well as outside the school environment that go beyond the intent of the specific behavioral objectives, (2) uncontrolled differences in the facilitating effects of teachers and other school personnel (usually motivational in origin), (3) inaccuracies in collecting, reading, analyzing, collating, and reporting of data, and (4) errors in research design and statistical methodology. In such situations, the wisdom and seasoned judgment of the trained evaluator are particularly helpful and necessary if meaningful, honest, and realistic conclusions are to be derived from the data obtained in the evaluation process.

A. FORMULATION OF A COMPREHENSIVE AND CONSISTENT SET OF BROAD GOALS AND SPECIFIC INSTRUCTIONAL OBJECTIVES

Development of a cohesive and comprehensive framework of broad goals and specific behavioral objectives (intended behavioral changes or outcomes) frequently arranged in a hierarchical order or taxonomy from general to specific outcomes (cognitive, affective, and psychomotor)

A-1 Broad educational objectives or goals, the social, institutional, and philosophical significance of which is determined by lay individuals and groups, professional individuals and groups (in education), and students and student groups

A-2 Specific behavioral (performance) objectives customarily stated by professional personnel in operational form to permit relatively objective measurement and/or empirical determination of the degree to which desired behavioral changes, or outcomes, have been attained in terminal performance

A-3 Developing judgmental criteria for defining relevance, significance, and appropriateness of objectives and for determining acceptable levels of measurable outcomes (behaviors) of these objectives within a framework of realistic priorities in relation to societal needs and expectations; learner–teacher readiness and capabilities; opportunity for student–teacher interaction and feedback to motivate and guide learning; availability of staff, financial, and physical resources; and opportunity to obtain or devise appropriate evaluative instruments

B. ENTERING BEHAVIORS (INTERNAL CONDITIONS) IN STUDENTS AND TEACHERS

Characteristics of students and teachers prior to instructional-learning activities and potentially interacting with one another

B-1 Students

Information customarily available from pretests, cumulative folders, or preliminary observations allowing teachers to modify instructional procedures relative to individual differences in abilities and aptitudes, readiness-maturation, previous relevant knowledge, existing cognitive and psychomotor skills, motivational patterns (attitudes, interests, values, needs, energy levels), learning sets and styles, social and cultural determinants, physical–physiological status, and specific disabilities (sensory, perceptual, intellectual, or psychomotor), if any

B-2 Teachers

Information not too readily available though obtainable regarding such characteristics as abilities and aptitudes, competencies in subject matter, motivational patterns, capabilities in learning diagnosis, teaching-style preferences, temperament patterns, empathy, physical-physiological status, and specific disabilities, if any

A four-stage teaching-learning-evaluation (TLE) model derived in part from the basic teaching model proposed by Robert Glaser ("Psychology and Instructional Technology" in TRAINING RESEARCH AND EDUCATION, Ed. R. Glaser. Pittsburgh: University of Pittsburgh Press, 1962, pp. 1–30) and elaborated upon by John P. DeCecco (THE PSYCHOLOGY OF LEARNING AND INSTRUCTION: EDUCATIONAL PSYCHOLOGY. Englewood Cliffs, N. J.: Prentice Hall, 1968) and in part from the evaluation paradigm prepared by Metfessel and Michael (1967, see page 174). Prepared by William B. Michael, San Marino, California, 1969.

C. INSTRUCTIONAL PROCEDURES (TEACHER INFORMATION, PROCESSING)

Implementation of teaching process-learning activities intended to result in relatively permanent changes in behavioral tendencies (capabilities or dispositions as inferred from performance measures and observable outcomes) in the following: simple association (stimulus-response) learning, verbal knowledge and skills, concept and principle acquisition (including discrimination and generalization), problem-solving capabilities necessitating positive transfer of learning (involving meaningful reception learning and expository teaching, discovery learning, and inquiry training), creative endeavor, social and affective learning (modifications in attitudes, interests, values, and perceptions of human relationships), and psychomotor skills

*Manipulative conditions in Stimulus Situation for
Modifying Learning Subject to Teacher Control and Decision-Making Capabilities*

C-1 Content Components

Selection and organization of content involving projected use of instructional materials: books, manuals, periodicals, films, film strips, tapes, programmed learning packages, laboratory-field exercises, lesson plans, independent study and research plans, and special equipment

C-2 Process Components

Selection, organization, and execution of teacher-behaviors (teaching acts) to facilitate student learning activities, and interaction or two-way feedback of teacher-learner behaviors as manifested, e.g., in lectures, question-and-answer periods, discussions, report writing, and direct and guided use of films, tapes, and programmed materials

C-3 External Conditions in Learning Situation which Teacher Takes into Account and Manipulates in Attaining Instructional Objectives

External conditions, which mediate between content and process components in C and which interact with internal conditions of the learner and teacher in B, being functionally related to characteristics of instructional materials and to teachers' planning students' meaningful exposure to and use of efficient activities with materials through the skillful application of principles of learning theory: contiguity, redintegration, amount and kind of practice (e.g., frequency; part vs. whole, massed vs. spaced practice), reinforcement, feedback, and arrangement of degree of similarity in stimuli (associated with positive transfer or interference as in retroactive and proactive inhibition)

D. EVALUATION OF PERFORMANCE WITH FEEDBACK LOOPS TO STEPS C, B, AND A

Determination of extent to which intended behavioral outcomes have been realized in terms of data furnished by tests, scales, observations, and other samplings of behaviors once judgmental standards have been set concerning what are considered desirable changes in levels of performance or desirable standings on criterion variables in the absence of pretest data needed to determine change—the effectiveness of the teaching-learning process (a) being judged in terms of the degree of congruence or correspondence between intended and observed levels of performance on specific objectives with some provision made for unexpected or creative outcomes and (b) being interpreted in relation to entering behaviors (step B) and instructional procedures including content and process components (step C); a judgment resulting in new decisions being made regarding possible alterations in nature and priorities of objectives, in revisions of or modifications in instructional materials and teaching behaviors, and in possible changes in expected levels of student performance

NEEDS ASSESSMENT

In the chart on page 5, the first step in a comprehensive evaluation model is to undertake a needs assessment, a process which determines the key needs to be addressed by the program. Once identified, these needs are translated into program goals that are eventually spelled out in the behavioral language of specific and attainable objectives. Pages 19 through 26 present selected outlines and checklists to illustrate both the different viewpoints regarding the definition of need and sample instruments that are available to assist in the needs assessment task.

Advantages and Disadvantages Accruing From Different Definitions of Need*

Definitions	Advantages	Disadvantages
Discrepancy View A need is a discrepancy between desired performance and observed or predicted performance.	○ is highly amenable to the use of norm-referenced and criterion-referenced tests as well as certification checklists ○ is generally accepted by school districts and state education departments	○ tends to concentrate needs assessment studies on those variables for which tests and norms are available ○ oversimplifies the criterion problem by attributing more validity than is deserved to norms, arbitrary standards and pronouncements by accrediting agencies ○ tends to reduce needs assessment to a simplistic mechanical process
Democratic View A need is a change desired by a majority of some reference group.	○ is easy to apply ○ has high public relations value ○ is democratic ○ tends to consider a wide range of variables ○ involves many people in the goal-setting process ○ provides useful information for determining the relative importance of potential need	○ confuses needs with preferences ○ depends heavily on the extent that the reference group is informed ○ tends to confound needs determinations with cost and comfort considerations ○ admits very real possibilities of forming invalid goals
Diagnostic View A need is something whose absence or deficiency proves harmful.	○ assumes that survival needs will not be overlooked ○ provides for the identification of met and unmet needs ○ uses logic and available research evidence to ascertain what deficiencies would be harmful ○ is amenable to the checklist approach	○ concentrates on basic survival needs to the exclusion of higher order needs ○ concentrates on removing the harmful effects of deprivation to the exclusion of seeking ways to improve on practice and performance that are already satisfactory ○ is highly subjective in practice, since research in education provides little evidence about the effects of various kinds of educational deprivation ○ is based on the questionable assumption that some needs are absolute
Analytic View A need is the direction improvement is predicted, given information about current status.	○ exhalts informed judgment and systematic problem solving ○ seeks full and complete description ○ focuses on improvement as opposed to remediation ○ does not depend on a prior statements of standards	○ is an abstraction that may be difficult to operationalize ○ requires highly skilled personnel

*Stufflebeam, Daniel L., *Needs Assessment in Evaluation,* presented at the AERA Evaluation Conference, San Francisco, California, September 23, 1977. Reproduced with permission of Daniel Stufflebeam.

SAMPLE CHECKLIST FOR A NEEDS ASSESSMENT*

Check one: **Parent**
Staff
Other (indicate role)

DIRECTIONS:

Below are listed sixteen areas of student growth to consider in planning next year's program. Select which four of the 16 you think are the most important *for a school to concentrate on,* and which are the four least important. Please place checks in the columns provided. There should be four checks in "most important," four checks in "least important," and eight areas which will have no checks. Obviously all 16 are important and plans will be made in each area. By completing this form *you are not suggesting that cuts should be made;* you are helping set priorities. The items are placed in this order so that later on responses can be easily tallied. DO NOT assume they are already in some order.

	Among 4 Most Important	Among 4 Least Important
1. A child is able to sound out words and understand what he or she has read.		
2. A child puts reading skills into practice; for example, reading books from a library and reading during leisure time.		
3. A child listens well and responds to others.		
4. A child uses speech in clear and accurate communication with others.		
5. A child writes, spells and punctuates using complete sentences.		
6. A child knows the basic math concepts and performs computation skills.		
7. A child puts mathematical facts and ideas into everyday life; for example, making change, telling time.		
8. A child knows how to think through a situation in order to understand it better and can apply scientific principles to better understand the environment.		
9. A child behaves in a way that shows that he or she is becoming a good citizen.		
10. A child knows about his or her own culture and about other cultures.		
11. A child shows pride in his or her own culture and shows awareness, understanding of, and respect for other people.		
12. A child understands and appreciates the value that art, music, dance, and drama have on our life style.		
13. A child knows the significance of the consumer in society and is aware of how one's career affects a life style.		
14. A child is physically healthy.		
15. A child feels positive about himself or herself and others.		
16. A child feels good about school in general.		

> **Place completed form in the enclosed envelope and return with your child.**

*Cox, Jim. The Needs Assessment: *A Guide for School Level Activities,* Downey, California: Office of the Los Angeles County Superintendent of Schools, July, 1979, p. 8. Reproduced with permission.

PRACTICAL GUIDELINES TO NEEDS ASSESSMENT*

The steps proposed for conducting a school's needs assessment are:

1. Identify the student-oriented goals.
2. Rank the importance of these goals without regard to performance levels.
3. Assess the level of performance for each of the goals.
4. Establish a priority for each student goal, considering both importance and performance.

Step 1: Identify the student-oriented goals

Student needs in any particular school are based upon the goals the school has for its students. Thus, the first step of a needs assessment is to identify these student-oriented goals.

Step 2: Rank the importance of the goals

Each group of people deemed significant to the planning process ranks the student goals in order of importance. It is not likely that equal attention will be needed or can be given to all areas. To keep the process simple, yet moving steadily toward the desired outcome, the importance of each goal is considered *without regard to current performance level;* e.g., a school might have very high reading achievement but still consider mastery of basic reading skills a high importance goal. Goals are categorized as high, moderate, or low importance.

Step 3: Assess the level of performance for each of the goals

Data are collected to identify how well students are performing in each goal area. The data should come from the best available source. For example, a profile of each student in reading or math, including a record of skill mastery, provides a far better source of information than does a questionnaire calling for teacher estimates of mastery. A general rule of thumb is to use those available data which stand the best chance of being accurate. The performance level for each goal is categorized as high, moderate, or low.

Step 4: Establish a priority for each student goal, considering both importance and performance

The goals are placed into one of the nine cells provided in the figure on page 22. Priorities are established, high to low, from upper left to lower right with cell number 1 being top priority. Cells numbered 2 have second-level priority; cells numbered 3 are third level; and cells 4 and 5 have least priority.

---

*Cox, Jim, *The Needs Assessment: A Guide for School Level Activities,* Downey, California: Office of the Los Angeles County Superintendent of Schools, July, 1979, pp. 2-3. Reproduced with permission.

The rationale for the procedure described is based in large measure upon procedures that Dr. Cox reports having learned in the early 1970's in interactive discussions with professional personnel at the Center for the Study of Evaluation, University of California, Los Angeles.

PERFORMANCE

	LOW	MODERATE	HIGH
HIGH	[1]	[2]	[3]
MODERATE	[2]	[3]	[4]
LOW	[3]	[4]	[5]

IMPORTANCE

The technique used for displaying the data is based on the following premises:

1. Findings of a needs assessment, in order to be useful, *must* establish priorities.
2. Importance of the goal and the performance level share equally in determining priorities.
3. Data are not useful unless the users understand, accept, and can *act* upon the information.

A CHECKLIST FOR DESIGNING NEEDS ASSESSMENT STUDIES*

A. *Preparation*

   1. Determine the *key elements* of the proposed needs assessment.

     _____ Identify the *purpose* to be served by the needs assessment.

     _____ Before proceding, insure that this is *defensible*, i.e., ethical and potentially viable.

     _____ Define the *client* and other *audiences*.

   2. Clarify the *reasons* for the study.

     _____ What are the *stated reasons* (e.g., selection of persons or groups to participate in a program, allocation of funds, modification of the curriculum, interpretation of program outcomes, or public relations)?

     _____ What possible *unstated reasons* exist (e.g., to justify a previous decision to cancel a program or to discharge certain personnel)?

     _____ Before proceding, insure that the reasons for the study are *honorable*.

*Stufflebeam, Daniel L., *Needs Assessment in Evaluation,* presented at the AERA Evaluation Conference, San Francisco, California, September 23, 1977. Reproduced with permission of Daniel Stufflebeam.

3. Make an initial approximation of the client's and audiences' *information needs.*

   _____ What are their *questions* (e.g., which students or schools most need assistance?)

   _____ What areas of the curriculum are most deficient? What knowledge and skills will students need after they graduate from a particular program?

   _____ What *information* do they think they need (e.g., teacher judgments, analysis of anecdotal records, test scores, and employer judgments)?

4. Secure and maintain *political viability.*

   _____ *Involve* members of key groups (such as school board members, administrators, teachers, students, and parents) in the design of the study.

   _____ Maintain *communication* with these groups throughout the study (through such means as a newsletter, news releases, public meetings, and an open door policy).

   _____ Determine and honor appropriate *protocol* (concerning such matters as entering and leaving school buildings, involving school personnel, obtaining clearance for data collection forms and procedures, and reviewing records).

5. Characterize the *subject(s)* of interest.

   _____ Decide on a definition of the *population* of interest.

   _____ *Describe* this population (in terms of such variables as number, age, sex, S.E.S., location, relevant experiences, and past achievements).

6. Identify other *variables* of interest.

   _____ What needs to be learned about the *setting* (e.g., its urban, rural, political, economic, and geographic character)?

   _____ What *program* variables are of particular interest (e.g., goals, procedures, budget, staff, and facilities)?

   _____ What *outcome* variables should be monitored (e.g., achievements in intellectual, emotional, physical, aesthetic, vocational, social, and moral areas)?

   _____ Are there any expected *negative side effects* of the program that should be monitored (e.g., potential lawsuits brought on by due process difficulties or reduced public support because of the revelation that students' needs have not been met)?

   _____ How about possible *positive side effects* (e.g., increased community understanding and parental involvement)?

   _____ Whose *judgments* about the existence and importance of needs should be obtained (e.g., those of program, staff, parents, students, and site visitors)?

   _____ What information should be obtained about *costs* of the program (e.g., developmental, maintenance, and opportunity costs)?

   _____ What about the *intrinsic qualifications* of the program (regarding especially its philosophical and conceptual adequacy)?

7. Formulate a general *design* for the study.

_____ Define *key terms* (especially need and needs assessment).

_____ State the primary and secondary *objectives* of the study (e.g., to assess and assign priorities to program goals, to select persons and institutions for compensatory service, to involve a broad reference group in goal setting, and/or to establish criteria for use in interpreting goal-free observations).

_____ Provide a *logical structure* for the study (e.g., present a list of concerns and issues drawn from prior investigations, or lists of possible learner and treatment needs given an analysis of the program under study).

_____ Describe the *procedures* to be used (such as surveys, document reviews, testing forecasts, and case studies).

_____ Summarize the *standards* that are viewed as appropriate for judging the study (e.g., *technical adequacy, use* by the client, *probity,* and *practicality*).

8. Develop a *management plan.*

_____ Present a detailed *schedule* of procedures (including the data gathering, analysis and reporting activities).

_____ Specify the *support* that will be needed to carry out the procedures (including staff, facilities, and finances).

_____ Describe any ways in which the study will contribute to *improved needs assessment practice* (especially in regard to training, development, and research).

9. Summarize the *formal agreements* that will govern the needs assessment.

_____ Clearly identify the *parties to the agreement* (including who will finance, conduct, and utilize the study).

_____ Delineate each participant's *responsibility and authority* for carrying out or facilitating the various parts of the study (especially in the data collection area).

_____ Specify the *reports and other products* that are to be produced (including their format, contents, and timing).

_____ Define the provisions covering *access to data* (such as a restriction against the review of personnel records or a provision for interviewing certain persons).

_____ Specify who will have *final editorial authority.*

_____ Specify who will have *authority to release the final report* including the conditions under which it may be released (e.g., the client may be assigned to release the report to the public, but only in an unedited form).

_____ Present the established *budget* (to include the schedule of payments and specified accounting and billing procedures).

_____ Define procedures for *reviewing and renegotiating* the formal agreements (e.g., if there are cost overruns in certain budget categories or if unforeseen factors make it desirable to modify the study design).

B. *Implementation*

    1. Acquire the needed *instrumentation.*

        _____ Specify the *sources* of information (e.g., relevant files, the professional litera-ture, the subjects, experts, policy groups, administrators, staff, the client, parents, and members of the community).

        _____ *Operationalize* the variables of interest (using techniques such as literature search, position papers, observation scales, rating scales, content analysis for-mat, questionnaires, interview schedules, norm-referenced tests, criterion-referenced tests, and applied performance tests).

        _____ Decide what to do about *critical levels* for each test (e.g., it may be appro-priate to decide that no advance designations are possible or desirable, or past practice or research may give direction for identifying useable cutting scores).

        _____ Select *critical comparisons* (such as the past or current performance of a local norm group, the past or current performance of an external norm group, or an accrediting agency's specifications).

    2. Collect the *data.*

        _____ Use appropriate *sampling techniques* (such as random, stratified random, matrix or systematic sampling).

        _____ Have *key groups* rate the *importance* of the variables of interest (e.g., teachers and parents might assign ratings of essential, desirable, neutral, and dysfunc-tional).

        _____ Obtain the *basic data* (which may include background, current status, and predicted status).

        _____ *Process* the obtained data (by verifying, coding, and storing it).

    3. *Analyze* and *synthesize* the obtained data.

        _____ *Describe the program* of interest as completely as the data permit (noting especially the program's goals, design, process, costs and results).

        _____ *Describe the subjects* of interests as completely as the data permit (especially in terms of their developmental levels and their attitudes toward the program).

        _____ List the *issues and concerns* that are revealed in the program and student data (e.g., weak administration, unrealistic goals, lackluster teaching, poor parental support, unmotivated students, inadequate finances, and unsafe conditions).

        _____ Search out *evidence* that would either *support* or *refute* the identified issues and concerns (such evidence may be in interview and observation protocols previously not scrutinized or in other data that have not been analyzed in detail; or it may be necessary to collect additional data on the questions of interest).

        _____ Perform *discrepancy analyses* if they are called for in the needs assessment design (e.g., such analyses may identify the percentages of students that per-formed above some critical level on a given instrument).

        _____ Perform *comparative analyses* if they are specified in the design (these may identify the percentages of students that are observed in each decile or quartile of a norm group distribution; they may give the position of a score, mean, or median in a percentile or standard score distribution for a norm group; or they may show the relative heights of a cumulative bar graph for each subject or group of subjects).

_____ Perform a *strengths analysis* (e.g., by searching out funding opportunities, and qualified persons that are available and may be applied to the validated issues and concerns).

_____ Formulate *conclusions* and *projections* (e.g., these may concern realized versus unrealized objectives, met and unmet needs, treatment sufficiencies and deficiencies, desirable or undesirable side effects, used, unused and misused opportunities, problems and tradeoffs, and possible alternative futures).

4. *Report* the findings.

_____ Establish appropriate *reporting levels* (e.g., summary, main and technical reports).

_____ Decide on report *contents* (such as purpose and design of the study, predilections of investigators, description of the program and subjects, identification and investigation of issues, discrepancy analysis, comparative analysis, strengths analysis, conclusions and projections, recommendations, limitations of the study, and the content that governed the study).

_____ Report the findings through some appropriate *media* (e.g., printed reports, newspaper accounts, oral presentations, public hearings, TV and radio presentations, and sociodramas).

C. *Application*

1. Assess the *merit of the study.*

_____ Check its *technical adequacy* (on such counts as defined object, defined setting, validity, reliability, and objectivity).

_____ Assess its *probity* (in terms of its full and open disclosure, contract fulfillment, and conflict of interest possibilities).

_____ Assess its *utility* (especially in regard to its timeliness, scope, relevance, dissemination, credibility, and importance).

_____ Assess its *practicality* (in regard to realistic design and cost considerations.

2. *Apply* the conclusions and projections.

_____ Assist the client and other audiences to *apply* the findings to their particular questions (focus on the preestablished questions but also help the audiences use the data to discover and address additional concerns).

_____ Help the audiences to make *full use* of the findings (e.g., to clarify objectives, set priorities, appropriate funds for development, write specifications for developmental efforts, assess program plans, assess outcome data, provide accountability reports, and to recycle the needs assessment process).

_____ Promote the use of the needs assessment study for purposes in addition to those for which the study was done (e.g., to provide *instruction* in needs assessment or to assist in generating and validating *new tools and strategies* for needs assessment work).

REFERENCES IN EVALUATION

General Contributions

Alkin, M. C., Daillak, R., White, P. *Using Evaluations: Does Evaluation Make a Difference?* Beverly Hills, California: Sage Publications, 1979.

Apple, M. W., Subkoviak, M. J., and Lufler, H. S., Jr. (Eds.). *Educational evaluation: Analysis and responsibility.* Berkeley, California: McCutchan, 1974.

Bellack, A. A. and Kliebard, H. M. (Eds.). Curriculum and evaluation. In M. C. Wittrock (Ed.), *Readings in educational research* (Vol. 7). Berkeley, California: McCutchan, 1977.

Bloom, B. S., Hastings, J. T., and Madaus, G. F. *Handbook on formative and summative evaluation of student learning.* New York: Mc-Graw-Hill, 1971.

Cooley, W. W. and Lohnes, P. R. *Evaluation research in education.* New York: Wiley, 1976.

Dressel, P. L. *Handbook of academic evaluation.* San Francisco: Jossey-Bass, 1976.

Guba, E. G. & Lincoln, Y. S. *Effective evaluation: Improving the usefulness of evaluation results through responsive and naturalistic approaches.* San Francisco: Jossey-Bass, 1981.

Mehrens, W. A. and Lehmann, I. J. *Measurement and evaluation in education and psychology* (2nd ed.). New York: Holt, Rinehart and Winston, 1978.

Patton, M. Q. *Qualitative evaluation methods.* Beverly Hills, California: Sage Publications, 1980.

Payne, D. A. (Ed.). *Curriculum evaluation: Commentaries on purpose, process, product.* Lexington, Massachusetts: D. C. Heath, 1974.

Popham, W. J. *Educational evaluation.* Englewood Cliffs, N. J.: Prentice-Hall, 1975.

Popham, W. J. *Evaluation in education: Current applications.* Berkeley, California: Mc-Cutchan, 1974.

Sax, G. *Principles of educational measurement and evaluation* (2nd ed.). Belmont, California: Wadsworth, 1980.

Stufflebeam, D. L., Foley, W. J., Gephart, W. J., Guba, E. G., Hammond, R. L., Merriman, H. O., and Provus, M. M. *Educational evaluation and decision making.* Itasca, Illinois: F. E. Peacock, 1971.

Wittrock, M. C. and Wiley, D. E. (Eds.). *The evaluation of instruction: Issues and problems.* New York: Holt, Rinehart and Winston, 1970.

Worthen, B. R. and Sanders, J. R. *Educational evaluation: Theory and practice.* Worthington, Ohio: Charles A. Jones, 1973.

Program Evaluation
(CSE Source)

The following set of eight books constitutes the *Program Evaluation Kit* that was prepared under the editorship of Lynn Lyons Morris and contributed to by members of the professional staff of the Center for the Study of Evaluation (CSE), University of California at Los Angeles. The kit was subsequently printed by Sage Publications in Beverly Hills, California. The references to be presented are in order of the volume listing rather than in alphabetical sequence by author.

1. Morris, L. L. and Fitz-Gibbon, C. T. Evaluator's handbook. In L. L. Morris (Ed.). *Program evaluation kit.* Beverly Hills, California: Sage Publications, 1978.

2. Morris, L. L. and Fitz-Gibbon, C. T. How to deal with goals and objectives. In L. L. Morris (Ed.). *Program evaluation kit.* Beverly Hills, California: Sage Publications, 1978.

3. Morris, L. L. and Fitz-Gibbon, C. T. How to design a program evaluation. In L. L. Morris (Ed.). *Program evaluation kit.* Beverly Hills, California: Sage Publications, 1978.

4. Morris, L. L. and Fitz-Gibbon, C. T. How to measure program implementation. In L. L. Morris (Ed.). *Program evaluation kit.* Beverly Hills, California: Sage Publications, 1978.

5. Henerson, M. E., Morris, L. L., and Fitz-Gibbon, C. T. How to measure attitudes. In L. L. Morris (Ed.). *Program evaluation kit.* Beverly Hills, California: Sage Publications, 1978.

6. Morris, L. L. and Fitz-Gibbon, C. T. How to measure achievement. In L. L. Morris (Ed.). *Program evaluation kit.* Beverly Hills, California: Sage Publications, 1978.

7. Morris, L. L. and Fitz-Gibbon, C. T. How to calculate statistics. In L. L. Morris (Ed.). *Program evaluation kit.* Beverly Hills, California: Sage Publications, 1978.

8. Morris, L. L. and Fitz-Gibbon, C. T. How to present an evaluation report. In L. L. Morris (Ed.). *Program evaluation kit.* Beverly Hills, California: Sage Publications, 1978.

Program Evaluation
(Other Sources)

Anderson, S. B. (Ed.). *New directions in program evaluation.* San Francisco: Jossey-Bass, 1978.

Borich, G. D. (Ed.). *Evaluating educational programs and products.* Englewood Cliffs, New Jersey: Educational Technology, 1974.

Cronbach, L. J. & Associates. *Toward reform of program evaluation: Aims, methods, and institutional arrangements.* San Francisco: Jossey-Bass, 1981.

Rutman, L. *Planning useful evaluations: evaluability assessment.* Beverly Hills, California: Sage Publications, 1980.

Thompson, M. *Benefit-Cost analysis for program evaluation.* Beverly Hills, California: Sage Publications, 1980.

Walberg, H. J. (Ed.). *Evaluating educational performance: A sourcebook of methods, instruments, and examples.* Berkeley, California: McCutchan, 1974.

Reference Works

Anderson, S. B., Ball, S., Murphy, R. T., and Associates. *Encyclopedia of educational evaluation.* San Francisco: Josey-Bass, 1975.

Struening, E. L. and Guttentag, M. (Eds.). *Handbook of evaluation research* (Vols. 1, 2). Beverly Hills, California: Sage Publications, 1975.

Periodicals

Phi Delta Kappa. *CEDR* [Quarterly: Spring, Summer, Fall, Winter]. Bloomington, Indiana: Author (8th and Union Streets).

Sage Publications. *Evaluation News (EN)* [Quarterly: February, May, August, November]. Beverly Hills, California: Author. (A publication of the professional organization, Evaluation Network, Robert Ingle, Treasurer, 571 Enderis Hall, University of Wisconsin—Milwaukee.)

The formulation of a problem is far more often essential than its solution, which may be merely a matter of mathematical or experimental skill. To raise new questions, new possibilities, to regard old problems from a new angle requires creative imagination and marks real advance in science.

A. Einstein and L. Infeld
THE EVOLUTION OF PHYSICS
Simon and Schuster, 1938

CHAPTER TWO

PLANNING RESEARCH STUDIES

Carrying out research investigations requires careful planning similar to that found in evaluation studies. Central to a research investigation is a clear-cut statement of the research problem. In this chapter attention is given to (a) steps to be taken in analyzing a problem situation and in formulating the problem statement, (b) citation of the advantages of completing the pilot study, (c) an enumeration of common mistakes often made by graduate students in research endeavors, and (d) planning stages to be undertaken by a computer in processing and analyzing data.

FORMULATION OF THE PROBLEM

"A question well-stated is a question half-answered."

Some common mistakes in problem-formulation:

1. Collecting data without a well-defined plan or purpose, hoping to make some sense out of it afterward.

2. Taking a "batch of data" that already exists and attempting to fit meaningful research questions to it.

3. Defining objectives in such general or ambiguous terms that your interpretations and conclusions will be arbitrary and invalid.

4. Undertaking a research project without reviewing the existing professional literature on the subject.

5. *Ad hoc* research, unique to a given situation, permitting no generalizations beyond the situation itself and making no contribution to the general body of educational research.

6. Failure to base research on a sound theoretical or conceptual framework, which would tie together the divergent masses of research into a systematic and comparative scheme, providing feedback and evaluation for educational theory.

7. Failure to make explicit and clear the underlying assumptions within your research so that it can be evaluated in terms of these foundations.

8. Failure to recognize the limitations in your approach, implied or explicit, that place restrictions on the conclusions and how they apply to other situations.

9. Failure to anticipate alternative rival hypotheses that would also account for a given set of findings and which challenge the interpretations and conclusions reached by the investigator.

STEPS IN PREPARING A RESEARCH INVESTIGATION[1]

A. PROBLEM-ANALYSIS PROCEDURES:

1. Select a problem that engages your attention and begs for a solution.
2. Accumulate the facts that might be related to the problem.
3. Settle by observation whether the facts are relevant.
4. Trace any relationships between facts that might reveal the key to the difficulty.
5. Propose various explanations (hypotheses) for the cause of the difficulty.
6. Ascertain through observation and analysis whether they are relevant to the problem.
7. Trace relationships between explanations that may give an insight into the problem solution.

---

1. Van Dalen, D. B. *Understanding Educational Research* (4th. ed.), McGraw-Hill, New York, 1966 (Rev.), Chapter 7.

8. Trace relationships between facts and explanations.
9. Question assumptions underlying the analysis of the problem.

B. EVALUATION OF A PROBLEM:

Personal Considerations

1. Is the problem in line with my goal expectations and the expectations of others?
2. Am I genuinely interested in this problem but free from strong biases?
3. Do I possess or can I acquire the necessary skills, abilities, and background knowledge to study this problem?
4. Do I have access to the tools, equipment, laboratories, and subjects necessary to conduct the investigation?
5. Do I have the time and money to complete it?
6. Can I obtain adequate data?
7. Does the problem meet the scope, significance, and topical requirements of the institution or periodical to which I will submit my report?
8. Can I obtain administrative support, guidance, and cooperation for the conduct of the study?

Social Considerations

1. Will the solution of this problem advance knowledge in the field appreciably?
2. Will the findings be of practical value to educators, parents, social workers, or others?
3. What will be the breadth of the application of the findings in terms of range of individuals, years of applicability, and areas of coverage?
4. Will the investigation duplicate the work that has been or is being done adequately by someone else?
5. If this topic has been covered, does it need to be extended beyond its present limits?
6. Is the topic sufficiently delimited to permit an exhaustive treatment yet sufficiently significant to warrant investigating it?
7. Will the conclusions of the study be of doubtful value because the tools and techniques available to conduct the inquiry are not adequately refined and sufficiently reliable?
8. Will the study lead to the development of other investigations?

TEN STEPS IN PLANNING GOOD RESEARCH[1]

1. *Basic difficulty*—What is it that has caught your interest or raised a question in your mind?

2. *Rationale and theoretical base*—Can this be fitted into a conceptual framework that gives a structured point-of-view? In other words, can you begin from a position of logical concepts, relationships, and expectations based on current thinking in this area?

---

1. Lefever, D. Welty. Criteria taken from seminar in research methods at University of Southern California.

Can you build a conceptual framework into which your ideas can be placed, giving definition, orientation, and direction to your thinking?

3. *Statement of the purpose or problem*—What is it that you plan to investigate? What are the general goals of the study? Define the problem.

4. *Questions to be answered*—When the research is finished, what are the questions to which reasonable answers can be expected?

5. *Statement of hypotheses or objectives*—Spell out the particular research hypotheses you will test or the specific objectives at which the research is aimed. Be concrete and clear, making sure that each hypothesis or objective is stated in terms of *observable behavior* allowing objective evaluation of the results.

6. *Design and procedure*—State who your subjects will be, how they will be selected, the conditions under which the data will be collected, treatment variables to be manipulated, what measuring instruments or data-gathering techniques will be used, and how the data will be analyzed and interpreted.

7. *Assumptions*—What assumptions have you made about the nature of the behavior you are investigating, about the conditions under which the behavior occurs, about your methods and measurements, or about the relationship of this study to other persons and situations?

8. *Limitations*—What are the limitations surrounding your study and within which conclusions must be confined? What limitations exist in your methods or approach—sampling restrictions, uncontrolled variables, faulty instrumentation, and other compromises to internal and external validity?

9. *Delimitations*—How have you arbitrarily narrowed the scope of the study? Did you focus only on selected aspects of the problem, certain areas of interest, a limited range of subjects, and level of sophistication involved?

10. *Definition of terms*—List and define the principal terms you will use, particularly where terms have different meanings to different people. Emphasis should be placed on operational or behavioral definitions.

ADVANTAGES OF A PILOT STUDY[1]

1. It permits a preliminary testing of the hypotheses that leads to testing more precise hypotheses in the main study. It may lead to changing some hypotheses, dropping some, and developing new hypotheses when called for.

2. It often provides the research worker with ideas, approaches, and clues not foreseen prior to the pilot study. Such ideas and clues greatly increase the chances of obtaining clear-cut findings in the main study.

1. Borg, Walter R., *Educational Research: An Introduction.* New York: David McKay Company, Inc., 1963, p. 185. By permission, (Items 1-5 and 7). Borg, W. R. and Gall, M. D. *Educational Research: An Introduction* (3rd ed.). New York: Longman, 1979, p. 70. By permission (Item 6).

3. It permits a thorough check of the planned statistical and analytical procedures, thus allowing an appraisal of their adequacy in treating the data. Needed alterations also may be made in the data-collecting methods, so that data in the main study may be analyzed more efficiently.

4. It greatly reduces the number of treatment errors, because unforeseen problems revealed in the pilot study may be overcome in redesigning the main study.

5. It may save the research worker a major expenditure of time and money on a research project that will yield nothing. Unfortunately, many research ideas that seem to show great promise are unproductive when carried out in the field or laboratory. The pilot study almost always provides enough data for the research worker to make a sound decision on the advisability of going ahead with the main study.

6. In many pilot studies it is possible to get feedback from research subjects and other persons involved that leads to important improvements in the main study although the pilot study should follow the main study procedure for the most part, variations such as trying alternative instruments and procedures and seeking feedback from subjects on the treatment, measures, and other aspects of research are usually desirable.[1]

7. In the pilot study, the research worker may try out a number of alternative measures, and then select those that produce the best results for the main study without some tentative evidence that they would be productive. If the student plans to continue beyond the Master's degree, his Master's research may sometimes serve as a pilot study for later research to be carried out as part of his doctoral program. The less research experience the student has, the more he is likely to profit from the pilot study. Because of this, the student should attempt a pilot study whenever possible, even if it must be limited to only a dozen or so cases.

COMMON MISTAKES MADE BY GRADUATE STUDENTS

A. COMMON ERRORS IN FORMULATING A RESEARCH STUDY[2]

1. Puts off selection of a problem until he has finished all or most of his courses.
2. Uncritically accepts the first research idea that he thinks of or that is suggested to him.
3. Selects a problem that is too vast or too vague to investigate meaningfully.
4. Prepares fuzzy or untestable hypotheses.
5. Fails to consider methods or analysis procedures in developing his tentative research plan.

---

1. From *Educational Research,* Third Edition, by Walter R. Borg and Meredith Damien Gall. Copyright © 1979 by Longman, Inc.
2. Borg, Walter R., *Educational Research: An Introduction.* David McKay Company, Inc., New York, 1963, p. 38. By permission.

B. COMMON ERRORS IN REVIEWING THE LITERATURE[1]

1. Carries out a hurried review of the literature in order to get started on the research project. This usually results in overlooking previous studies containing ideas that would have improved the student's project.
2. Relies too heavily upon secondary sources.
3. Concentrates on research findings when reading research articles, thus overlooking valuable information on methods, measures, and so forth.
4. Overlooks sources other than education journals, such as newspapers and popular magazines which often contain articles on educational topics.
5. Fails to define satisfactorily the topic limits of his review of the literature. Searching too broad an area often leads to the student's becoming discouraged or doing a slipshod job. Searching too narrow an area causes him to overlook many articles that are peripheral to his research topic but contain information that would help him design a better study.
6. Copies bibliographic data incorrectly and is then unable to locate the reference needed.
7. Copies far too much material onto note cards. This often indicates that the student does not have a clear understanding of his project and thus cannot separate important from unimportant information.

C. COMMON ERRORS IN GATHERING RESEARCH DATA[2]

1. Pays insufficient attention to establishing and maintaining rapport with his subjects. This often leads to refusals to cooperate or to a negative attitude that can reduce the validity of tests and other measures.
2. Weakens his research design by making changes for the administrative convenience of the schools from which he draws his subjects.
3. Fails to explain the purposes of measures used in the research to teachers and administrators. If a teacher thinks a test or measure is silly or worthless, her attitude is quickly sensed by pupils and leads to poor cooperation.
4. Fails to evaluate available measures thoroughly before selecting those to be used in his research. This often leads to the use of invalid or inappropriate measures.
5. Selects measures to use in his research of such low reliability that true differences are hidden by the errors of the measure.
6. Selects measures to use in his research that he is not qualified to administer and score.

D. COMMON ERRORS IN USE OF STANDARD MEASURING INSTRUMENTS[3]

1. Fails to check the content validity of achievement measures in the situation in which the research is to be carried out.
2. Fails to standardize or control the teacher's role in the data collection situation, therefore introducing bias resulting from nonstandard instructions, coaching of some of the pupils involved in the study, and variations in degree of assistance given pupils during test.
3. Checks overall validity and reliability of measures selected but fails to check

1. Borg, Walter R., *Educational Research: An Introduction*. David McKay Company, Inc., New York, 1963, p. 67. By permission.
2. Ibid, p. 94
3. Ibid, p. 94

validity and reliability data on subtest scores even though these scores are to be employed in the research analysis.

4. Uses personality inventories and other self-reporting devices in situations in which the subject might be expected to fake his replies in order to create a desired impression.

5. Assumes that standard tests measure what they claim to measure without making a thorough evaluation of validity data available.

6. Attempts to use measures that he is not sufficiently trained to administer, analyze, or interpret.

7. Fails to make optimum use of the testing time he has available by administering long tests when shorter ones are available that meet the requirements of the research project equally well.

8. Does not carry out a pretrial of his measuring instruments and, as a result, makes blunders in the administration procedures during the collection of his first data, thus introducing bias.

E. COMMON ERRORS IN USE OF STATISTICAL TOOLS[1]

1. Selects statistical tool that is not appropriate or correct for proposed analysis.

2. Collects research data, and then tries to find a statistical technique that can be used in analysis.

3. Uses only one statistical procedure when several can be applied to the data. This often leads to overlooking results that could have made a significant contribution to the thesis.

4. Uses statistical tools in situations in which the data grossly fail to meet the assumptions upon which the tools are based. Most statistical tools will give reasonably accurate results unless assumptions are seriously violated.

5. Overstates the importance of small differences that are statistically significant.

6. Student avoids correlational analysis if the standard product-moment correlation cannot be applied.

7. Uses the incorrect correlation technique—such as, using the biserial correlation when the widespread biserial correlation is called for.

8. Uses the product-moment correlation significance tables to interpret non-Pearsonian correlations. Because most non-Pearsonial correlations have a larger standard error than the product-moment correlation, this mistake leads to overestimating the significance of coefficients so interpreted.

9. Uses correction for attenuation in situations where it is not appropriate in order to make the results appear more significant.

F. COMMON ERRORS IN RESEARCH DESIGN AND METHODOLOGY[2]

1. Student fails to define his research population.

2. Uses a sample too small to permit analysis of the performance of interesting subgroups.

3. Attempts to conduct his research using volunteer subjects.

4. Changes his design in ways that weaken the research in order to make data collection more convenient for the schools involved.

1. Borg, Walter R., *Educational Research: An Introduction.* David McKay Company, Inc., New York, 1963, pp. 145 and 164. By permission.
2. Ibid, p. 186.

5. In an attempt to collect as much data as possible, he makes excessive demands upon his subjects that lead to their refusal to cooperate.
6. Attempts to carry out a study in one semester that would require two/three years to do satisfactorily.
7. Fails to plan his data collection in sufficient detail to avoid excessive treatment errors.
8. Starts collecting his research data without carrying out a pilot study or adequately testing his measures and procedures.

G. COMMON ERRORS IN HISTORICAL RESEARCH[1]

1. A research area is selected in which sufficient evidence is not available to conduct a worthwhile study or test the hypotheses adequately.
2. Excessive use of secondary sources of information is frequently found in studies not dealing with recent events.
3. Attempts to work on a broad and poorly defined problem.
4. Fails to evaluate adequately his historical data.
5. Allows personal bias to influence his research procedures.
6. The student's report recites facts but does not synthesize or integrate these facts into meaningful generalizations.

H. COMMON ERRORS IN DESCRIPTIVE RESEARCH[2]

1. Student does not formulate clear and specific objectives.
2. Relates his data-gathering procedure to his objectives in only a general way and thereby fails to get quantitative data specific to his problem.
3. Selects his sample on the basis of convenience rather than attempting to obtain a random sample.
4. Does not plan his analysis until after his data are collected.
5. Structures his data collecting devices (questionnaires, interview guides, observation forms, and so on) so that biased results are obtained.

I. COMMON ERRORS IN QUESTIONNAIRE STUDIES[3]

1. Student uses a questionnaire in working with problems that can be better studied with other research techniques.
2. Gives insufficient attention to the development of his questionnaire and fails to pretest it.
3. Asks too many questions, thus making unreasonable demands on the respondent's time.
4. Overlooks details of format, grammar, printing, and so on that, if observed, give the respondent a favorable first impression.
5. Fails to check a sample of nonresponding subjects for possible bias.

J. COMMON ERRORS IN INTERVIEW STUDIES[4]

1. Student does not adequately plan the interview or develop a detailed interview guide.

---

1. Borg, Walter R., *Educational Research: An Introduction*. David McKay Company, Inc., New York, 1963, pp. 196–198. By permission.
2. Ibid, p. 233.
3. Ibid, pp. 233–234.
4. Ibid p. 234.

2. Does not conduct sufficient practice interviews to acquire needed skills.
3. Fails to establish safeguards against interviewer bias.
4. Does not make provisions for calculating the reliability of his interview data.
5. Uses language in the interview that is not understood by the respondents.
6. Asks for information that the respondent cannot be expected to have.

K. COMMON ERRORS IN OBSERVATIONAL STUDIES[1]

1. Student does not sufficiently train his observers and thus obtains unreliable data.
2. Uses an observation form that demands too much of the observer.
3. Fails to take adequate safeguards against the observer disturbing or changing the situation he is to observe.
4. Attempts to evaluate behavior that occurs so infrequently that reliable data cannot be obtained through observations.

L. COMMON ERRORS IN CONTENT ANALYSIS[2]

1. Student selects content that is easily available but does not represent an unbiased sample of all content related to the research objectives.
2. Fails to determine the reliability of his content-analysis procedures.
3. Uses classification categories that are not sufficiently specific and comprehensive.

M. COMMON ERRORS IN THE STUDY OF RELATIONSHIPS[3]

1. Student assumes the results of causal-comparative or correlational research to be proof of a cause-and-effect relationship.
2. Uses sample in causal-comparative research that differs on so many pertinent variables that comparisons of groups can yield no interpretable results.
3. Attempts to study possible causes of a broadly defined behavior pattern that actually includes a number of unlike subgroups. This usually leads to a jumble of confused and contradictory results with no clear relationships emerging.
4. Tries to build a correlational study around conveniently available data instead of collecting the data needed to do a worthwhile study.
5. Selects variables for correlation that have been found unproductive in previous studies.
6. Fails to make use of educational and psychological theory in selecting variables for study in correlation research.
7. Uses simple correlation techniques in studies where partial correlation or multiple correlation is needed to obtain a clear picture of the way the variables are operating.
8. Applies tables giving significance levels of Pearsonian correlation coefficients to non-Pearsonian correlations, which often leads to reporting nonsignificant relationships as being significant.
9. Uses the "shotgun" approach in exploratory relationship studies.
10. Fails to develop satisfactory criterion measures for use in correlation studies of complex skills or behavior patterns.

1. Borg, Walter R., *Educational Research: An Introduction.* David McKay Company, Inc., New York, 1963, p. 260. By permission.
2. Ibid, p. 260.
3. Ibid, pp. 286–287.

PLANNING FOR COMPUTER ANALYSIS
AND DATA PROCESSING

The role of the computer in processing and analyzing research data is now a major consideration in studies involving complex calculations and large amounts of data. The advantages
of a computer are speed and volume. As a result, the actual cost of computer time is quite
reasonable, since seconds or minutes are involved to process data that would require weeks
or months to perform with a standard desk calculator.

The economy and efficiency of the computer, however, depends upon some practical
contingencies: (1) The data must be coded to meet computer input requirements. Ordinarily,
this follows the format restrictions of the IBM punch card (10 rows × 80 columns) with all
entries assigned alpha-numerical values (i.e., letters or numerals). Someone must then enter
the raw data correctly on the cards using a key punch machine and following the logic of the
particular set of coding instructions. (2) The data are processed and analyzed by a computer
program. If you can match your own design and analysis requirements to *existing* computer
programs, you will not incur additional costs involved in having new programs written or old
ones modified; therefore, it is important to investigate the availability of both computer
facilities and computer programs specific to your particular needs before including plans for
computer analysis of your data.

Suggestions for recording data—Final advice for the collection and recording of data with
computer processing in mind should always be obtained from the staff of the computer
facility with which you will be dealing. In general, each item of data should be coded to
represent the column or columns on the IBM punch card corresponding to the category of
that entry. It would be wise to do a pilot run of your data recording and processing procedures to work out any difficulties.

Some cautions about computer analysis of research data—The power and prestige of
modern computers can easily mislead the inexperienced researcher. Two cautions are worth
listing:

1.   *Errors*—While the actual mechanism and circuitry of an operational computer
tend to be highly reliable, human errors can be introduced in a number of ways: the IBM
punch card can have one or more incorrect entries; an error can exist in the computer program itself (program errors can be extremely obscure—appearing irregularly or only under
certain conditions); the special "instruction" decks that support the particular computer
program can be in error; and magnetic tapes on which the computer programs are stored
can be mishandled. Confidence is gained if the IBM punch cards are carefully checked for
errors and if the computer program has been well validated with use.

2.   *The "Black Box" problem*—To the typical researcher, the technicalities of computers, computer programs, and their statistical manipulations amount to a "black box"—
he cannot see the inside workings and must take on faith what the computer printouts yield
as well as what the computer experts say about the whole mysterious process. For many
research purposes, this presents no problem but in exploratory research it is important to
keep close to the data—to "have a feel for it" that can only come through processing the
data by hand. One of the consultants to this handbook reported that he always parallels
computer analysis of his data with the hand analysis of a small subsample. In this way, he
stays closer to his data and frequently uncovers errors in the particular analysis program.

The tragedies of science are the slayings of beautiful hypotheses by ugly facts.

T. H. Huxley

CHAPTER THREE

GUIDE TO RESEARCH DESIGNS, METHODS, AND STRATEGIES

When the research study has been formulated, the next step is to construct the research design. This is the plan of attack: what approach to the problem will be taken? what methods will be used? what strategies will be most effective?

Design decisions depend on the purposes of the study, the nature of the problem, and the alternatives appropriate for its investigation. Once the purposes have been specified, the study should have explicit scope and direction, and attention can be focused on a delimited target area. The nature of the problem then plays the major role in determining what approaches are suitable. Design alternatives can be organized into nine functional categories based on these differing problem characteristics:[1]

1. Historical
2. Descriptive
3. Developmental
4. Case or Field
5. Correlational
6. Causal-comparative
7. True experimental
8. Quasi-experimental
9. Action

The most obvious characteristics of each of these categories are summarized in the chart on the next two pages. Each category, then, is individually presented in the series of pages following the chart (pages 44–55).

---

1.   Because authorities differ in their classification criteria, the above scheme is arbitrary and overlapping. "Descriptive" research, for instance, is commonly used in a much broader sense encompassing everything except "historical" and "experimental" research. To avoid the complication of subcategories under main categories, "descriptive" research is used here in its more literal and narrow sense. This makes possible a list of single categories as if each was separate and distinct. Actually, there are as many similarities as differences and the categories are not always mutually exclusive, crossing over under many conditions. The reader is urged to examine the more complete information within this section and to compare the scheme presented here with others in current textbooks on research.

NINE BASIC METHODS OF RESEARCH

METHOD	PURPOSE
HISTORICAL	To reconstruct the past objectively and accurately, often in relation to the tenability of an hypothesis.
DESCRIPTIVE	To describe systematically a situation or area of interest factually and accurately.
DEVELOP-MENTAL	To investigate patterns and sequences of growth and/or change as a function of time.
CASE AND FIELD	To study intensively the background, current status, and environmental interactions of a given social unit: an individual, group, institution, or community.
CORRE-LATIONAL	To investigate the extent to which variations in one factor correspond with variations in one or more other factors based on correlation coefficients.
CAUSAL-COMPARATIVE or "EX POST FACTO"	To investigate possible cause-and-effect relationships by observing some existing consequence and searching back through the data for plausible casual factors.
TRUE EXPERI-MENTAL	To investigate possible cause-and-effect relationships by exposing one or more experimental groups to one or more treatment conditions and comparing the results to one or more control groups not receiving the treatment (random assignment being essential).
QUASI-EXPERI-MENTAL	To approximate the conditions of the true experiment in a setting which does not allow the control and/or manipulation of all relevant variables. The researcher must clearly understand what compromises exist in the internal and external validity of his design and proceed within these limitations.[1]
ACTION	To develop new skills or new approaches and to solve problems with direct application to the classroom or other applied setting.

1. For a discussion of the concept of "control" see pages 80–81; "internal and external validity" are discussed on pages 59–63

EXAMPLES

A study reconstructing practices in the teaching of spelling in the United States during the past fifty years; tracing the history of civil rights in the United States education since the civil war; testing the hypothesis that Francis Bacon is the real author of the "works of William Shakespeare."

Population census studies, public opinion surveys, fact-finding surveys, status studies, task analysis studies, questionnaire and interview studies, observation studies, job descriptions, surveys of the literature, documentary analyses, anecdotal records, critical incident reports, test score analyses, and normative data.

A longitudinal growth study following an initial sample of 200 children from six months of age to adulthood; a cross-sectional growth study investigating changing patterns of intelligence by sampling groups of children at ten different age levels; a trend study projecting the future growth and educational needs of a community from past trends and recent building estimates.

The case history of a child with an above average IQ but with severe learning disabilities; an intensive study of a group of teenage youngsters on probation for drug abuse; an intensive study of a typical suburban community in the Midwest in terms of its socio-economic characteristics.

To investigate relationships between reading achievement scores and one or more other variables of interest; a factor-analytic study of several intelligence tests; a study to predict success in college based on intercorrelation patterns between college grades and selected high school variables.

To identify factors related to the "drop-out" problem in a particular high school using data from records over the past ten years; to investigate similarities and differences between such groups as smokers and nonsmokers, readers and nonreaders, or delinquents and nondelinquents, using data on file.

To investigate the effectiveness of three methods of teaching reading to first grade children using random assignments of children and teachers to groups and methods; to investigate the effects of a specific tranquilizing drug on the learning behavior of boys identified as "hyperactive" using random assignment to groups receiving three different levels of the drug and two control groups with and without a placebo, respectively.

Most so-called field experiments, operational research, and even the more sophisticated forms of action research which attempt to get at causal factors in real life settings where only partial control is possible; e.g., an investigation of the effectiveness of any method or treatment condition where random assignment of subjects to methods or conditions is not possible.

An inservice training program to help teachers develop new skills in facilitating class discussions; to experiment with new approaches to teaching reading to bilingual children; to develop more effective counseling techniques for underachievers.

BASIC STEPS IN THE PLANNING
AND CONDUCT OF RESEARCH

1. Identify the problem area.

2. Survey the literature relating to it.

3. Define the actual problem for investigation in clear, specific terms.

4. Formulate testable hypotheses and define the basic concepts and variables.[1]

5. State the underlying assumptions which govern the interpretation of results.

6. Construct the research design to maximize internal and external validity.[2]

   a. Selection of subjects.

   b. Control and/or manipulation of relevant variables.

   c. Establishment of criteria to evaluate outcomes.

   d. Instrumentation—selection or development of the criterion measures.

7. Specify the data collection procedures.

8. Select the data analysis methodology.

9. Execute the research plan.

10. Evaluate the results and draw conclusions.

HISTORICAL RESEARCH

Purpose:

To reconstruct the past systematically and objectively by collecting, evaluating, verifying, and synthesizing evidence to establish facts and reach defensible conclusions, often in relation to particular hypotheses.

---

1. Variables can be classified into three categories:
    a. *Independent (input, manipulated, treatment,* or *stimulus) variables,* so-called because they are "independent" of the outcome itself; instead, they are presumed to cause, effect, or influence the outcome.
    b. *Dependent (output, outcome,* or *response) variables,* so-called because they are "dependent" on the independent variables: the outcome presumably depends on how these input variables are managed or manipulated.
    c. *Control (background, classificatory,* or *organismic) variables,* so-called because they need to be controlled, held constant, or randomized so that their effects are neutralized, cancelled out, or equated for all conditions. Typically included are such factors as age, sex, IQ, SES (socio-economic status), educational level, and motivational level; it is often possible to redefine these particular examples as either independent or dependent variables, according to the intent of the research.

    A fourth category often is cited having to do with conceptual states within the organism: *intervening variables (higher order constructs).* These cannot be directly observed or measured and are hypothetical conceptions intended to explain processes between the stimulus and response. Such concepts as learning, intelligence, perception, motivation, need, self, personality, trait, and feeling illustrate this category.

2. See pages 60–63.

Examples:

A study of the origins of grouping practices in elementary schools in the United States to understand their basis in the past and relevance to the present; to test the hypothesis that Francis Bacon was the real author of "the works of William Shakespeare."

Characteristics:

1. Historical research depends upon data observed by others rather than by the investigator. Good data result from painstaking detective work which analyzes the authenticity, accuracy, and significance of source material.

2. Contrary to popular notions, historical research must be rigorous, systematic, and exhaustive; much "research" claiming to be historical is an undisciplined collection of inappropriate, unreliable, or biased information.

3. Historical research depends upon two kinds of data: *primary sources* where the author was a direct observer of the recorded event, and *secondary sources* where the author is reporting the observations of others and is one or more times removed from the original event. Of the two, primary sources carry the authority of firsthand evidence and have priority in data collection.

4. Two basic forms of criticism weigh the value of the data: *external criticism* which asks, "Is the document or relic authentic?" and *internal criticism* which asks, "If authentic, are the data accurate and relevant?" Internal criticism must examine the motives, biases, and limitations of the author which might cause him to exaggerate, distort, or overlook information. This critical evaluation of the data is what makes true historical research so rigorous—in many ways, more demanding than experimental methods.

5. While historical research is similar to the "reviews of the literature" which precede other forms of research, the historical approach is more exhaustive, seeking out information from a larger array of sources. It also tracks down information that is much older than required by most reviews and hunts for unpublished material not cited in the standard references.

Steps:

1. Define the problem. Ask yourself these questions: Is the historical approach best suited for this problem? Are pertinent data available? Will the findings be educationally significant?

2. State the research objectives and, if possible, the hypotheses that will give direction and focus to the research.

3. Collect the data, keeping in mind the distinction between primary and secondary sources. An important skill in historical research is note-taking—small file cards (3×5, 4×6), each containing one item of information and coded by topic, are easy to rearrange and convenient to file.

4. Evaluate the data, applying both internal and external criticism.

5. Report the findings, including a statement of the problem, a review of source material, a statement of underlying assumptions, basic hypotheses, and methods used to test the hypotheses, the findings obtained, the interpretations and conclusions reached, and a bibliography.

DESCRIPTIVE RESEARCH

Purpose: To describe systematically the facts and characteristics of a given population or area of interest, factually and accurately.

Examples:

1. A public opinion survey to assess the pre-election status of voter attitudes toward a school bond election.
2. A community survey to establish the needs for a vocational education program.
3. A study and definition of all personnel positions in an education center.
4. A report of test score results in a school district.

Characteristics:

1. Descriptive research is used in the literal sense of describing situations or events. It is the accumulation of a data base that is solely descriptive—it does not necessarily seek or explain relationships, test hypotheses, make predictions, or get at meanings and implications, although research aimed at these more powerful purposes may incorporate descriptive methods. Research authorities, however, are not in agreement on what constitutes "descriptive research" and often broaden the term to include all forms of research except historical and experimental. In this broader context, the term *survey studies* is often used to cover the examples listed above.

2. Purpose of Survey Studies:[1]
   a. To collect detailed factual information that describes existing phenomena.
   b. To identify problems or justify current conditions and practices.
   c. To make comparisons and evaluations.
   d. To determine what others are doing with similar problems or situations and benefit from their experience in making future plans and decisions.

Steps:

1. Define the objectives in clear, specific terms. What facts and characteristics are to be uncovered?
2. Design the approach. How will the data be collected? How will the subjects be selected to insure they represent the population to be described? What instruments or observation techniques are available or will need to be developed? Will the data collection methods need to be field-tested and will data gatherers need to be trained?
3. Collect the data.
4. Report the results.

---

1. Based in part on Van Dalen, D. B. *Understanding educational research* (4th ed.). New York: McGraw-Hill, 1979.

DEVELOPMENTAL RESEARCH

Purpose: To investigate patterns and sequences of growth and/or change as a function of time.

Examples:

1. Longitudinal growth studies directly measuring the nature and rate of changes in a sample of the same children at different stages of development.

2. Cross-sectional growth studies indirectly measuring the nature and rate of these same changes by drawing samples of different children from representative age levels.

3. Trend studies designed to establish patterns of change in the past in order to predict future patterns or conditions.

Characteristics:

1. Developmental research focuses on the study of variables and their development over a period of months or years. It asks, "What are the patterns of growth, their rates, their directions, their sequences, and the interrelated factors affecting these characteristics?"

2. The sampling problem in the longitudinal method is complicated by the limited number of subjects it can follow over the years; any selective factor affecting attrition biases the longitudinal study. If the threat of attrition is avoided by sampling from a stable population, this introduces unknown biases associated with such populations. Furthermore, once underway, the longitudinal method does not lend itself to improvements in techniques without losing the continuity of the procedures. Finally, this method requires the continuity of staff and financial support over an extended period of time and typically is confined to university or foundation centers that can maintain such an effort.

3. Cross-sectional studies usually include more subjects, but describe fewer growth factors than longitudinal studies. While the latter is the only direct method of studying human development, the cross-sectional approach is less expensive and faster since the actual passage of time is eliminated by sampling different subjects across age ranges. Sampling in the cross-sectional method is complicated because the same children are not involved at each age level and may not be comparable. To generalize intrinsic developmental patterns from these sequential samples of children runs the risk of confusing differences due to development with other differences between the groups that are artifacts of the sampling process.

4. Trend studies are vulnerable to unpredictable factors that modify or invalidate trends based on the past. In general, long-range prediction is an educated guess while short-range prediction is more reliable and valid.

Steps:

1. Define the problem or state the objectives.

2. Review the literature to establish a baseline of existing information and to compare research methodologies including available instruments and data collection techniques.

3. Design the approach.

4. Collect the data.

5. Evaluate the data and report the results.

CASE AND FIELD STUDY RESEARCH

Purpose: To study intensively the background, current status, and environmental interactions of a given social unit: an individual, group, institution, or community.

Examples:

1. Piaget's studies of cognitive growth in children.

2. An in-depth study of a pupil with a learning disability by a school psychologist or a student on probation by a social worker.

3. An intensive study of the "inner city" culture and living conditions in a large metropolitan environment.

4. An anthropologist's exhaustive field study of cultural life on a remote Indian reservation in the Southwest.

Characteristics:

1. Case studies are in-depth investigations of a given social unit resulting in a complete, well-organized picture of that unit. Depending upon the purpose, the scope of the study may encompass an entire life cycle or only a selected segment; it may concentrate upon specific factors or take in the totality of elements and events.

2. Compared to a survey study which tends to examine a small number of variables across a large sample of units, the case study tends to examine a small number of units across a large number of variables and conditions.

Strengths:

1. Case studies are particularly useful as background information for planning major investigations in the social sciences. Because they are intensive, they bring to light the important variables, processes, and interactions that deserve more extensive attention. They pioneer new ground and often are the source of fruitful hypotheses for further study.

2. Case study data provide useful anecdotes or examples to illustrate more generalized statistical findings.

Weaknesses:

1. Because of their narrow focus on a few units, case studies are limited in their representativeness. They do not allow valid generalizations to the population from which their units came until the appropriate follow-up research is accomplished, focusing on specific hypotheses and using proper sampling methods.

2. Case studies are particularly vulnerable to subjective biases. The case itself may be selected because of its dramatic, rather than typical, attributes; or because it neatly fits the researchers preconceptions. To the extent selective judgments rule certain data in or out, or assign a high or low value to their significance, or place them in one context rather than another, subjective interpretation is influencing the outcome.

Steps:

1. State the objectives. What is the unit of study and what characteristics, relationships, and processes will direct the investigation?

2. Design the approach. How will the units be selected? What sources of data are available? What data collection methods will be used?

3. Collect the data.

4. Organize the information to form a coherent, well-integrated reconstruction of the unit of study.
5. Report the results and discuss their significance.

CORRELATIONAL RESEARCH

Purpose: To investigate the extent to which variations in one factor correspond with variations in one or more other factors based on correlation coefficients.

Examples:
1. A study investigating the relationship between grade point average as the criterion variable and a number of other variables of interest.
2. A factor-analytic study of several personality tests.
3. A study to predict success in graduate school based on intercorrelation patterns for undergraduate variables.

Characteristics:
1. Appropriate where variables are very complex and/or do not lend themselves to the experimental method and controlled manipulation.
2. Permits the measurement of several variables and their interrelationships simultaneously and in a realistic setting.
3. Gets at the degrees of relationship rather than the all-or-nothing question posed by experimental design: "Is an effect present or absent?"
4. Among its limitations are the following:
   a. It only identifies what goes with what—it does not necessarily identify cause-and-effect relationships.
   b. It is less rigorous than the experimental approach because it exercises less control over the independent variables.
   c. It is prone to identify spurious relational patterns or elements which have little or no reliability or validity.
   d. The relational patterns are often arbitrary and ambiguous.
   e. It encourages a "shot-gun" approach to research, indiscriminately throwing in data from miscellaneous sources and defying any meaningful or useful interpretation.

Steps:
1. Define the problem.
2. Review the literature.
3. Design the approach:
   a. Identify the relevant variables.
   b. Select appropriate subjects.
   c. Select or develop appropriate measuring instruments.
   d. Select the correlational approach that fits the problem.
4. Collect the data.
5. Analyze and interpret the results.

CAUSAL-COMPARATIVE RESEARCH [1]

Purpose: To investigate possible cause-and-effect relationships by observing some existing consequence and searching back through the data for plausible causal factors. This is in contrast to the experimental method which collects its data under controlled conditions in the present.

Examples:

1. To identify factors characterizing persons having either high or low accident rates, using data in insurance company records.

2. To determine the attributes of effective teachers as defined, for example, by their performance evaluations and other data in the personal files. Teacher records over the past ten years are then examined, comparing these data to the amount of summer school attendance or to each of several other factors.

3. To look for patterns of behavior and achievement associated with age differences at the time of school entrance, using descriptive data on behavior and achievement test scores in the cumulative pupil records of children currently in the sixth grade.

Principal Characteristics:

Causal-comparative research is "ex post facto" in nature, which means the data are collected after all the events of interest have occurred. The investigator then takes one or more effects (dependent variables) and examines the data by going back through time, seeking out causes, relationships, and their meanings.

Strengths:

1. The causal-comparative method is appropriate in many circumstances where the more powerful experimental method is not possible:
   a. When it is not always possible to select, control, and manipulate the factors necessary to study cause-and-effect relations directly.
   b. When the control of all variations except a single independent variable may be highly unrealistic and artificial, preventing the normal interaction with other influential variables.
   c. When laboratory controls for many research purposes would be impractical, costly, or ethically questionable.

   Note: The *experimental method* involves both an experimental and a control group. Some treatment "A" is given the experimental group, and the result "B" is observed. The control group is not exposed to "A" and their condition is compared to the experimental group to see what effects "A" might have had in producing "B." In the *causal-comparative method*, the investigator reverses this process, observing a result "B" which already exists and searches back through several possible causes ("A" type of events) that are related to "B."

2. It yields useful information concerning the nature of phenomena: what goes with what, under what conditions, in what sequences and patterns, and the like.

---

1. The authors are indebted to Van Dalen, D. B. *Understanding educational research* (4th ed.). New York: McGraw-Hill, 1979, for much of this material.

3. Improvements in techniques, statistical methods, and designs with partial control features, in recent years, have made these studies more defensible.

Weaknesses:

1. The main weakness of any ex post facto design is the lack of control over independent variables. Within the limits of selection, the investigator must take the facts as he finds them with no opportunity to arrange the conditions or manipulate the variables that influenced the facts in the first place. To reach sound conclusions, the investigator must consider all the other possible reasons or *plausible rival hypotheses* which might account for the results obtained. To the extent that he can successfully justify his conclusions against these other alternatives, he is in a position of relative strength.
2. The difficulty in being certain that the relevant causative factor is actually included among the many factors under study.
3. The complication that no single factor is the cause of an outcome but some combination and interaction of factors go together under certain conditions to yield a given outcome.
4. A phenomenon may result not only from multiple causes but also from one cause in one instance and from another cause in another instance.
5. When a relationship between two variables is discovered, determining which is the cause and which the effect may be difficult.
6. The fact that two, or more, factors are related does not necessarily imply a cause-and-effect relationship. They all simply may be related to an additional factor not recognized or observed.
7. Classifying subjects into dichotomous groups (e.g., "Achievers" and "Nonachievers"), for the purpose of comparison, is fraught with problems, since categories like these are vague, variable, and transitory. Such investigations often do not yield useful findings.
8. Comparative studies in natural situations do not allow controlled selection of subjects. Locating existing groups of subjects who are similar in all respects except for their exposure to one variable is extremely difficult.

Steps:

1. Define the problem.
2. Survey the literature.
3. State the hypotheses.
4. List the assumptions upon which the hypotheses and procedures will be based.
5. Design the approach:
    a. Select appropriate subjects and source materials.
    b. Select or construct techniques for collecting the data.
    c. Establish categories for classifying data that are unambiguous, appropriate for the purpose of the study, and capable of bringing out significant likenesses or relationships.
6. Validate the data-gathering techniques.
7. Describe, analyze, and interpret the findings in clear, precise terms.

TRUE EXPERIMENTAL RESEARCH

Purpose: To investigate possible cause-and-effect relationships by exposing one or more experimental groups to one or more treatment conditions and comparing the results to one or more control groups not receiving the treatment.

Examples:

1. To investigate the effects of two methods of teaching a twelfth grade history program as a function of class size (large and small) and levels of student intelligence (high, average, low), using random assignment of teachers and students-by-intelligence-level to method and class size.

2. To investigate the effects of a new drug abuse prevention program on the attitudes of junior high school students using experimental and control groups who are either exposed or not exposed to the program, respectively, and using a pretest-posttest design in which only half of the students randomly receive the pretest to determine how much of an attitude change can be attributed to pretesting or to the educational program.

3. To investigate the effects of two methods of pupil evaluation on the performance of children in the twenty-three elementary schools of a given suburban district. N in this study would be the number of classrooms, rather than children, and the method would be assigned by stratified random techniques such that there would be a balanced distribution of the two methods to classrooms across grade levels and socio-economic locations of schools.

Characteristics of Experimental Designs:

1. Requires rigorous management of experimental variables and conditions either by direct control/manipulation or through randomization. (See pages 80–81.)

2. Typically uses a control group as a baseline against which to compare the group(s) receiving the experimental treatment.

3. Concentrates on the control of variance:[1,2]
   a. To maximize the variance of the variable(s) associated with the research hypotheses.
   b. To minimize the variance of extraneous or "unwanted" variables that might affect the experimental outcomes, but are not themselves the object of study.
   c. To minimize the error or random variance, including so-called errors of measurement.
   Best solution: Random selection of subjects, random assignment of subjects to groups, and random assignment of experimental treatments to groups.

4. Internal validity is the *sine qua non* of research design and the first objective of experimental methodology. It asks the question: Did the experimental manipulation *in this particular study* really make a difference? (See pages 60–61.)

---

1. Based on Kerliner, Fred N. *Foundations of Behavioral Research.* New York: Holt, Rinehart, and Winston, 1973.

2. See page 80 for a discussion of the control of variance.

5. External validity is the second objective of experimental methodology. It asks the question: How *representative* are the findings and can the results be *generalised* to similar circumstances and subjects? (See pages 62–63.)

6. In classic experimental design, all variables of concern are held constant except a single treatment variable which is deliberately manipulated or allowed to vary. Advances in methodology such as factorial designs and the analysis of variance now allow the experimenter to permit more than one variable to be manipulated or varied concurrently across more than one experimental group. This permits the simultaneous determination of (1) the effects of the principal independent variables (treatments), (2) the variation associated with classificatory variables, and (3) the interaction of selected combinations of independent and/or classificatory variables. (See page 44.)

7. While the experimental approach is the most powerful because of the control it allows over relevant variables, it is also the most restrictive and artificial. This is a major weakness in applications involving human subjects in real world situations, since human beings often act differently if their behavior is artifically restricted, manipulated, or exposed to systematic observation and evaluation.[1]

Seven Steps in Experimental Research:[2]

1. Survey the literature relating to the problem.
2. Identify and define the problem.
3. Formulate a problem hypothesis, deducing the consequences, and defining basic terms and variables.
4. Construct an experimental plan:
    a. Identify all nonexperimental variables that might contaminate the experiment, and determine how to control them.
    b. Select a research design.
    c. Select a sample of subjects to represent a given population, assign subjects to groups, and assign experimental treatments to groups.
    d. Select or construct and validate instruments to measure the outcome of the experiment.
    e. Outline procedures for collecting the data, and possibly conduct a pilot or "trial run" test to perfect the instruments or design.
    f. State the statistical or null hypothesis.
5. Conduct the experiments.
6. Reduce the raw data in a manner that will produce the best appraisal of the effect which is presumed to exist.
7. Apply an appropriate test of significance to determine the confidence one can place on the results of the study.

---

1. The debate between experimental precision versus its artificiality, on the one hand, and between naturalistic realism versus its imprecision, on the other, is largely a matter of appreciating what is possible and appropriate in a given set of circumstances. Both can make valuable contributions and the strengths of one often counterbalance the weaknesses of the other.

2. Van Dalen, D. B. and Meyer, W. J. *Understanding Educational Research.* New York: McGraw-Hill, 1966 (Rev.).

QUASI-EXPERIMENTAL RESEARCH[1]

Purpose: To approximate the conditions of the true experiment in a setting which does not allow the control and/or manipulation of all relevant variables. The researcher must clearly understand what compromises exist in the internal and external validity of his design and proceed within these limitations.

Examples:

1. To investigate the effects of spaced versus massed practice in the memorizing of vocabulary lists in four high school foreign language classes without being able to assign students to the treatment at random or to supervise closely their practice periods.

2. To assess the effectiveness of three approaches to teaching basic principles and concepts in economics to primary grade children when some of the teachers inadvertently were allowed to volunteer for one of the approaches because of its impressive-looking materials.

3. Educational research involving a pretest-posttest design in which such variables as maturation, effects of testing, statistical regression, selective attrition, and stimulus novelty or adaptation, are unavoidable or overlooked.

4. Most studies of the social problems of delinquency, rioting, smoking, or instances of heart disease, where control and manipulation are not always feasible.

Characteristics:

1. Quasi-experimental research typically involves applied settings where it is not possible to control all the relevant variables but only some of them. The researcher gets as close to the true experimental rigor as conditions allow, carefully qualifying the important exceptions and limitations. Therefore, this research is characterized by methods of partial control based on a careful identification of factors influencing both internal and external validity listed on pages 59–63.

2. The distinction between true and quasi-experimental research is tenuous, particularly where human subjects are involved as in education. A careful study of the paradigms presented on pages 63–76 will clarify the relative nature of this distinction as a matter of approximation on a continuum between "one shot case studies" of an action research nature to experimental-control group designs with randomization and rigorous management of all foreseeable variables influencing internal and external validity.

3. While action research (see opposite page) can have quasi-experimental status, it is often so unformalized as to deserve separate recognition. Once the research plan systematically examines the validity question, moving out of the intuitive and exploratory realm, the beginnings of experimental methodology are visible.

Steps in Quasi-experimental Research: The same as with true experimental research, carefully recognizing each limitation to the internal and external validity of the design.

---

1. The term "quasi-experimental" was first introduced into the literature in 1957 by Donald T. Campbell and reiterated in subsequent work with Julian C. Stanley.

ACTION RESEARCH

Purpose: To develop new skills or new approaches and to solve problems with direct application to the classroom or working world setting.

Examples: An inservice training program to help train counselors to work more effectively with minority group children; to develop an exploratory program in accident prevention in a driver's education course; to solve the problem of apathy in a required high school "orientation" class; to test a fresh approach to interesting more students in taking vocational education courses.

Characteristics:

1. Practical and directly relevant to an actual situation in the working world. The subjects are the classroom students, the staff, or others with whom you are primarily involved.
2. Provides an orderly framework for problem-solving and new developments that is superior to the impressionistic, fragmentary approach that otherwise typifies developments in education. It also is empirical in the sense that it relies on actual observations and behavioral data, and does not fall back on subjective committee "studies" or opinions of people based on their past experience.
3. Flexible and adaptive, allowing changes during the trial period and sacrificing control in favor of responsiveness and on-the-spot experimentation and innovation.
4. While attempting to be systematic, action research lacks scientific rigor because its internal and external validity is weak (see pages 59–63). Its objective is situational, its sample is restricted and unrepresentative, and it has little control over independent variables. Hence, its findings, while useful within the practical dimensions of the situation, do not directly contribute to the general body of educational knowledge.

Steps:

1. Define the problem or set the goal. What is it that needs improvement or that might be developed as a new skill or solution?
2. Review the literature to learn whether others have met similar problems or achieved related objectives.
3. Formulate testable hypotheses or strategies of approach, stating them in clear, specific, pragmatic language.
4. Arrange the research setting and spell out the procedures and conditions. What are the particular things you will do in an attempt to meet your objectives?
6. Establish evaluation criteria, measurement techniques, and other means of acquiring useful feedback.
6. Analyze the data and evaluate the outcomes.

DIFFERENCES AMONG FORMAL EDUCATIONAL RESEARCH, ACTION RESEARCH, AND THE CASUAL APPROACH TO PROBLEM SOLVING IN EDUCATION[1]

Area	Formal Educational Research	Action Research	Casual or "Common Sense" Approach
1. Training required	Extensive training in measurement, statistics, and research methods is needed. Much of the scientific research done in education is weak because of deficiencies of the researchers in these areas.	Only a limited training in statistics and research methods is needed because rigorous design and analysis are not usually necessary. More training in educational measurement is needed than most teachers possess. Even if teacher's research skills are low, good action research can be carried out with the aid of a consultant.	No training is needed. This is the same method used since pre-historic times to achieve faulty solutions to ill defined problems.
2. Goals	To obtain knowledge that will be generalizable to a broad population and to develop and test educational theories.	To obtain knowledge that can be applied directly to the local classroom situation, and to give the participating teachers inservice training.	To make changes in the current procedure that appear likely to improve the situation.
3. Locating the research problem	Problems identified by a wide range of methods. Research worker must understand the problem, but is usually not directly involved in it.	Problems identified in the school situation that are causing the research worker trouble or are interfering with the efficiency of his teaching.	Problems identified in same manner as action research.
4. Hypotheses	Highly specific hypotheses are developed that employ operational definitions and are testable.	A specific statement of the problem usually serves as the research hypothesis. Ideally, action research hypotheses should approach rigor of formal research.	Specific hypotheses not established. Participants rarely progress beyond a fuzzy and ill-defined concept concerning the nature of the problem.

1. From Borg, Walter R., *Educational Research.* New York: David McKay Company, 1963, pp. 319–322. By permission.

DIFFERENCES AMONG FORMAL EDUCATIONAL RESEARCH, ACTION RESEARCH, AND THE CASUAL APPROACH TO PROBLEM SOLVING IN EDUCATION (cont.)[1]

Area	Formal Educational Research	Action Research	Casual or "Common Sense" Approach
5. Review of the literature	An extensive review of primary source material is usually carried out, giving the research worker a thorough understanding of the current state of knowledge in the research area. This enables him to build upon the knowledge accumulated by others.	A review of available secondary sources gives the teacher a general understanding of the area to be studied. Exhaustive review of primary sources is almost never done.	Usually no review of the literature is carried out, although one or two secondary sources may be checked.
6. Sampling	Research worker attempts to obtain a random or otherwise unbiased sample of the population being studied, but is usually not completely successful.	Pupils available in the class of the teacher or teachers doing the research are used as subjects.	Some casual observation of pupil behavior may be made by the teacher after the change decided upon has been in effect for a while.
7. Experimental design	Design is carefully planned in detail prior to start of the study and adhered to as closely as possible. Major attention is given to maintaining comparable conditions and reducing error and bias. Control of extraneous variables is important.	Procedures are planned in general terms prior to start of study. Changes are made during the study if they seem likely to improve the teaching situation. Little attention is paid to control of the experimental conditions or reduction of error. Because participating teachers are ego-involved in the research situation, bias is usually present.	If classroom testing of the decision is attempted, procedures are planned only in the most general terms. No attempt is made to establish common definitions or procedures among participating teachers.

1. From Borg, Walter R., *Educational Research*. New York: David McKay Company, 1963, pp. 319–322. By permission.

DIFFERENCES AMONG FORMAL EDUCATIONAL RESEARCH, ACTION RESEARCH, AND THE CASUAL APPROACH TO PROBLEM SOLVING IN EDUCATION (cont.)[1]

Area	Formal Educational Research	Action Research	Casual or "Common Sense" Approach
8. Measurement	An effort is made to obtain the most valid measures available. A thorough evaluation of available measures and a trial of these measures usually precedes their use in the research.	Less rigorous evaluation of measures than in scientific research. Participants often lack training in the use and evaluation of educational measures, but can do a satisfactory job with help of a consultant.	Usually no evaluation is made except for the casual observations of the teachers participating. The teacher's opinion as to whether the new procedure is an improvement or not depends almost entirely on whether the teacher approves the change.
9. Analysis of data	Complex analysis often called for. Inasmuch as generalizability of results is a goal, statistical significance is usually emphasized	Simple analysis procedures usually are sufficient. Practical significance rather than statistical significance is emphasized. Subjective opinion of participating teachers is often weighted heavily.	Subjective opinion of the participants is usually the only procedure used. No attempt made at objective analysis.
10. Application of results	Results are generalizable, but many useful findings are not applied in educational practice. Differences in training and experience between research workers and teachers generate a serious communication problem.	Findings are applied immediately to the classes of participating teachers and often lead to permanent improvement. Application of results beyond the participating teachers is usually slight.	Decisions reached are applied immediately in classes of participating teachers. Even if the decision leads to improvement, it is often changed later because no evidence is available to support its continuance. This approach leads to educational fads and "change for the sake of change."

1. From Borg, Walter R., *Educational Research.* New York: David McKay Company, 1963, pp. 319–322. By permission.

OVERVIEW: INTERNAL AND EXTERNAL VALIDITY IN AN EXPERIMENTAL DESIGN[1]

Internal Validity asks the question: did, in fact, the experimental treatments make a difference *in this specific instance?* *External Validity* asks the question: to what populations, settings, treatment variables, and measurement variables can this effect be *generalized?* While *internal validity* is the *sine qua non*, and while the question of *external validity* like the question of inductive inference is never completely answerable, the selection of designs strong in both types of validity is obviously the ideal. This is particularly true in education, in which generalization is to applied settings of known character.

Internal Validity—Eight classes of extraneous variables which, if not controlled in the experimental design, may produce effects becoming confounded with the effect of the experimental variable:

1. HISTORY—specific events occurring between the first and second measurement in addition to the experimental variable.
2. MATURATION—processes within the subjects operating as a function of the passage of time, per se (growing older, hungrier, fatigued, or less attentive).
3. TESTING—the effects of testing upon the scores of a subsequent testing.
4. INSTRUMENTATION—changes in obtained measurement due to changes in instrument calibration or changes in the observers or judges.
5. STATISTICAL REGRESSION—a phenomenon occurring when groups have been selected on the basis of extreme scores.
6. SELECTION—biases resulting from the differential selection of subjects for the comparison groups.
7. EXPERIMENTAL MORTALITY—the differential loss of subjects from the comparison groups.
8. SELECTION-MATURATION INTERACTION, Etc.—interaction effects between the aforementioned variables which can be mistaken for the effects of the experimental variable.

External Validity (*Representativeness*)—Four jeopardizing factors:

1. INTERACTION effects of SELECTION biases and the experimental variable.
2. REACTIVE or INTERACTION effect of PRETESTING—The pretesting modifies the subject in such a way that he responds to the experimental treatment differently than will unpretested persons in the same population.
3. REACTIVE effects of experimental procedures—effects arising from the experimental setting which will not occur in nonexperimental settings.
4. MULTIPLE-TREATMENT INTERFERENCE—effects due to multiple treatments applied to the same subjects where prior treatments influence subsequent treatments in the series because their effects are not erasable.

---

1. Campbell, Donald T. and J. C. Stanley, *Experimental and Quasi-experimental Designs for Research.* Chicago: Rand McNally and Company, 1966.

INTERNAL VALIDITY[1]

When checking the internal validity of his design, an experimenter asks: Did the independent variable X really produce a change in the dependent variable? Before claiming that it did, he must make certain that some of the following extraneous variables have not produced an effect that can be mistaken for the effect of X.

1. *Contemporary history.*

   Sometimes the subjects experience an event—in or out of the experimental setting—besides the exposure to X, that may affect their dependent variable scores. If X is television instruction and the dependent variable is healthful practices of the students, the advent of an epidemic in the community rather than X may cause pupils to change some of their health practices. The simultaneous advent of the epidemic would be said to confound X. (An experimenter uses the term "confound" to indicate that an effect can be attributed to two or more variables, and the portion due to each cannot be determined.)

2. *Maturation processes.*

   Biological and psychological processes within the subjects may change during the progress of the experiment which will affect their responses. The subjects may perform better or worse on T_2 not because of the effect of X, but because they are older, more fatigued, or less interested than when they took T_1. Their age, fatigue, or interest would confound the interpretation of the effect of X.

3. *Pretesting procedures.*

   T_1 (pretest) may serve as a learning experience that will cause the subjects to alter their responses on T_2 (posttest) whether or not X is applied.

4. *Measuring instruments.*

   Changes in the testing instruments, human raters, or interviewers can affect the obtained measurements. If T_2 is more difficult than T_1, or a different person rates subjects on the rating scales, these factors rather than X can cause the difference in the two scores. Slight fluctuations in mechanical measuring instruments can also cause the difference. If the same person judges the performance of two groups in succession or the same groups before and after the application of X, his judgment may vary because he becomes more experienced and discriminating, or more fatigued and careless.

5. *Statistical regression.*

   In some educational research, particularly in remedial education, groups are selected on the basis of their extreme scores. When this selection procedure is employed, the effect of what is called "statistical regression" may be mistaken for the effect of X. Suppose that students who do exceptionally poor or exceptionally well on one test are selected to receive an experimental treatment. The mean (average score) of either of these groups will move toward the mean of the parent population on the second test whether or not X is applied. If the mean for the top ten subjects in a class is 90, the

---

1. Adapted in part from Van Dalen, D. B. *Understanding educational research* (4th ed.). New York: Mc-Graw-Hill, 1979. (Adapted from Campbell, D. T., and Stanley, J. C., *Experimental and quasi-experimental designs for research,* Rand McNally and Company, Chicago, 1966.)

scores of these subjects will fan out on the retest—some will be higher and some will be lower—but the mean of the group will be almost inevitably lower. Similarly, the mean for the lowest ten subjects on the second test will be almost inevitably higher.

Upon retesting, low initial means go up toward the population mean and high initial means go down toward the population mean. Why? Regression toward the mean occurs because of random imperfections in measuring instruments. The less-than-perfect capacity of T_1 and T_2 to measure knowledge will cause a variation of subjects' performances. Pupils are likely to vary within a given range because there is a less-than-perfect correlation between the two tests. The more deviant (extreme) pupils' scores are from the population mean, the more they are likely to vary. Random instability in the population may also account for regression toward the mean. Some subjects may obtain low scores on T_1 because they were upset or careless on that day. On the second test they may have better "luck," feel better, or strive harder to bring themselves up to their natural level. As a result, their higher scores will pull up the mean of their group on the second test.[1]

6. *Differential selection of subjects.*

If the experimental and control groups are exposed to X, a method of teaching spelling and afterward a test given, the test results may reflect a pre-X difference in the two groups rather than the effect of X. Perhaps the experimental group could spell better than the control group before X was applied.

7. *Differential experimental mortality.*

If a particular type of subject drops out of one group after the experiment is underway, this differential loss may affect the findings of the investigation. Suppose that the subject in the experimental group who receive the lowest T_1 scores drop out after taking the test. The remainder of the experimental group may show a greater gain on T_2 than the control group, not because of its exposure to X but because the low scoring subjects are missing.

8. *Interaction of selection and maturation, selection and history, etc.*

When the experimental and control groups have the same T_1 scores, some other differences between them—such as, intelligence or motivation —rather than X may cause one of them to get higher T_2 scores. Because of this type of interaction, studies that compare volunteers (self-selected groups) with nonvolunteers must always be questioned. Suppose that an experimenter locates forty children from impoverished homes who are poor readers and twenty of them volunteer to participate in a cultural enrichment program. The volunteers may improve in reading more without X and benefit more from X than the nonvolunteers because they are different initially—they are motivated more highly toward self-improvement to begin with.

---

1. If two samples are drawn randomly from *two different populations*, so that there is no pairing or matching on a one-to-one basis, statistical regression is no longer involved.

EXTERNAL VALIDITY[1]

Discussion thus far has been confined to checking the internal validity of the design. An experimenter gives this task primary consideration, but he is also concerned about external validity—the generalizability or representativeness of the experimental findings. Consequently, he asks: What relevance do the findings concerning the effect of X have beyond the confines of the experiment? To what subject populations, settings, experimental variables, and measurement variables can these findings be generalized?

When checking the design of an experiment, an experimenter may ask: Can the findings be generalized to all college students? All students attending Harvard University? All Harvard freshmen who are enrolled in a particular course? Or must the findings be limited to the particular Harvard freshmen who participated in the experiment? An experimenter can strengthen the external validity of his design if he describes the population to which the results will apply *before* he conducts the experiment. If he draws a random sample from this predetermined population (say, Harvard freshmen) and exposes the sample to X, he can make the following generalization: The effect that X had on the sample population (fifty Harvard freshmen) will be the same for the population that the sample represents (all Harvard freshmen).

An investigator is concerned not only about the generalizability of his findings with respect to a subject population, but also with respect to settings, independent variables, and measurement variables. Will the findings be representative of other geographical areas, sizes of schools, times of day, or time of year? Will the findings provide information about situations in which one X, no X, variations of X, or more than one X is present? Will the findings be representative of situations in which one or several types of criterion measurement are used?

The representativeness of the setting that is selected for an experiment will determine how extensively the findings can be applied. If the findings of a study are derived from data that are obtained in a deprived rural area, an experimenter cannot claim that they will hold true for wealthy metropolitan areas. If objective tests are used to measure the effect of a new teaching method, an experimenter cannot claim that the same effect would have been observed if essay tests or oral participation had been used as the measuring instruments.

When examining the external validity of a design, the experimenter checks the following threats to representativeness:

1. *Interaction effects of selection biases and X.*

    The characteristics of the subjects who are selected to participate in an experiment determine how extensively the findings can be generalized. A random sample of seventh-grade students from one school will not be representative of all seventh-grade students. The intelligence, socioeconomic status, or some other characteristic of these particular students may cause X to be more effective for them than for other seventh-grade students. If X is a new textbook, it may produce excellent results in Dort School where most students have high IQs. But an experimenter cannot generalize that X will produce the same results in all seventh-grade classes, for the textbook may not be equally effective in Friar School where most students have low IQs.

---

1. Adapted in part from Van Dalen, D. B. *Understanding educational research* (4th ed.). New York: McGraw-Hill, 1979. (Adapted from Campbell, D. T., and Stanley, J. C., *Experimental and quasi-experimental designs for research,* Rand McNally and Company, Chicago, 1966.)

2. *Reactive or interaction effect of pretesting.*

Giving a pretest may limit the generalizability of the experimental findings. A pretest may increase or decrease the experimental subjects sensitiveness to X: it may alert them to issues, problems, or events that they might not ordinarily notice. Consequently, these subjects may be no longer representative of the unpretested population from which they came. Suppose that fifty Harvard freshmen are exposed to X, a romantic film with a racial-prejudice theme. Their responses on T_2 may not reflect the effect of the film as much as the increased sensitivity to racial prejudice that taking T_1 produced. The effect of the film for the experimental subjects may not be representative of its effect for Harvard freshmen who see the romantic film without being pretested.

3. *Reactive effects of experimental procedures.*

The experimental procedures may also produce effects that limit the generalizability of the experimental findings. If the presence of observers and experimental equipment makes pupils and teachers aware of the fact that they are participating in an experiment, they may alter their normal behavior. If they alter the very behavior that is being measured, the experimenter cannot claim that the effect of X for the sample population will be the same for subjects who are exposed to X in nonexperimental situations.

4. *Multiple-treatment interference.*

When the same subjects are exposed repeatedly to two or more Xs, the effects of the previous Xs are not usually erasable; hence, the findings may be generalized only to persons who experience the same sequence of treatments repeatedly. If subjects are exposed to three types of music throughout the day, they may be more productive when marching music is played; but they might not respond in the same way if marching music were played continuously.

A "POOR" RESEARCH DESIGN (NO CONTROL): THE "ONE-SHOT CASE STUDY":[1]

Treatment	Posttest
X	T_2

Design procedures (using example of determining whether or not a new teaching method will increase reading speed):

1. Expose subjects to X, the new teaching method, for a given period of time.
2. Administer T_2, the posttest, to measure mean reading speed *after* exposure to X.

Internal validity:

1. Disadvantages:
    a. There is a complete absence of control and no internal validity. The "quick

---

1. Adapted in part from Van Dalen, D. B. *Understanding educational research* (4th ed.). New York: Mc-Graw-Hill, 1979. (Adapted from Campbell, D. T., and Stanley, J. C., *Experimental and quasi-experimental designs for research,* Rand McNally and Company, Chicago, 1966.)

and easy" nature of this approach, often used as a basis for a change or innovation in education, is entirely misleading.

b. No provision for comparison exists except implicitly, intuitively, and impressionistically. (*Note:* basic to science is the process of comparison and securing scientific evidence involves making at least one comparison.)

c. This approach usually involves the "error of misplaced precision,"—a great deal of care given to the collection of data about which our conclusions can only be impressionistic and imprecise.

d. The attempt to use standardized tests in lieu of a control group is misguided, since rival sources of difference other than X are so numerous as to render the standardization group useless as a "control" group.

2. Advantage: This method may be useful in exploring for researchable problems or developing ideas or devices, as in action research. It simply is not a basis from which we can reach defensible *conclusions* in research. The danger is that we will go this far, and no farther—that we will justify what we are doing in terms of impressionistic evidence alone.

DESIGN 1—(MINIMAL CONTROL): ONE-GROUP PRETEST–POSTTEST DESIGN[1]

Pretest	Treatment	Posttest
T_1	X	T_2

Design procedures—(using the example of determining whether or not a new teaching method will increase reading speed):

1. Administer T_1, the pretest, to measure mean reading speed of a single group *before* exposure to the new teaching method.

2. Expose subjects to X, the new teaching method, for a given period of time.

3. Administer T_2, the posttest, to measure mean reading speed *after* exposure to X. Compare T_1 and T_2 to determine what difference, if any, the exposure to X has made.

4. Apply an appropriate statistical test to determine whether the difference is significant.

Internal Validity

1. Advantages: the pretest provides a comparison between performances by the same group of subjects *before* and *after* exposure to X (the experimental treatment). It also provides a control for *selection* and *mortality* variables, if the same subjects take T_1 and T_2.

1. Adapted in part from Van Dalen, D. B. *Understanding educational research* (4th ed.). New York: McGraw-Hill, 1979. (Adapted from Campbell, D. T., and Stanley, J. C., *Experimental and quasi-experimental designs for research,* Rand McNally and Company, Chicago, 1966.)

2. Disadvantages:
    a. No assurance that X is the only or even the major factor in a $T_1 - T_2$ difference.
    b. Plausible rival hypotheses ("probable error"):
        (1) History—e.g., if some subjects are fitted for glasses between T_1 and T_2.
        (2) Maturation—the fact that they are growing older, or more tired, or are less enthusiastic, or less attentive.
        (3) Testing effects—the experience of T_1, by itself, may increase motivation, alter attitudes, induce learning sets, or stimulate self-pacing.
        (4) Changing effects of instrumentation—any changes in the test, its scoring, the observation or interview techniques, or calibration of an automated teaching device, that make T_1 and T_2 different events.
        (5) Statistical regression—an inevitable effect when an extreme group is being compared on pretest and posttest measures (see page 65).
        (6) Selection biases and mortality—if the same subjects did not take both T_1 and T_2, differences may be due to uncontrolled characteristics or factors related to this difference alone.

DESIGN 2—RANDOMIZED CONTROL-GROUP PRETEST–POSTTEST DESIGN[1]

Group	Pretest	Treatment	Posttest
Experimental Group (R)*	T_1	X	T_2
Control Group (R)	T_1	.	T_2

* Random assignment

Design Procedure

1. Select subjects from a population by random methods.
2. Assign subjects to groups and the treatment (X), or nontreatment $(.)$, to groups by random methods.
3. Pretest the groups on the dependent variable (T_1), finding the mean pretest score for both the experimental and control groups.
4. Keep all conditions the same for both groups, except for exposing *only* the experimental group to X, the experimental treatment (independent variable) for a specified period of time.
5. Test the groups on T_2, the dependent variable, and find the mean posttest score for both groups.

---

1. Adapted in part from Van Dalen, D. B. *Understanding educational research* (4th ed.). New York: Mc-Graw-Hill, 1979. (Adapted from Campbell, D. T., and Stanley, J. C., *Experimental and quasi-experimental designs for research,* Rand McNally and Company, Chicago, 1966.)

6. Find the difference between the T_1 and T_2 means for each group separately $(T_2 - T_1)$.

7. Compare these differences to determine whether the application of X is associated with a change favoring the experimental group over the control group (which was not exposed to X).

8. Apply an appropriate statistical test to determine whether the difference in the scores is significant—that is, if the difference is large enough to reject the null hypothesis that the difference is simply a chance occurrence.

Design 2 can be extended to the study of two or more variations of the independent variable—for example, two methods of teaching reading:

First Experimental Group (R)	T_1	X_a (Method a)	T_2
Second Experimental Group (R)	T_1	X_b (Method b)	T_2
Control Group (R)	T_1		T_2

In this case, conclusions can be reached about the differential effects of Method a and Method b, *without* the control group. However, a more powerful conclusion can be made about both methods with a control group comparison.

Internal Validity:

1. In general, internal validity gains strength in Design 2. Between-session variations (extraneous variables that occur between T_1 and T_2) are controlled since they affect both groups equally.

2. Within-session variations, however, pose problems. Such variations involve differences that the experimental and control groups may experience when they are tested and treated separately. For example, differences in room conditions, personalities of the teachers, or wording of instructions. *Solution:* test or treat subjects individually or in small groups, randomly assigning subjects, times, and places to experimental and control conditions. The effects of any unwanted situational factors are thus randomly distributed among the subgroups, allowing them to be ignored.

3. To control for within-session instrument differences, it is necessary also to assign mechanical instruments, teachers, observers, and raters to sessions—or preferably to a single session. Ideally, if observers or judges are involved, they should remain unaware of which groups are being used for control or experimental purposes, since they may have subtle biases that could influence their observations.

---

1. Adapted in part from Van Dalen, D. B. *Understanding educational research* (4th ed.). New York: McGraw-Hill, 1979. (Adapted from Campbell, D. T., and Stanley, J. C., *Experimental and quasi-experimental designs for research,* Rand McNally and Company, Chicago, 1966.)

Assignment

4. *Differential selection* is controlled by random selection methods, *maturation* and *pretesting* effects occur equally for all groups, *differential mortality* can be assessed for nonrandom patterns, and *statistical regression* is controlled when extreme scorers from the same population are randomly assigned to groups (statistical regression will occur but it will occur equally with all groups).

External validity: Do the results allow valid generalizations to other persons and situations for which the subjects and settings of this study are presumably representative? More specifically, can extraneous variables interact with the experimental treatment and make the subjects unrepresentative of the population from which they were selected? Can the claim be made that the effect which X had on the subjects will be the same for other members of the population who did not participate in the experiment?

1. *Interaction* of *pretesting* and X—Design 2 does not control for this possibility. If the pretesting somehow sensitizes or alters the subject so that he responds to X differently than if no pretesting had taken place, then the external validity will have been compromised. (See Design 3 for solution.)

2. *Interaction* of *selection* and X—If the subjects in the experiment are different in any particular way from persons to whom one wishes to generalize, biased influences can arise. If subjects are from a university community, or if they come from only a few schools that were willing to cooperate out of many schools approached, subtle factors can enter the picture which compromise the generalization.

3. Interaction of X with such factors as *history* can compromise external validity. If an experiment coincides with a dramatic event or an atypical condition (e.g., war, depression, scandal, and local strife) subjects may respond to X differently than during normal circumstances.

4. The *reactive effects* of *experimental procedures* may hamper generalization. If subjects know they are in an experiment they may react differently (put forth unusual effort or cooperate to an unnatural degree.) Solution: either avoid letting the subjects know they are in an experiment or treat both the experimental and control groups with equal attention so that they are unable to distinguish which is which. Many times T_1 and T_2 measures can be part of routine school testing or evaluation with X presented as part of the normal instructional or counseling program. The question of ethical practices must, of course, be carefully examined and proper authorization secured in advance.

---

1. Adapted in part from Van Dalen, D. B. *Understanding educational research* (4th ed.). New York: Mc-Graw-Hill, 1979. (Adapted from Campbell, D. T., and Stanley, J. C., *Experimental and quasi-experimental designs for research,* Rand McNally and Company, Chicago, 1966.)

DESIGN 3—RANDOMIZED SOLOMON FOUR-GROUP DESIGN[1]

Group	Pretest	Treatment	Posttest	Difference*
1—Pretested (R)**	T_1	X	T_2	$1D = T_1, X, M, H$
2—Pretested (R)	T_1	.	T_2	$2D = T_1, M, H$
3—Unpretested (R)		X	T_2	$3D = X, M, H$
4—Unpretested (R)		.	T_2	$4D = M, H$

* D—The difference between T_1 and T_2 mean scores represents the effects of various combinations of variables, such as: pretesting T_1, independent variable X, history H, maturation M. To find *the effect of X alone*, subtract $4D$ from $3D$. To find *the effect of pretesting alone*, subtract $4D$ from $2D$. To find *the effect of the interaction of pretesting and X*, add $2D$ and $3D$ and subtract the sum for $1D$.

** (R): Random assignment.

Design 3 overcomes the external validity weakness in Design 2. When pretesting may affect the subjects in an experiment such that they become sensitized to X in a way that they respond differently than unpretested subjects, external validity is compromised and one cannot generalize the experimental findings from the sample to the population. Design 3 solves this problem by adding two "Unpretested" groups (3 and 4) to the study.

Design 3 requires that the subjects be assigned at random to the four groups. The random assignment of subjects makes it possible to assume that the pretest scores for groups 3 and 4 would have been similar to the pretest scores attained by groups 1 and 2. But since groups 3 and 4 are not pretested, no interaction between X and the effects of T_1 can be reflected in their T_1 scores.

Design validity—Design 3 permits the control and measurement of both (1) the *main effects of pretesting* and (2) the *interaction effects* of *pretesting* and X. Furthermore, the combined effects of *maturation* and *history* can be measured if the T_2 mean for group 4 is compared with the T_2 means. This design actually amounts to doing the experiment twice (once with pretests and once without). Consequently, if the results of the "two experiments" are consistent, greater confidence can be placed in the findings than would otherwise be possible.

Supplementary matching procedures may be used with Designs 3 and 4. If matching is employed, the subjects are matched on some factor other than the dependent variable. If T_1 and T_2 are reading achievement tests, for example, the matching may be done on IQ scores, but not the reading scores. In general, matching without random assignment is not recommended.

---

1. Adapted in part from Van Dalen, D. B. *Understanding educational research* (4th ed.). New York: McGraw-Hill, 1979. (Adapted from Campbell, D. T., and Stanley, J. C., *Experimental and quasi-experimental designs for research,* Rand McNally and Company, Chicago, 1966.)

DESIGN 4—RANDOMIZED CONTROL-GROUP POSTTEST ONLY DESIGN[1]

	Pretest	Treatment	Posttest
Experimental Group $(R)*$		X	T_2
Control Group (R)		.	T_2

* Random assignment

Design Procedures—Design 4 consists of the last two groups in the Solomon design: the two unpretested groups.

As in all rigorously controlled designs, prior to the application of X the subjects are assigned at random to the experimental and control groups. Why can the experimenter omit the pretest? Because randomization techniques permit him to declare that at the time of assignment the groups were equal. The probability theory tells him to what extent the randomly assigned subjects in the two groups might have been expected to differ by chance on T_1, and the test of significance takes account of such chance differences.

After the subjects are assigned at random to groups, the experimental group is exposed to X, such as a film with a racial-prejudice theme, and the control group is not. During or after the exposure to X, the two groups are tested for the first time. Their scores are compared to ascertain the effect of X, and an appropriate test of significance is applied to determine whether this difference is greater than might have occurred by chance.

Design validity—Design 4 is superior to Design 2 because no interaction effect of pretesting and X can occur. Groups are assumed to be equivalent on the basis of random selection. It controls for, but does not measure the effects of, history, maturation and pretesting. It is particularly useful when pretests are unavailable, inconvenient, or too costly; when subjects anonymity must be kept; and when a pretest may interact with X. (Note: Design 2 is superior to Design 4 when the sample size is small and a check on equivalence is appropriate. Also, if T_1 information is routinely available, Design 2 is probably preferable.)

DESIGN 5—NONRANDOMIZED CONTROL-GROUP PRETEST-POSTTEST DESIGN[1]

	Pretest	Treatment	Posttest
Experimental Group	T_1	X	T_2
Control Group	T_1	.	T_2

Design Procedures—Same as Design 2, except subjects are not assigned to groups at random. Preassembled groups that are as similar as availability permits are selected and are given pretests. Pretest means and standard deviations are then compared for similarity.

---

1. Adapted in part from Van Dalen, D. B. *Understanding educational research* (4th ed.). New York: Mc-Graw-Hill, 1979. (Adapted from Campbell, D. T., and Stanley, J. C., *Experimental and quasi-experimental designs for research,* Rand McNally and Company, Chicago, 1966.)

Internal Validity:

1. Fairly satisfactory if groups have similar means and standard deviations on pretest.

2. Control group insures against mistaking effects of history, pretesting, maturation, and instrumentation, for the main-effects of X.

3. Differences in within-session history and instrumentation can be sources of contamination, if not carefully checked, however.

4. Mortality effects are controlled by checking pretest and posttest records.

5. Main threats to internal validity arise from interaction between such variables as selection and maturation, selection and history, or selection and testing. In the absence of randomization, the possibility always exists that some critical difference, not reflected in the pretest, is operating to contaminate the posttest data. For example, if the experimental group consists of volunteers, they may be more highly motivated; or if they happen to have a different experience background which affects how they interact with the experimental treatment—such factors rather than X by itself, may account for the differences.

6. Statistical regression can be avoided but should be checked. For example, if two different schools have substantially different means on a criterion test, one might match students from both schools to insure a sample of "equal" ability so that the lower school is not "penalized." However, on the posttest, both groups will regress toward the mean of their respective schools, creating an artificial difference.

External Validity: The same general questions apply here as with Design 2. Design 5 has some practical advantages, since it deals with intact classes and does not disrupt the school's program. By involving a wide variety of classes from several settings it is possible to achieve an even higher degree of external validity. This is especially true for *interaction* of *selection* and X. The *reactive effects of experimental procedures* may hamper generalizations, but to a lesser extent than in Design 2. Conducting an authorized experiment without the subjects being aware of it is easier with intact classes than when subjects are assigned at random to treatment groups.

---

1. Adapted in part from Van Dalen, D. B. *Understanding educational research* (4th ed.). New York: McGraw-Hill, 1979. (Adapted from Campbell, D. T., and Stanley, J. C., *Experimental and quasi-experimental designs for research,* Rand McNally and Company, Chicago, 1966.)

DESIGN 6—COUNTERBALANCED DESIGN[1]

Application: when random assignment of subjects is not possible and intact groups must be used. Advantages over Design 5: when a limited number of subjects is available, no pretest is given, and more than one variation of X is tested.

Treatment Variations

Replication	X_a	X_b	X_c	X_d
1	A	B	C	D
2	B	D	A	C
3	C	A	D	B
4	D	C	B	A

Column Mean Scores:

Design Procedures:

1. Each group of subjects (A, B, C, or D) is exposed to each variation of X (or absence of X, if a control group is used) at different times during the experiment. In the above example, there are four variations of X applied to four different groups in such a way that: (a) a different X is presented to each group each time, and (b) each X precedes and follows each other X an equal number of times.

2. After all the experimental sessions are completed, the column mean for each variation of X is computed. A column mean represents the average score for all groups when exposed to the particular X in the column heading. A comparison of these column mean scores reveals what effect the different Xs have upon group performance.

Design Validity:

1. Design 6 controls for weakness inherent in Design 5—namely, the possibility that the nonrandomized groups might not be equivalent in all important respects, introducing differences that are mistaken for the effects of X. The Counterbalanced Design rotates out these subjects' differences by exposing all variations of X to all groups, at the same time controlling for order-of-presentation effects. If one group happens to be more intelligent than the others, each X will profit from this superiority.

2. Interaction effects can contaminate the findings if, for example, one group fatigues dramatically on one trial (*selection-maturation interaction*), or if the interaction for

---

1. Adapted in part from Van Dalen, D. B. *Understanding educational research* (4th ed.). New York: Mc-Graw-Hill, 1979. (Adapted from Campbell, D. T., and Stanley, J. C., *Experimental and quasi-experimental designs for research,* Rand McNally and Company, Chicago, 1966.)

some reason affects a different group each time over several replications.

3. Primary weakness of Design 6 for education: does not control for the effect of an exposure to one X if it carries over and combines with measurements of the next X. When the possibility of carry-over effects exists, sufficient time should elapse between replications to permit these effects to dissipate. If the assumption that there are no residual or carry-over effects operating cannot be satisfied, Design 6 will not be appropriate. (Example of carry-over effects: In a drug experiment, the effect of a given drug may remain in the body and combine with the effect of a subsequent drug. The measurement of the effect of the second drug is now contaminated by the first. Another illustration highly relevant to education is the transfer of training effect where cognitive processes are involved.)

DESIGN 7—ONE-GROUP TIME-SERIES DESIGN[1]

This design is the same as Design 1, except that several measurements are taken before and after the introduction of X:

	Pretest			Treatment	Posttest			
T_1	T_2	T_3	T_4	X	T_5	T_6	T_7	T_8

Internal Validity:

1. The several tests given over a period of time provide more control over possible sources of internal invalidity than Design 1. If, for example, there is no appreciable difference in the first four T scores, the difference between the T_4 and T_5 scores cannot reasonably be due to *maturation, testing,* or *regression.* Changes in *instrumentation,* or effects of *selection* or *mortality* can be largely controlled, or accounted for, also.

2. The chief potential source of internal invalidity is *contemporary history*—for instance, the coincidence (with X) of some influential event such as the simultaneous appearance of a televised program related to the experimental instruction, an environmental change (such as weather, public scandal) or cyclic variation (e.g., weekend, end-of-semester examinations). The role of such factors must be carefully observed and assessed.

External Validity:

1. Generalization of findings of Design 7 depends upon the experimental conditions. An *interaction* between *pretesting* and X can occur if the pretesting introduces factors which somehow modify the subjects so that they are no longer representative of the population from which they were drawn. Atypical tests, for example, might induce an attitude or set in the subjects which will never be experienced by the general population of subjects. Standardized achievement tests, on the other hand, are common experiences to nearly all subjects.

---

1. Adapted in part from Van Dalen, D. B. *Understanding educational research* (4th ed.). New York: McGraw-Hill, 1979. (Adapted from Campbell, D. T., and Stanley, J. C., *Experimental and quasi-experimental designs for research,* Rand McNally and Company, Chicago, 1966.)

2.   A *selection-X interaction* can occur if not carefully avoided. For example, if the subjects are volunteers, or come from groups with special characteristics, or if the repetition of the unique *T*s cause selective absenteeism, they may not represent the general population of possible subjects.

DESIGN 8—CONTROL-GROUP TIME-SERIES DESIGN[1]

Design 8 follows from Design 7 by simply adding a control group, thus controlling for the effects of *contemporary history*, the main weakness within Design 7. If the control group fails to show a gain from T_4 to T_5 and the experimental group yields a gain, the plausibility of some contemporary event accounting for the gain is greatly reduced, since both groups have experienced this particular event.

	Pretest				Treatment	Posttest			
Experimental Group:	T_1	T_2	T_3	T_4	X	T_5	T_6	T_7	T_8
Control Group:	T_1	T_2	T_3	T_4	$\cdot$	T_5	T_6	T_7	T_8

This design is also superior to Design 5 by controlling for *selection-maturation interaction*. If one group shows a greater rate of gain than the other, this accelerated gain would also appear in the pre-*X* testing.

The multiple posttests employed in Designs 7 and 8 can be the source of vital information that a single posttest design will not reveal. For instance, if *X* is a short-term influence which tends to disappear with time, these designs will pick up this trend. Or, one variation of *X* may have strong but *short-term* effects while another variation of *X* may have mild but *long-term* effects.

An alternative design strategy to control for the effects of maturation, pretesting, regression, and contemporary history (Cf. Design 8) begins with several groups which are pretested at the same time but which are posttested at different intervals of time:

Group A:	T_1	X	T_2		
Group B:	T_1	X		T_2	
Group C:	T_1	X			T_2
Group D:	T_1	X			T_2
Group E:	T_1	X			T_2

By adding a control group with the same pretest and posttest pattern, but without the treatment, the effects of the treatment can be assessed. This strategy is particularly appropriate where maturational factors are involved and where the effects of serial testing within groups should be minimized.

---

1.   Adapted in part from Van Dalen, D. B. *Understanding educational research* (4th ed.). New York: McGraw-Hill, 1979. (Adapted from Campbell, D. T., and Stanley, J. C., *Experimental and quasi-experimental designs for research,* Rand McNally and Company, Chicago, 1966.)

A COMPARISON OF THE EIGHT EXPERIMENTAL DESIGNS

DESIGN 1
One-Group Pretest-Posttest

$$T_1 \quad X \quad T_2$$

DESIGN 2
Control-Group Pretest-Posttest

$$E_R \quad T_1 \quad X \quad T_2$$
$$C_R \quad T_1 \quad . \quad T_2$$

DESIGN 3
Randomized Solomon Four-Group Design

$$E_{R_1} \quad T_1 \quad X \quad T_2$$
$$C_{R_1} \quad T_1 \quad . \quad T_2$$
$$\overline{\phantom{C_{R_2}}}$$
$$C_{R_2} \qquad \quad X \quad T_2$$
$$C_{R_2} \qquad \quad . \quad T_2$$

DESIGN 4
Randomized Control-Group Posttest Only

$$E_R \quad X \quad \quad T_2$$
$$C_R \quad . \quad T_2$$

DESIGN 5
Nonrandomized Control-Group Pretest-Posttest

$$E \quad T_1 \quad X \quad T_2$$
$$C \quad T_1 \quad . \quad T_2$$

DESIGN 6
"Counterbalanced" Treatments

	X_a	X_b	X_c	X_d
1	A^*	B	C	D
2	B	D	A	C
3	C	A	D	B
4	D	C	B	A

* A, B, C, and D represent each of four *groups* of subjects, respectively.

DESIGN 7
One-Group Time-Series

$$T_1 \; T_2 \; T_3 \; T_4 \; X \; T_5 \; T_6 \; T_7 \; T_8$$

DESIGN 8
Control-Group Time-Series

$$T_1 \; T_2 \; T_3 \; T_4 \; X \; T_5 \; T_6 \; T_7 \; T_8$$
$$T_1 \; T_2 \; T_3 \; T_4 \; . \; T_5 \; T_6 \; T_7 \; T_8$$

LEGEND:
X—Experimental treatment (independent variable)
X_a, X_b, X_c, X_d (Design 6)—Treatment variations
.—No treatment
T_1—Pretest (Designs 1–5)
T_2—Posttest (Designs 1–5)
T_1, T_2, T_3, T_4—Pretesting (Design 7–8)
T_5, T_6, T_7, T_8—Posttesting (Designs 7–8)
E—Experimental group
C—Control group
$_R$—Random selection

Table Indicating Correspondence Between Handbook Design Designations and Notations and the Original Campbell and Stanley Design Designations and Notations*

ISAAC AND MICHAEL HANDBOOK

Design Number	Designation & Notation	Pages
1.	One-Group Pretest-Posttest $T_1 \ x \ T_2$	64-65
2	Randomized Control-Group Pretest-Posttest $E_R \ T_1 \ x \ T_2$ $C_R \ T_1 \ . \ T_2$	65-67
3	Randomized Soloman Four-Group $E_{R1} \ T_1 \ x \ T_2$ $C_{R1} \ T_1 \ . \ T_2$ $E_{R2} \quad x \ T_2$ $C_{R2} \quad . \ T_2$	68
4	Randomized Control-Group Posttest Only $E_R \quad x \ T_2$ $C_R \quad . \ T_2$	69
5.	Nonrandomized Control-Group Pretest-Posttest $E \quad T_1 \ x \ T_2$ $C \quad T_1 \ . \ T_2$	69-70
6.	Counterbalanced $x_a \ x_b \ x_c \ x_d$ 1 A B C D 2 B D A C 3 C A D B 4 D C B A	71-72
7	One-Group Time Series $T_1 \ T_2 \ T_3 \ T_4 \ T_5 \ T_6 \ T_7 \ T_8$	72-73
8.	Control-Group Time Series $T_1 \ T_2 \ T_3 \ T_4 \ x \ T_1 \ T_2 \ T_3 \ T_4$ $T_1 \ T_2 \ T_3 \ T_4 \ . \ T_5 \ T_6 \ T_7 \ T_8$	73

CAMPBELL AND STANLEY

Design Number	Designation & Notation	Pages
2.	One-Group Pretest-Posttest $O_1 \ x \ O_2$	7-12
4.	Pretest-Posttest Control Group $RO_1 \ x \ O_2$ $RO_2 \quad O_4$	13-24
5.	Soloman Four-Group $R \ O_1 \ x \ O_2$ $R \ O_3 \quad O_4$ $R \quad x \ O_5$ $R \quad x \ O_6$	24-25
6.	Posttest-Only Control Group $R \quad x \ O_1$ $R \quad O_2$	25-27
10.	Nonequivalent Control Group $\underline{O \quad x \quad O}$ $O \ - \ - \ O$	47-50
11.	Counterbalanced 1 2 3 4 $A \ x_1O \ x_2O \ x_3O \ x_4O$ $B \ x_2O \ x_4O \ x_1O \ x_3O$ $C \ x_3O \ x_1O \ x_4O \ x_2O$ $D \ x_4O \ x_3O \ x_2O \ x_1O$	50-52
7.	Time-Series Experiment $O_1 \ O_2 \ O_3 \ O_4 \ O_5 \ O_6 \ O_7 \ O_8$	37-43
14.	Multiple Time-Series $O \ O \ O \ O \ x \ O \ O \ O \ O$ $O \ O \ O \ O \quad O \ O \ O \ O$	55-57

*Campbell, Donald T., and Stanley, Julian C., *Experimental and Quasi-Experimental Designs for Research*, Rand McNally and Company, Chicago, 1966.

FACTORS JEOPARDIZING THE VALIDITY OF EXPERIMENTAL DESIGNS[1]

Sources of Invalidity	EXPERIMENTAL DESIGNS*							
	Little Control	Rigorous Control			Partial Control			
	1	2	3	4	5	6	7	8
Internal validity								
Contemporary history	—	+	+	+	+	+	—	+
Maturation processes	—	+	+	+	+	+	+	+
Pretesting procedures	—	+	+	+	+	+	+	+
Measuring instruments	—	+	+	+	+	+	?	+
Statistical regression	?	+	+	+	?	+	+	+
Differential selection of subjects	+	+	+	+	+	+	+	+
Experimental mortality	+	+	+	+	+	+	+	+
Interaction of selection and maturation, etc.	—	+	+	+	—	?	+	+
External validity								
Interaction of selection and X	—	?	?	?	?	?	?	—
Interaction of pretesting and X	—	—	+	+	—	?	—	—
Reactive experimental procedures	?	?	?	?	?	?	?	?
Multiple-treatment interference								—

* Names of Designs 1 to 8 are:
1. One-group Pretest-Posttest
2. Randomized Control-group Pretest-Posttest
3. Randomized Solomon Four-group
4. Randomized Control-group Posttest only
5. Nonrandomized Control-group Pretest-Posttest
6. Counterbalanced
7. One-group Time-series
8. Control-group Time-series

Note: A plus symbol indicates control of a factor, a minus indicates lack of control, a question mark suggests there is some source for concern, and a blank indicates that the factor is not relevant.

FACTORIAL DESIGNS

Classical experimental design allows the variation of a single X at a time, holding all other conditions constant. Complex behavior, however, usually will not be fitted into such an artificial situation. Furthermore, factors influencing behavior frequently *interact* to produce differences that do not occur when only one factor is free to vary at a time. For example, there might be an interaction between intelligence and method of teaching such that authoritarian methods work better with low intelligence subjects and democratic methods work better with high intelligence subjects. A study of the two teaching methods which holds

---

1. Material on this page and on the preceding page is adapted in large measure from Van Dalen, D.B. *Understanding educational research* (4th ed.). New York: McGraw-Hill, 1979, pp. 279-280.

intelligence constant will lead to misleading conclusions, just as would a study allowing intelligence to vary but holding the teaching method constant. To permit research studies where more than one factor is free to vary at a time, *factorial designs* have become increasingly prominent. They have several advantages over the classical experimental design:

1. They permit the testing of several hypotheses simultaneously, rather than having to conduct a series of single X experiments to study the effects of different Xs on, for example, learning.

2. They permit the conduct of only one experiment to answer several complex questions at once, such as: What effect does X_1-type teacher have on learning achievement when using X_2-type methods in X_3-length classes with X_4-type students?

3. Where *interaction* between two or more variables simultaneously makes a difference, it reveals this difference.

4. Where the classical experimental control of all variables but one is impractical or impossible.

Note: The basic statistical technique used to test the null hypothesis in factorial designs is analysis of variance (see pages 182-183).

THE 2 × 2 FACTORIAL DESIGN[1]

Length of Period (X_2)

	50′	30′	Mean	Difference
Lecture	A 59.0	B 58.0	58.5	−1.0
Discussion	C 82.0	D 84.0	83.0	+2.0
Mean:	70.5	71.0		
Difference	+23.0	+26.0		

Teaching Method (X_1)

This is the simplest factorial design, permitting the study of the effects of two Xs (treatments), each of which is varied in two ways (levels or values).

Example:

1. Let X_1 represent two teaching methods and X_2 represent two lengths of time for a class period.

2. Assign subjects at random to each of the four possible combinations of experi-

---

1. Adapted from Van Dalen, D. B. *Understanding educational research* (4th ed.), pp. 256-262. (Adapted from Campbell, D. T., and Stanley, J. C., *Experimental and quasi-experimental designs for research,* Rand McNally and Company, Chicago, 1966.)

mental treatment. Group A is exposed to 50-minute lecture periods, Group B to 30-minute lecture periods, Group C to 50-minute discussion periods, and Group D to 30-minute discussion periods.

3. After a predetermined period of time, the achievement of each subject is measured and the mean scores of each of the groups are recorded in their appropriate cells (e.g., Group A = 59.0, Group B = 58.0, etc.).

4. Mean scores are also computed for the pairs of groups exposed to the lecture method (A and B = 58.5) and the discussion method (C and D = 83.0); the 50-minute period (A and C = 70.5) or the 30-minute period (B and D = 71.0). These combined means are placed in their respective row or column margins.

Design Information:

1. What is the main effect of teaching method (X_1) on achievement scores? Answer: A comparison of the mean score of the two lecture groups (58.5) with that of the two discussion groups (83.0) appears to favor the latter as more effective.

2. What is the main effect of length of class (X_2) on achievement scores? Answer: A comparison of the mean score of the two groups with 50-minute periods (70.5) and the two groups with 30-minute periods (71.0) suggests no particular difference.

3. What is the interaction effect, if any, of teaching method and length of class period on the achievement scores? Answer: If there is an interaction, the effect that a teaching method has on the achievement scores will differ for 30- and 50-minute classes. If the discussion method, for example, is more effective with one length of class than it is with the other, there is an interaction. If there is no interaction, the effect of a teaching method on achievement scores will be the same for both lengths of class periods. The data in the above example, therefore, reveal no appreciable interaction effect.

EXTENDED FACTORIAL DESIGNS

Factorial designs more complex than the 2 × 2 model are often employed. For example:

2 × 3 Design—two independent variables: one varied in two ways; the other varied in three ways. Example:

First variable: Sex (*male* or *female*)

Second variable: Method of teaching reading (*reading experience approach, phonics approach,* and *word recognition approach*).

3 × 3 Design—three independent variables: each varied three ways. Example:
First variable: Intelligence (*Above* 110 *IQ, Between* 90–110 *IQ,* and *Below* 90 *IQ*)
Second variable: Problem-solving approach (*individual, small group,* and *large group*) Third variable: Time allotment (2 *hours without interruption,* 2 1-*hour sessions with a* 1 *hour break,* 2 1-*hour sessions with a* 24-*hour break*).

2 × 2 × 2 Design: three independent variables: each varied two ways. Example:
First variable: Age (12 *year olds* and 15 *year olds*)
Second variable: Sex (*boys* and *girls*)
Third variable: Counseling atmosphere (*directive* or *nondirective*)
Note: this design requires eight treatment groups (2 × 2 × 2 = 8) and can answer

the following seven questions: What is the main effect on (for example) achievement scores of (1) X_1, (2) X_2, and (3) X_3? What is the interaction effect on the achievement scores of (4) X_1 and X_2, (5) X_1 and X_3, (6) X_2 and X_3, and (7) X_1, X_2, and X_3?

Designs of greater complexity than the above illustrations are possible, though they tend to be unwieldy and highly sophisticated.

An important characteristic of factorial designs is that several hypotheses can be tested simultaneously, releasing researchers from the rigidity of classical designs. Whereas classical designs allowed only the study of a single variable at a time, factorial designs permit several variables to be investigated in one experiment. An example of this multi-factor approach would be an experiment investigating simultaneously the following question: What effect does teacher personality (X_1) have on student achievement when using a particular teaching method (X_2) in a particular classroom situation (X_3) with students of particular ability level (X_4)?

ADDITIONAL CONCERNS, STRATEGIES, AND PITFALLS IN THE DESIGN OF RESEARCH

The payoff in research studies comes in reaching significant and useful conclusions after the data have been collected and analyzed within the *framework of the design.* Good planning and careful design anticipate which questions will be open to investigation and establish the conditions under which conclusions can be defensibly drawn.

The major difficulty, discussed earlier in this section, arises from the role of *plausible rival hypotheses* which the design must minimize if the results are to be meaningful. In other words, can the findings be explained for reasons other than those advanced by the research hypotheses? Subtle biases, contaminating factors, inadequate controls and numerous oversights and oversimplifications conspire to waylay the obvious interpretation which seems to follow so directly from the research framework.[1]

In essence, then, the goal of good design is to maximize internal and external validity and minimize error. To bolster the probability of this outcome, the remaining pages of this

---

1. Varying degrees of "confirmation" are conferred upon a theory by examining the number of *plausible rival hypotheses* available to account for the data. As the number of such rival hypotheses decreases, confirmation increases. Equally important, the more numerous and independent the ways in which the experimental effect is demonstrated, the less numerous and less plausible any single rival hypothesis becomes. The appeal is to parsimony. If several sets of differences can all be explained by a single hypothesis claiming that X has an effect, while several distinct uncontrolled-variable effects otherwise must be hypothesized, a different one for each observed difference, then the effect of X becomes the most tenable. In other words, a general finding among several studies, which is contested on different grounds from one study to another, is strengthened by that fact alone. (From Donald T. Campbell and Julian C. Stanley, *Experimental and Quasi-experimental Designs for Research.* Chicago: Rand McNally, 1966.)

section summarize further concerns, strategies, and pitfalls often neglected in unsophisticated or carelessly designed research. They are organized under the following topical headings:

1. Control—a key concept in experimental design
2. Confounding and cancellation of effects: two pitfalls of interaction
3. Generalizability of research findings
4. Interaction between variables
5. Some common sources of error
6. Making meaningful comparisons
7. Reactive versus nonreactive measures
8. Measurement: single versus multiple outcomes—*triangulation*
9. Statistical regression effects
10. Short-term and long-term studies
11. Five points about research design
12. Large samples versus small samples
13. Individual differences
14. Matching as a control technique: some disadvantages

CONTROL—A KEY CONCEPT IN EXPERIMENTAL DESIGN[1]

Research design has two basic purposes: first and most obvious, to provide answers to research questions and, second, to *control variance* (variability).[2] There are three kinds of variance that must be controlled according to the following set of "minimax" principles if answers to research questions are to be valid:

1. *Maximize the experimental variance*—the systematic effects of the variable(s) associated with the research hypotheses. This is done by designing, planning, and conducting research so that the experimental conditions are as different as possible, emphasizing their importance.

2. *Control the extraneous variance*—the effects of other systematic but "unwanted" variables that might influence the experimental outcomes but are not themselves the object of study. There are five ways to do this:
   a. Simply prevent the variation of an extraneous variable such as IQ by holding it *constant*. For example, choose subjects that are homogeneous on this variable by holding IQs within a range between 90–110.
   b. The most powerful technique is *randomization* which controls for all possible extraneous variables simultaneously. Ideally, this means randomly selected subjects

1. Adapted from Kerlinger, Fred N. *Foundations of behavioral research* (2nd ed.). New York: Holt, Rinehart, and Winston, 1973, Chapter 17.
2. "Variance" is a statistical way of looking at the variability of scores or means. "Control of variance" is taking into account all factors which systematically contribute to the generation of individual differences in scores or measures on the outcome or dependent variable.

who are randomly assigned to groups which, in turn, are randomly assigned the treatment or control conditions.

c. Build the extraneous variables right into the design as if they were independent variables. This achieves control and yields additional information about their effect on the dependent variable and their possible interactions with other independent or classificatory variables.

d. Perhaps the most commonly used method for controlling extraneous variables is *matching* the subjects on one or more variables. Matching has many disadvantages and is now generally discouraged (see page 99), but it occasionally remains useful if a substantial correlation ($\geqslant$ .50) between the matching variable(s) and the dependent variable exists.

e. The final method of control is *statistical* and is inherent in all research design since it is inseparable from other control techniques. The method of analysis of covariance is particularly useful in place of matching, but still requires randomization.

3. *Minimize the error variance*—the effects of random fluctuations including so-called errors of measurement. This is achieved largely by careful control of the measurement conditions and by increasing the reliability of the measures themselves. While error variance is unpredictable and self-cancelling around a mean of zero, if it is sizable it can swallow up the systematic variance of the experimental variables just as a signal is lost in a high noise background. Sampling error is minimized by increasing the sample size.

CONFOUNDING AND CANCELLATION OF EFFECTS: TWO PITFALLS OF INTERACTION

The interaction between variables, intentional or incidental, poses at least two difficulties for research design, if unforeseen.

Confounding. Confounding exists when the variance of one or more independent variables, usually outside the focus of the research, mixes with the variance arising from the independent variable(s) built into the research problem. Consequently, it is unclear whether the relationship found is between the independent/ classificatory and dependent variables in the research design, or between the extraneous independent/ classificatory variables and the dependent variable, or both. Succinctly, whenever the effects of the independent variables cannot be evaluated unambiguously, confounding probably is present.[1]

EXAMPLE: Two groups of students, A, the control group, and B, the treatment group, obtain the following mean performance scores:

Group A	Group B
$M = 60$	$M = 69$

If the mean scores between the two groups are taken at their face value, assuming their difference is statistically significant, we would conclude that the treatment was

---

1. Kerlinger, F. N. *Foundations of behavioral research* (2nd ed.). New York: Holt, Rinehart and Winston, 1973.

effective. Suppose, however, we learn afterward that Group A had a mean IQ of 109 and Group B, a mean IQ of 115. Because the treatment and intelligence were unwittingly *confounded*, it is no longer clear which made the difference.

Cancellation of effects. Sometimes, instead of finding a difference whose source is confounded, a difference will be hidden from view because the design failed to identify and/or distinguish between variables whose effects counteract each other or, within a single variable, failed to compare contrasting levels or amounts resulting in the same cancellation of effect.

EXAMPLE: Consider an investigation of the differential effects of either small or large steps in programmed instruction, in terms of mean terminal achievement test scores, yielding these results:

	Group I small steps	Group II large steps	
High IQ	70	90	$\overline{M}$ Ach.score = 80
Low IQ	50	30	$\overline{M}$ Ach.score = 40
	$\overline{M}$ Ach.score = 60	$\overline{M}$ Ach.score = 60	

If the original analysis dealt only with randomly selected subjects, with no distinction between levels of IQ, no differences between Group I and Group II would have been observed, since means of 60 were reported for both groups. A differential analysis of the data, on the other hand, reveals an interaction between IQ and step size such that High IQs do better with large steps and Low IQs with small steps. Obviously, if the IQ levels are indiscriminately combined, their differential effects are cancelled and remain hidden.

GENERALIZABILITY OF RESEARCH FINDINGS[1]

Generalizability is the problem of external validity. Having done research with satisfactory internal validity, to what other situations do the results apply? In educational research, generalizability of the results is often the crucial practical question—what is learned in a single research setting ought to apply generally to many actual classroom settings. Here are three useful considerations to increase the generalizability of results:

1. *Generalizability of Results and Selection of Subjects:*

   Oftentimes, a researcher casts about for a school in which to conduct a study until he finds one willing to cooperate. If several schools have turned him down, it is reasonable to suspect that the cooperating school may not be representative of schools in general. Sampling biases often occur because of the inertia of researchers to assure representa-

1. Adapted from Donald T. Campbell and Julian C. Stanley. *Experimental and Quasi-experimental Designs for Research*. Chicago: Rand McNally, 1966.
2. Based on a suggestion by William B. Michael of the University of Southern California.

tiveness in their selection procedures which, in turn, assures generalizability of the findings to the largest number of schools.

Solution No. 1: Select subjects at random from a variety of classes and/or schools, rather than taking entire classes from a single school or school district. This minimizes the impact on any given school and maximizes the representativesness of the educational sample. This strategy is also apt to be more economical, less conspicuous, less disruptive to the classroom, and reduces overtesting (if testing only involves the sample).

Solution No. 2: Use classrooms as the unit and randomly select these from a representative population of school districts to which generalizations of the findings would be appropriate.

2. *Generalizability of Results and Variation of the Input or Stimulus Source:*

Contrary to a prevalent notion about the importance of *exact* replications of the stimulus source in experimental design (e.g., providing exactly the same recorded stimulus to all groups), varying the stimulus source may actually increase the generalizability of the results. This is particularly true when the task is to communicate effectively the main point of a message or treatment to new users. With the taped interview, for example, repeated each time are the same irrelevant features which may account for the effect rather than the message, per se. By varying the stimulus source, but keeping the intended communication intact, the conclusion that the source of effects lies in the message is strengthened.

Another example of this principle is to have every teacher using every treatment within the research design, thus distributing all specific irrelevancies across all treatments and preventing the confounding of any particular irrelevancy with any particular treatment. While this design feature enhances the generalizability of the results, it frequently is impractical because of the obvious burden it places on the participating teachers.

3. *Generalizability among observations:*

Just as any given treatment carries with it irrelevant characteristics which may turn out to cause the effect, so any given observation or measuring instrument is imbedded among characteristics irrelevant to the intended assessment but which may be mistaken for it.

Solution: Use multiple measures of outcomes: e.g., essay examinations, objective tests, and indices of classroom participation. (see p. 92.)

---

1. Adapted from Donald T. Campbell and Julian C. Stanley. *Experimental and Quasi-experimental Designs for Research.* Chicago: Rand McNally, 1966.

INTERACTION BETWEEN VARIABLES

Patterns of Interaction

The current emphasis in behavioral research is upon interactions between variables. The old questions, What method works best? or What factor is most important? have given way to questions specifying, What variables? In what combinations and amounts? Under what conditions? With what subjects? and To meet what objectives?

Interaction-proneness

Some factors are more interaction-prone than others. It is important to look for the interaction between variables, combining them to optimize outcomes.

Main Effects Versus Interactions[1]

In cases of ignorance, however, a main effect of one variable is to be judged more likely than the interaction of two other variables. More generally, main effects are more likely than interactions. If every highest order interaction is significant, if every effect is specific to certain values on all other potential treatment dimensions, then a science is not possible. If generalizations are ever possible, it is because the great bulk of potential determining factors can be discarded.

Use of Inappropriate Independent Variables[2]

It is useful to select independent variables such that they are relevant and arranged in realistic combinations with each other to take into account the interaction relationships. If one questions whether he has defined his variables properly, he is likely to discover new things. Often the researcher selects what appear to be obvious and important variables as if they were independent of the others. If an interaction relationship exists between two or more of these independent variables, however, he is apt to overlook highly important and useful information.

Examples: Class size is an important independent variable only in relationship with different teaching methods; to consider it separately is to miss its relevance to teaching. Another example of interaction between independent variables comes from Gage's research on the Minnesota Teacher Attitude Inventory (MTAI). This is a well-developed test based on the conception that teachers who are warm, gentle, democratic, and child-centered, have a superior relationship with the class and it has validity ratings near .40. However, when

---

1.   Adapted from D. T. Campbell and J. C. Stanley. *Experimental and Quasi-experimental Designs for Research.* Chicago: Rand McNally, 1966.
2.   Based on notes by Stephen Isaac of suggestions made by Lee J. Cronbach at a California Educational Research Association meeting, c.1960.

Gage developed another test of cognitive versus emotional orientation and compared "interpersonal relations-valuing" classes with "cognitive learning-oriented" classes—classes where the teacher and pupil are collaborating in a learning enterprise—MTAI predictive validities remained around .40 for the former but fell to zero in the latter case. Thus, an oversimple conception of the independent variable led apparently to a false interpretation of previous results.

The fixed treatment assumption[1]

In the validation of tests involving personality categories, evidence is typically sought to match these personality categories with success in particular treatment outcomes. For example, Strong's Vocational Interest Test is used to fit the client's answers to similar patterns in various occupations. The end effect of this orientation is to select persons of a single type for any given occupation, leading to social stereotyping. Other research suggests that atypical patterns predict success for some of the less common pathways within a particular vocational field.

Solution: Allow for the relationship between personality characteristics and validation criteria in a flexible, rather than a fixed, fashion. Instead of predicting whether type A does better than type B in a given treatment, look for ways to change the treatment to fit individuals of different kinds. It is important to ask: What teaching methods work best for what kinds of students under what conditions?

SOME COMMON SOURCES OF ERROR

THE HALO EFFECT

This is the tendency for an irrelevant feature of a unit of study to influence the relevant feature in a favorable or unfavorable direction. Typically, a strong initial positive or negative impression of a person, group, or event tends to influence ratings on all subsequent observations. Impressions formed early in a series of observations often affect later observations; or impressions based on high or low status attributes of the unit of study affect observations on unrelated attributes—quoting a celebrity's opinion on an educational issue or associating

---

1. Based on notes by Stephen Isaac of suggestions made by Lee J. Cronbach at a California Educational Research Association meeting, c.1960.

emotionally-loaded labels with candidates in a hotly contested school board election. The more vague and impressionistic the variable to be rated, the more powerful is the effect; the more specific and clearly defined the variable, the less evident is the effect.

RATING ERRORS

In addition to the halo effect, three other tendencies plague the validity of ratings:
1. The over-rater error—rating subjects in general on the side of leniency or favorableness.
2. The under-rater error—rating subjects in general on the side of severity or unfavorableness.
3. The central tendency error—rating subjects toward the middle of the scale. This often occurs when the observer is unfamiliar with or uncertain about what is being rated.

THE HAWTHORNE EFFECT

In an industrial efficiency study performed at the Hawthorne Plant of Western Electric in Chicago during the 1920's it was observed that to single out a group of workers for a special research project makes them feel and act differently compared to regular workers. The effect of this was to bring about a *consistent increase in productivity* in spite of changes in the working conditions intended both to increase and decrease efficiency. Explanations for this effect point to the factors of: (1) novelty; (2) awareness that one is a participant in an experiment; (3) a modified environment involving observers, special procedures, and new patterns of social interaction; and (4) knowledge of results in the form of daily productivity figures and other feedback, ordinarily not systematically available.

THE EXPERIMENTER BIAS EFFECT OR "SELF-FULFILLING PROPHECY" IN RESEARCH

Well documented in articles by Dr. Robert Rosenthal of Harvard, this is the bias a researcher is inclined to project into his methodology and treatment that subtly shapes the data in the direction of his foregone conclusions. What the researcher "expects to see," where he directs his attention, what he ignores or forgets, what he remembers or records, and even the way he interacts with subjects to alter their own expectations and motivational states, all can influence the results to fit his preconceptions.

THE "JOHN HENRY" EFFECT

The phenomenon in a research study involving human subjects assigned to experimental and control groups, when those who are identified as "controls" discover their status and, by that fact, are determined "to show the experimental group a thing or two," actually outperforming them.

THE PLACEBO EFFECT

A placebo is an inert or neutral stimulus given to subjects as if it were the active treatment variable itself. In medical research the placebo often is an injection of sterile water or a chemically inert pill administered so that the subject cannot distinguish between the neutral and the active ingredient. This allows the observer to separate treatment effects from psychological reactions induced by the treatment situation involving, in particular, the patient's expectations and suggestibility. For this reason, background elements in an educational research setting often turn out to be the agents of change in addition to the active treatment variable. For example, in a research study to examine the effects of videotape playback on increasing participation in class discussions using treatment and control groups, it might turn out that the presence of videotape recording equipment and any operators or observers were of equal or greater importance in contrast to the actual videotape playback. Unless the same equipment and personnel are present in at least some of the control classes as a placebo condition, the actual effectiveness of the playback may be misconstrued.

THE POST HOC ERROR

"After this, therefore because of this." Many events follow one another without having a cause-and-effect relationship. The reasons for this vary all the way from simple coincidence to complex relationships with other factors. For example, an increase in the ocean's temperature is directly related to the number of drownings along the California coast. We do not conclude that the warmer surf, per se, is more dangerous but that it attracts larger numbers of swimmers, exposing more people to the probability of drowning.

ERROR OF MISPLACED PRECISION

To collect data with great care and precision but within the framework of a faulty design, invalidates the findings and the painstaking work that produced them. When properly evaluated, this is also demoralizing to the staff associated with the project.

BEWARE OF "TYPICAL" CASE STUDIES

Studies based on "typical" cases are usually biased and nonrepresentative. Such cases too often are more ideal than typical, or better fit the reporter's biases than others which might have been cited. A defendable alternative would be to select and review several cases *at random*, a procedure rarely followed.

THE LAW OF THE INSTRUMENT

This refers to the human inclination to become attached to a certain instrument or procedure and apply it as an across-the-board solution to every problem. As one pair of authors put it, "If you give a small boy a hammer, he will find that everything he encounters needs pounding!" [1] Most of the popular devices, innovations, and panaceas in education are vulnerable to this overreaction. In such instances, the focus is on the instrument or procedure and not the problem, placing the cart before the horse. This error is avoided by examining the problem first and then seeking appropriate instruments and procedures that best fit the properties of the problem.

---

1. Paul E. Resta and Robert L. Baker. *Formulating the Research Problem.* Inglewood, California: Southwest Regional Laboratory for Educational Research and Development, 1967.

MAKING MEANINGFUL COMPARISONS

BASELINE DATA[1]

To observe changes in behavior, it is first necessary to establish baseline data against which to make meaningful comparisons. Such data establish what the subjects were like before the treatments and/or observations began. To be valid, baseline data must allow appropriate adaptation periods to any unusual modifications of the research setting such as television cameras, observers in the room, new equipment, and other noticeable changes in the environment. Common procedures for gathering baseline data are the *pretest* and the *control group*. The latter is important where there is an expected treatment effect and the absence of treatment is the baseline. Control groups are also necessary where the baseline is a subjective judgment in a rater's head which is likely to change with experience.

PITFALL OF "DO NOTHING" CONTROL GROUPS[2]

Control groups ordinarily should experience *all things* in common with the treatment group *except* the critical factor, per se. Control groups that "do nothing" are apt to differ from the treatment groups in more ways than just the isolated treatment variable. For example, if technicians or observers are present in the classrooms of treatment groups, they should also be present for the control groups since their presence may account for the effect rather than the treatment itself. The same is true for special equipment, visitors, interruptions, and other events that tend to single out treatment groups but ignore control groups.

EXPERIMENTAL DESIGN AND RANDOM ASSIGNMENT[3]

The most rigorous means of making meaningful comparisons is the controlled experiment with random assignment of subjects, occasions, and treatment conditions. While many research problems do not lend themselves to this technique, many more opportunities exist than are used.

USE OF INDEX NUMBERS[4]

Irrelevant sources of variance in raw data can be controlled by transforming these data into weighted, compensated, or counter-balanced aggregates. Intelligence quotients, the "labor force," and "real wages" are examples where such adjustments make meaningful comparisons possible. Such transformations are particularly critical in historical or longitudinal comparisons.

For example, the problem of measuring "mental ability" or "intelligence" across age ranges so that younger children of a given ability level could be equated to older children of the same comparative ability level, was solved by inventing the concept of *mental age*. Categories of test items, each serially ordered in difficulty, were given to children representing various chronological age intervals. The average score for each of these intervals became the "mental age" level for that corresponding chronological age level. By dividing the child's obtained mental age by his chronological age, and multiplying the resulting ratio by 100 to clear decimals, an index was devised called the intelligence quotient, or IQ, allowing direct comparisons, independent of chronological age differences. (For a restriction on this procedure, see page 95, "Two Statistical Points, item 1.")

1,2.   Based on notes taken at a Field Studies Workshop given by staff members of the Far West Regional Laboratory, Berkeley, California, 1968.
3,4   Adapted from E. J. Webb, D. T. Campbell, R. D. Schwartz, and L. Sechrest. *Unobtrusive Measures.* Chicago: Rand McNally, 1966.

ELIMINATION OF PLAUSIBLE RIVAL HYPOTHESES[1]

These ask the question: What other plausible interpretations are allowed by the research setting and the measurement processes? The fewer of these, and the more implausible each is, the more validly interpretable is the comparison.

INITIAL DIFFERENCES BETWEEN CONTROL AND EXPERIMENTAL GROUPS[2]

It is often misleading to determine *critical ratio* or *t tests* on a before-and-after basis, without first comparing initial differences between control and experimental groups. There are two solutions:

1. *Gain scores:*[3] For each group, compute pretest-posttest gain scores and then calculate a *t* between gain scores for the experimental and control groups.

2. *Covariance:* A better solution than simple gain score comparisons is to carry out randomized "blocking" or "leveling" on pretest scores or perform an analysis of covariance with the pretest scores as the covariate. Random assignment is essential.

Caution: The use of matched pairs to avoid initial differences seldom is a satisfactory alternative. See page 99.

THE RETROSPECTIVE PRETEST[4]

Sometimes a researcher would like to have pretest information on groups of subjects after it is too late to collect it. A possible solution is the "retrospective pretest:" subjects simply are asked to *reflect* on their attitudes or behavior prior to some given event on which they are being compared.

This procedure was validated in a military setting when white soldiers in all-white or mixed-race units evidenced no differences in their pre-military attitudes toward Negroes, whereas whites in the mixed-race units revealed more favorable attitudes toward Negroes after their experiences with military integration. Suprisingly, though experience with Negroes led to these more favorable attitudes on the part of whites, this same experience apparently did not exercise a "halo effect" upon their recollections of how they felt before the integration experience.

PITFALL IN "METHOD" STUDIES

In method-of-teaching studies, it is dangerous to assume that two teachers are actually teaching with the same method. Observers often report critical differences that suggest two versions of a given method. Such an interaction is crucial in making meaningful interpretations.

1,4   Adapted from D. T. Campbell and J. C. Stanley. *Experimental and Quasi-experimental Designs for Research.* Chicago: Rand McNally, 1966.
2.   Based on notes by Stephen Isaac of suggestions made by Lee J. Cronbach at a California Educational Research Association meeting c.1960.
3.   Gain scores often are highly unreliable and hazardous to use. For an authoritative discussion of this problem see: Lord, Frederic M., "The Measurement of Growth," EDUCATIONAL AND PSYCHOLOGICAL MEASUREMENT, Vol. 16, No. 4 (Winter), 1956, pp. 421–427. Also see Cronbach, Lee J. and Furby, Lita, "How We Should Measure 'Change'—Or Should We?" PSYCHOLOGICAL BULLETIN, Vol. 74, No. 1. (July), 1970, pp. 68–80.

REACTIVE VERSUS NONREACTIVE MEASURES

REACTIVE MEASURES[1]

A measurement is reactive whenever the subject is directly involved in a study and he is *reacting* to the measurement process itself. The risk of introducing changes peculiar to the measurement process takes several forms:

1. *The guinea pig effect:* To the extent that one feels he is a "guinea pig" and must do his best or that the method of data collection starts trains of thought not previously characteristic of the subject or makes him defensive, antagonistic or unusually co-operative, the measuring process itself changes the respondent and biases the research results.

2. *Role selection:* When approached as a respondent in a research study, an individual tends to assume a role of "the kind of person he thinks he should be" in this situation. To the extent that this assumed role differs from his natural behavior in situations similar to, but outside the research setting, validity decreases.

3. *Measurement as change agent:* The *preamble effect* described by Cantril[2] indicates that the instructions to a test or questionnaire induce certain attitudes or sets in the respondent which even persist beyond the research situation. Initial "don't know" answers on opinion surveys frequently set into motion opinion-forming processes which otherwise would not have happened. *Practice effects* are also observed where exercise on the pre-test accounts for gains on the posttest. "Testwise" subjects who develop skills in test-taking exhibit this same change tracing back to the measurement act.

4. *Response sets:* This is the tendency of subjects to respond to questions in certain predictable ways. The *acquiescence response set* describes the phenomenon that respondents will more frequently endorse a positive statement than disagree with its opposite. Respondents more often than not will prefer strong statements to moderate or inconclusive ones. Sequences of questions presented in a similar format lead to response patterns affecting items in the last half of a test differently than in the first half, possibly because the respondent becomes aware of his adaptation pattern by the middle of the instrument and shifts to a variation to avoid monotony or conformity. The *social desirability response set* refers to items where one alternative is more acceptable socially than another.[3]

5. *Interviewer effects:* The sex, age, race, manner of dress, and speech patterns or accents, of the interviewer all interact with the attitudes or expectations of the respondent toward these characteristics.

6. *Change in the research instrument:* Differences often appear *within* the same interviewer or panel of judges over time; increasing skill, sensitivity, sophistication, fatigue, boredom, or a shifting adaptation level modifies the interviewer and his effect as a "stimulus" upon the subject. If the instrument is a record-keeping system which changes over the years with new ways of collecting and classifying information, then impressions of changing behavior may be nothing more than artifacts of an altered measurement process. For example: an apparent increase in the suicide rate resulting from improved reporting procedures.

1. Adapted from E. J. Webb, D. T. Campbell, R. D. Schwartz, and L. Sechrest. *Unobtrusive Measures.* Chicago: Rand McNally, 1966.
2. Cantril, H., *Gauging Public Opinion,* Princeton, Princeton Univ. Press, 1944.
3. Edwards, A. L., *The Social Desireability Variable in Personality Assessment and Research,* New York: Dryden Press, 1957.

NONREACTIVE MEASURES[1]

A measurement is nonreactive when it does not change that which is being measured. It is a passive or unobtrusive measure of behavior and does not introduce stimulus factors to which the subject might otherwise react. Nonreactive measures have been categorized into the following types:

1. *Physical traces:*
    a. Erosion—For example, examination of library books for physical "wear and tear" as an index of their actual use.
    b. Accretion—For example, measuring the amount of campus litter before and after an administration-sponsored "cleanup campaign" as an index of student attitude toward administrative authority.
2. *Archives and records:* actuarial, governmental, mass media, industrial, personnel, and miscellaneous running records, public and private. For example, changes in library withdrawal patterns as an index of the effectiveness of a reading appreciation program in a high school.
3. *Unobtrusive observation:* expressive behavior, physical activity, language behavior, conversion sampling, time duration, and time sampling of behavior. An example is counting the number of time students raise their hands, smile, or participate in class discussions as indices of their interest in a particular instructional program.

Nonreactive measures are vulnerable to sampling biases and other non-representative distortions that influence kinds and rates of physical change, record keeping procedures, and observable human behavior patterns. In ridding a measurement of its reactive characteristics, the risk of even more serious consequences is not eliminated. A reasonable measurement strategy is *triangulation:* incorporate more than one measure of the phenomena in question. For example, to measure the effectiveness of a particular reading program, obtain: (1) scores on a standardized reading achievement test; (2) school attendance record patterns; and (3) their preference for books in their free time compared with nonreading activities. This would combine one reactive with two nonreactive measures of the program's effect. (See page 92.)

MAKING CLASSROOM RESEARCH NONREACTIVE[2]

To reduce the Hawthorne or guinea pig effect which causes subjects to respond differently from that under normal classroom conditions, the following inconspicuous strategies are suggested:

1. Build the research measures into the regular classroom examinations or through tests presented as regular examinations and similar in content.
2. Involve alternative teaching procedures presented without announcement or apology in the regular teaching process.
3. Use the regular staff to conduct experimentation within schools, especially where findings are to be generalized to other classroom situations.

---

1. Based on discussion from E. J. Webb, D. T. Campbell, R. D. Schwartz, and L. Sechrest. *Unobtrusive Measures.* Chicago: Rand McNally, 1966.
2. Based on discussion from Donald T. Campbell and Julian C. Stanley. *Experimental and Quasi-experimental Designs for Research.* Chicago: Rand McNally, 1966.

MEASUREMENT: SINGLE VERSUS MULTIPLE OUTCOMES – *TRIANGULATION*

The operational definition of a concept, leading to its measurement in behavioral terms, has led to the self-defeating practice of arbitrarily selecting a single measurement criterion or class of observations. For example, the questionnaire or interview technique together account for about 90 percent of research in the social sciences. Operationalism is better served by *multiple measures* of a given concept or attribute, each sharing a portion of the theoretically relevant components but each having different loadings of irrelevant factors or "noise." Once a proposition has been confirmed by two or more independent measurement processes, the uncertainty of its interpretation is greatly reduced. The *triangulation of measurement* process is far more powerful evidence supporting the proposition than any single criterion approach.[1] Two problems are raised:

1. Multiple measures of a given concept are often disappointing and inconsistent, pointing to the gravity of the measurement problem in the social sciences and the risks of false confidence where single criterion methods are employed. Such results are also awkward to report coherently.

2. Since all components of a multi-method approach may not deserve equal weighting, they ideally should be weighted according to the amount of extraneous variation each is known to have and then taken in combination according to its independence from similar sources of bias.

For example:[2] In a study of the effect of praise or blame on the outcome of reading instruction, no significant differences were found among the various groups on the criterion of *gain in reading*. If a second criterion had been used, such as *attitudes toward reading*, a highly significant treatment difference might have been found. Most research of this kind looks at an achievement or skill outcome rather than the development of attitudes. The failure of people to choose to read following their formal education, or to choose mathematics in their higher education, given the skill development to do both, strongly suggests that a counter-current of *negative attitudes* to avoid these experiences, lies hidden underneath.

Using more than one outcome measure or criterion simply means the selection of more than one *dependent variable*, such as achievement *plus* attitudes *plus* transfer to a new process. If no differences are obtained on one criterion, differences on another may prove equally valuable and relevant. Cronbach reports a study by Brownell of four methods of teaching subtraction; he found only small differences both on a skill criterion and on a retention criterion but clearly superior results favoring one method over all the others when he measured transfer to a new process. There are serious risks in making recommendations based on a single criterion which fails to consider the whole outcome of an educational process.[2]

---

1. Adapted from E. J. Webb, D. T. Campbell, R. D. Schwartz, and L. Sechrest, *Unobtrusive Measures*. Chicago: Rand McNally, 1966.
2. Notes by Stephen Isaac based on a talk by L. J. Cronbach, Invited Address, California Educational Research Association, c.1960.

STATISTICAL REGRESSION EFFECTS

Subjects selected because they are particularly high or low on some variable, on an equivalent form of the variable will tend to regress toward the mean because of imperfect correlation between the two measures of the variable. Since children are selected into special programs on the basis of extreme scores ("gifted," "retarded," "slow readers," etc.), there is a danger that the role of statistical regression will be overlooked in the outcomes. Thus, a Booster Reading Program for the "bottom 25 percent" of third graders on a standardized reading achievement test will be assured of increased scores on a posttest, by that fact alone. The same youngsters probably will not place so low a second time because the same set of penalizing chance factors will not operate to make all of them so "unlucky" again.

Statistical regression involves several considerations:[1]

1. Extreme groups, on a second testing or posttest, behave as if the bright subjects are becoming less bright and the dull subjects are becoming less dull.

2. The greater the deviation of the extreme scores, the greater the regression to the mean.

3. The lower the correlation, the greater the regression toward the mean.

4. Groups selected for independent reasons, but which just happen to have extreme scores on a given variable, will tend not to regress so much on the retest as they would on a measure highly correlated with the selection variable. (The random or extraneous sources of variance have been allowed to affect the initial scores in *both* directions.)

5. Groups selected on the basis of extreme scores on one variable but evaluated on an unrelated dependent variable should be reasonably free of the regression effect on that second variable.

6. An indirect pseudo-gain can occur when subjects are selected on some criterion other than the pretest (e.g., "failing scores on a class examination"). Because the class examination and the pretest are closer to each other in time, they tend to correlate higher than does the class examination and the posttest administered much later. If the treatment is a "How to Study" program, and with more regression to the mean on the posttest because of the somewhat lower correlation with the class examination, a pseudo-gain may be mistaken for an actual gain. The lower the correlation, the greater will be the regression.

7. When subjects are matched according to a pretest criterion, there is risk of regression effects if the matching involves two different populations. Suppose, for example, pairs are made up from two schools representing middle and lower socioeconomic levels, respectively, but "equating" the subjects by matching them on the basis of IQ scores. Since the two schools probably have different mean population IQs, students from each school will tend to regress toward their respective population means on a second intelligence test, yielding a difference which may be only a statistical artifact.[2]

---

1. Based on discussion from Donald T. Campbell and Julian C. Stanley, *Experimental and Quasi-experimental Designs for Research*. Chicago: Rand McNally, 1966.
2. For a most enlightening discussion of regression artifacts see the contribution by Donald T. Campbell and Albert Erlebacher, "How Regression Artifacts in Quasi-experimental Evaluations Can Mistakenly Make Compensatory Education Look Harmful," in J. Hellmuth (Ed.) *Compensatory Education: a National Debate*, Vol. III of THE DISADVANTAGED CHILD, New York: Brunner/Mazel.

SHORT-TERM AND LONG-TERM STUDIES

1. *Short-term and Long-term Effects:*[1]

   Short-term and long-term effects tend to differ both quantitatively and qualitatively. For example, research by Hovland has shown that long-range effects are greater than immediate effects for general attitudes, although weaker for specific attitudes. To check for such differences extended over time, serial posttests such as one month later, six months later, and one year later, might be designed into the study. In the short-duration studies, the possibility of getting significant results depends upon the power of the treatment variable. Strong stimuli (e.g., operant conditioning techniques) yield results very early in the treatment. Weak stimuli tend to get lost in the error variance of the environmental surroundings.

2. *Three Points are Necessary to Define a Function:*

   Two-point before-and-after designs have a serious fault when investigating behavior related to underlying growth or change functions. Such functions require a minimum of three measurement points in order to determine whether they resemble a simple linear function or a curvilinear one. To get at still more complex functions involving periodic fluctuations, cycles, accelerations and decelerations, temporary effects, step-like patterns or delayed reactions, more than three points are required. A longitudinal design may be necessitated.

   For example, in many Headstart programs initial gains achieved during a special summer program disappear after a few months unless they are systematically maintained by an ongoing treatment program. Also, studies of intelligence have shown that the IQ undergoes a complex series of accelerations and decelerations during childhood and adolescence. Learning curves often are complex functions with step-like characteristics combining ascending and descending slopes with plateaus.

3. *Possible Experimental Design:*

   A design strategy to get at changing functions and to control for the effects of maturation, pretesting, regression, and contemporary history (see page 73) begins with several groups which are pretested at the same time but whch are posttested at different time intervals, respectively:

Group A:	T_1	X	T_2		
Group B:	T_1	X		T_2	
Group C:	T_1	X			T_2
Group D:	T_1	X			T_2
Group E:	T_1	X			T_2

   By adding a control group with the same pretest and posttest pattern, but without the treatment, the effects of the treatment can be assessed. This strategy is particularly appropriate where maturational factors are involved and where the effects of serial testing within groups should be minimized.

---

1. Adapted from D. T. Campbell and J. C. Stanley, *Experimental and Quasi-experimental Designs for Research.* Chicago: Rand McNally, 1966.

FIVE POINTS ABOUT RESEARCH DESIGN[1]

1. Measurement of multiple outcomes is preferable to single outcomes. In other words, use more than one *dependent variable:* for example, achievement, attitudes, and transfer to a new process. Result: if no differences are obtained on one, differences on another may prove equally valuable and relevant.

2. Begin with *dependent variables* each having sufficient criterion reliability to minimize the probability that measurement error, per se, will mask a significant difference actually present in the outcomes.

3. Select appropriate *independent variables* such that they are relevant and are arranged in realistic combination with each other to take advantage of interaction relationships. For example, it makes little sense to study class size as a variable unless one also brings in its relationship to teaching method, pupil characteristics, and other factors.

4. Allow for the relationship between personality characteristics and validation criteria in a flexible, rather than a fixed, fashion. For instance, rather than using the Strong Inventory to select medical school candidates across the board, look for the additional subpatterns which fall outside the "typical" medical interest profile but would predict success in some of the less prominent specialty fields as medical research, and medical school instruction. Otherwise, there is a risk of selecting out potentially successful candidates and creating professional stereotypes that are absolute rather than relative.

5. Emphasize the interaction between individual differences and particular learning principles or methods. Too much reliance has been placed on randomization, equated groups and formal statistical controls; too little reliance on controls by individual differences. In other words, instead of seeking general principles of education applying to everyone, seek empirically established principles about how to deal with people of particular types.

TWO STATISTICAL POINTS[1]

1. When matching is appropriate, avoid matching groups on the basis of IQ. Equating should be done on the basis of mental age, achievement, or some other nonrelative measure. Pupils of a given IQ are not at all alike if their ages are different.[2]

2. Analysis of covariance is greatly neglected as a means of controlling for individual differences. When the assumptions underlying covariance cannot be met, there is a simple nonparametric analogue available. It permits adjustment for initial differences between groups that arise by chance. (Valid application of analysis of covariance requires that groups have been randomly chosen; in effect, analysis of covariance adjusts for usually relatively small differences in pretest or covariate means that have arisen as a function of random sampling error.)

---

1. Based on notes by Stephen Isaac of an address by Lee J. Cronbach to the California Educational Research Association, c.1960.
2. For a discussion of the disadvantages of matching see page 99.

LARGE SAMPLES VERSUS SMALL SAMPLES[1]

The advantages of using *large samples* in educational research have been enhanced with computer technology. Large-sample statistics involve smaller sampling errors, greater reliability, and increase the power of a statistical test applied to the data. Other things being equal, large samples are preferable to small samples. Despite the advantages of using large representative samples, there are, however, several arguments favoring research with small samples under certain conditions:

1. *Small Sample Economy:*

   When it is not economically feasible to collect or analyze large sample data, small samples will be appropriate. Small-sample statistics assure the researcher of acceptable reliability in estimating sampling error before making decisions about his data.

2. *Computer Monitoring:*[2]

   Even when large samples are being used and the data are being analyzed by computer programs, there are problems:
   a. *Errors*—Preparing and processing data in a computer environment risks many sources of error: incorrectly coded or punched input cards, program errors, often obscure and complex; errors in the special instruction decks controlling the programs; and mishandled magnetic tapes.
   b. *The "black box" problem*—The complexities of a constantly changing computer technology usually force the researcher to accept the printout of final results on faith. A helpful safeguard is to draw a small sample of data and run a parallel analysis by hand. This illuminates the mechanics of the statistical analysis and serves as an independent check against errors.

3. *Exploratory Research and Pilot Studies:*[3]

   To find promising leads or alternatives in research, it is essential to stay close to data. Samples with *N*'s between 10 *and* 30 have many practical advantages:
   a. A quick, convenient sample size with which to work.
   b. Provides easy multipliers and divisors, facilitating calculations.
   c. Samples of this size are large enough to test the null hypothesis, yet small enough to overlook weak treatment effects. Remembering that statistically significant findings for any relevant variable appear simply by increasing the sample size toward the universe, such findings are not apt to be *educationally significant* since the variable in question is too diluted to make a practical difference.

4. *N in Large Studies:*[4]

   In large educational studies, *N* actually equals the number of classrooms, not the number of individuals. This distinction increases in importance as the number of classrooms approaches 20 to 30, and is a critical consideration in analyzing and interpreting the data, since it involves the distinction between large and small sample statistics.

---

1. See page 68 for instances when large samples are necessary.
2. See page 40.
3. Suggested by Dr. Harry Munsinger, University of California at San Diego.
4. Based on notes taken at a Field Studies Workshop given by staff members of the Far West Regional Laboratory, Berkeley, California, 1968.

INDIVIDUAL DIFFERENCES

INDIVIDUAL DIFFERENCES AND LAWS
OF BEHAVIOR[1,2]

Most research in education concerns groups with conclusions based on group averages. The risk in this approach is the loss of important information about *laws of behavior* and individual differences. Consider the following learning plots where each dotted line represents a different individual and the solid line the group mean:

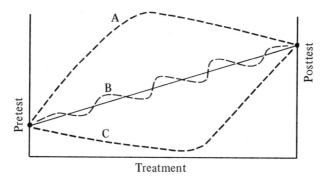

From the group data alone, it might be erroneously concluded that, since the three learners began and ended at the same levels, the learning was equivalent. The individual learning plots, based on serial measures, tell a strikingly different story of three quite distinct events. Learner A made the most initial progress but peaked early and actually lost ground at the end. Learner B made consistent progress with many minor plateaus. Learner C was a slow starter but came through with an impressive spurt at the last minute. Clearly, three different learning events were taking place and no meaningful "law of learning" ever would be discovered using the group data.

Each of the differences between individuals points to a difference in how a behavioral law or laws might be operating at that moment, and that is the crucial question. It is conceivable, for instance, that the above individual differences are all functions of a single reinforcement principle operating in similar ways but at different times and in varying amounts. If so, the discovery of this function depends upon the discrete observations of individuals. Also, to discover *functions* more than two observations are needed, a condition not met by the typical before-and-after paradigm and one that increases in importance if the function is cyclical. Individual serial observations, as often as practical, are essential in research designed

---

1.   Based on notes taken at a Field Studies Workshop given by staff members of the Far West Regional Laboratory, Berkeley, California, 1968.
2.   See item 2, page 94.

to reveal the shape of learning functions. If the three individual learning plots are not variations of a single reinforcement factor but represent complex differences between the three learners and what causes them to learn, this again is the only method that will isolate the kinds of determinants, their characteristics, and the manner of their interaction.

PATTERNS AMONG INDIVIDUALS AND THE USEFULNESS OF SUBGROUPS

Between the overall group average and the infinity of individual differences, it is reasonable to expect meaningful and useful inter-mediate patterns. Consider this commonplace example: In a before-and-after evaluation design involving a class of 33 children, the teacher notes that the posttest mean is 7 points higher than the pretest mean and concludes that "the class improved and her teaching methods are working." Suppose, however, that closer examination of the data reveals a disconcerting fact: while 22 of the children had higher posttest scores, 11 actually had lower scores. Because the children who gained outnumbered the children who lost, there was a deceptive net gain overall. Besides overlooking the losses, the mean gain of 7 points is misleadingly low for those who did improve. More realistic analysis would have reported a mean gain of 17.5 points for the 22 who improved and a mean loss of 14 points for those who regressed. Underneath these several ob-servations lies the problem of test unreliability and the regression effect between the two testings. A conscientious teacher armed with these considerations might ask herself such questions as: What caused two-thirds of my students to do better on the posttest and one-third to do worse? What do children in each category have in common? Do I interact differently with these two groups? Do my methods affect the two groups differently? Or, are my tests reliable enough to give me the answers I seek?

Types of people, styles of learning, and background factors such as socio-economic and cultural differences invite research asking questions about patterns and interactions. For instance, the researcher might want to know what teaching methods work best for what kinds of students, or what kinds of teachers interact more effectively with what kinds of students, or what kinds of learning environments interact favorably with these patterns.

MATCHING AS A CONTROL TECHNIQUE: SOME DISADVANTAGES[1,2]

1. *In general,* the technique of matching subjects to form pairs for later comparison tends to create more control problems than it solves. Therefore, the matching technique is coming under increasing criticism and should generally be set aside in favor of control by random selection and assignment methods. Random assignment is also required when the technique of *analysis of covariance* is applied. This statistical tool allows the adjustment of posttest scores to compensate for a lack of equivalence between control and experimental groups observed on a pretest or initial measure correlated with a post-test. See footnote 2, however, for another option. Also, see page 81, item 2d.

2. *Matching with identical twins using random assignment:* Nature provides an excellent control situation in the case of identical twins, though their relatively rare occurrence poses serious practical limitations on their use. The rule of *random assignment* to treatments or groups must still be observed.

3. *Matching with ordinary subjects on a T_1 variable using random assignment:* While there is some validity in using ordinary subjects matched on some pretest (T_1) criterion (e.g., IQ, achievement, age, or socioeconomic status) and where random assignment to treatments or groups is still observed, certain problems are created. For example:

   a. The problem of deciding on *which* variables to base the matching.

   b. The problem of obtaining satisfactory measures of variables which influence the dependent variable, so that they can be reliably and validly used. Many such variables reported in the literature are too vague, ill-defined, or over-determined to identify or measure objectively.

   c. The problem of statistical regression when matching subjects or groups which turn out to represent different populations with respect to the matching variable(s). Suppose, for example, pairs are made up to represent two different schools, matching subjects on the basis of IQ scores. If the two schools have different mean population IQs, students from each school will tend to regress toward their respective school means on a second intelligence test, creating a difference which may be only a statistical artifact.

   d. The problem of discarding subjects who do not fit the matching criteria, especially if extreme scores are involved or if matching is based on two or more variables. Depending on the number and restrictiveness of the matching variables, the ratio of matching pairs to discards quickly becomes a costly one—twenty acceptable matchings perhaps running into hundreds or even thousands of subjects.

---

1. Adapted in part from Van Dalen, D. B. *Understanding educational research* (4th ed.). New York: Mc-Graw-Hill, 1979. (Adapted from Campbell, D. T., and Stanley, J. C., *Experimental and quasi-experimental designs for research,* Rand McNally and Company, Chicago, 1966.)
2. A solution for avoiding the problems of matched pairs is *matched groups,* grouping subjects into blocks on the basis of their expected homogeneous response on some dependent variable, in the absence of treatment effects, compared to an expected heterogeneous response of subjects selected completely at random. The advantage of matched groups over randomized groups is an expected smaller error mean square in the analysis of variance, for the same number of observations. See Edwards, Allen, L., *Experimental Design in Psychological Research,* Holt, Rinehart, and Winston, Inc., New York, 3rd. Ed., 1968, Chapter 9: "Randomized Block Designs."

If a thing exists, it exists in some amount. If it exists in some amount, it can be measured.

E. L. Thorndike

CHAPTER FOUR

INSTRUMENTATION AND MEASUREMENT

In reaching conclusions in research and evaluation studies it is necessary, first, to establish the *criteria* upon which such conclusions will be based and, second, to provide *measurements* of these criteria.

Instrumentation is the process of selecting or developing measuring devices and methods appropriate to a given evaluation problem. While a variety of approaches to the problem of measurement have been developed, two principal questions confront them all:

1. Is it *reliable?* Is it an accurate, consistent, and stable measuring instrument?

2. Is it *valid?* Is it really measuring what it claims to measure? and, Is it relevant?

Note to the reader: This chapter, more than the others, tends to be a series of relatively autonomous exhibits and may seem disjointed. No attempt is made to create an impression of continuity but the various topics covered were selected on the basis of their utility and representativeness.

A FORM FOR EVALUATING TESTS[1]

1. Title
2. Author
3. Publisher
4. Forms and groups to which applicable
5. Practical features
6. General type
7. Date of publication
8. Cost, booklet; answer sheet
9. Time required
10. Purpose for which evaluated
11. Description of test, items, scoring
12. Author's purpose and basis for selecting items
13. Adequacy of directions; training required to administer
14. Mental functions or traits represented in each score
15. Comments regarding design of test
16. Predictive validation (criterion, number and type of cases, result)
17. Concurrent validation (criterion, number, and type of cases, result)
18. Other empirical evidence indicating what the test measures
19. Comments regarding validity for particular purposes
20. Equivalence of forms or internal consistency (procedure, cases, result)
21. Stability over time (procedure, time interval, cases, result)
22. Norms (type of norms, cases)
23. Comments regarding adequacy of reliability and norms for particular purpose
24. Comments of reviewers
25. General evaluation
26. References

---

1. Cronbach, Lee J., *Essentials of Psychological Testing,* (2nd Ed.). New York: Harper & Brothers, 1960, p. 148.

CHART COMPARING VARIOUS TEST SCORES
AND THEIR CORRESPONDENCE TO EACH OTHER[1]

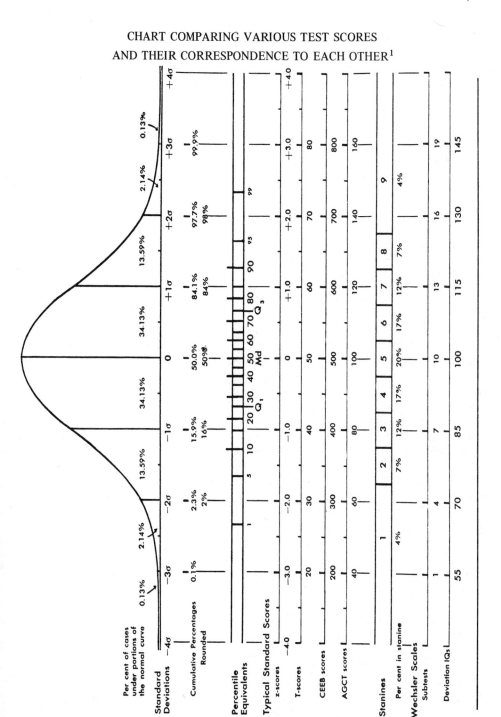

1. Test Service Bulletin Number 48, The Psychological Corporation, 304 East 45th Street, New York, New York 10017.

INTERPRETING TEST SCORES

To interpret a test score, two things must be known:

1. The nature of the score itself—what kind of scoring or scaling system was used in its calculation?

2. The basis for comparison underlying the score—what reference population or norm group does it represent, if any?

TYPES OF TEST SCORES

1. *Raw Scores*—Simply the total number of points an individual earns on a test before it is converted to any formal or standardized scoring system. A raw score, by itself, is uninterpretable, since there is no way of knowing how it compares with anything else.

> EXAMPLE: A high school student obtains the following raw scores: English— first test, 35; second test, 70; and Algebra—96. By these facts alone we have no idea idea how the student is doing. Which of these scores are above average? below average? Which score is actually the highest? the lowest? Compared to his first test in English, did the student do twice as well on the second test? With the limited information provided in the absence of any frame of reference, none of these questions is answerable.

2. *Percentile (Centile) Ranks* and *Percentiles (Centiles)*—Raw scores begin to have meaning when they are rank ordered from high to low. Because this procedure ignores the sample size, a convenient solution is to convert the scores into percentage values. There are two statistics used for this purpose: (1) the *percentile (centile) rank* of any given score, which is a number between 0 and 100 indicating the percent of cases in a norm group falling at or below that score; and, conversely, (2) the *percentile (centile)*, which is a point on a scale of scores at or below which a given percent of the cases falls. For example, an individual obtaining a score on a test with a percentile rank of 68, or whose score lies at the 68th percentile, can be said to be doing *as well as, or better than,* 68 percent of the persons to whom he is being compared. Percentiles of 25, 50, and 75 divide a distribution of scores into four quarters and are called the first, second, and third *quartiles,* respectively. The 50th percentile, or second quartile, is also the *median* or the point on the scale of scores, above and below which lies the top 50 percent and bottom 50 percent of cases, respectively. It is important to remember, however, that each quartile is a *point* on a scale and is not a quarter of the distribution. A score cannot lie *within* any quartile; rather, it lies between two quartiles, below the first quartile, or above the third quartile. Occasionally, a score will fall exactly *at* a particular quartile. If the term *quarter* is used, then it is correct to say a score falls within, for example, the bottom quarter of the distribution.

Percentile ranks and percentiles have three important advantages: (1) they are easily understood by lay audiences; (2) they allow exact interpretation; and (3) they are more appropriate for markedly skewed data than scores based on the normal probability curve. There are also some disadvantages. Because a percentile scale consists of 100 points, it is misleading to report results in percentage terms when the sample size is under 100, a distortion which increases as the sample size approaches zero. Furthermore, percentile ranks and percentiles only permit statements about rank (greater than, equal to, or less than) and the intervals between units are not equal (the interval between the 60th and 70th percentiles is not equal to the interval between the 80th and 90th percentiles). Because the intervals are unequal, their values are misleading near the center of a distribution where they exaggerate small differences (the raw score difference between the percentiles of 50 and 55 may be infinitesimal) and especially misleading at the extremes of a distribution (the raw score difference between the percentiles of 98 and 99 may be quite large). The distortion is apt to be greatest when dealing with several percentiles reported as 99 where raw score score differences can vary tremendously (a "brilliant" student may answer twice as many questions as a "bright" student, but both might be reported as having percentiles of 99, if the two performances fall in the top óne percent of the reference group). The same is true at the opposite end of the scale. As a general rule of thumb, percentiles between 10 and 90 reflect minimal distortion; beyond these limits in either direction they should be interpreted with the distortion factor in mind.

3. *Stanine Scores*—Stanine ("standard nine") scores combine the understandability of percentages with the properties of the normal curve of probability. A scale is created with nine intervals, each interval representing half of a standard deviation. The middle interval (5th stanine) straddles the midpoint of the distribution, encompassing the middle 20 percent of cases. The 4th, 3rd, 2nd, and 1st stanines, moving from the center to the extreme lower end of the distribution in increments of one-half of a standard deviation, encompass respectively, 17, 12, 7, and 4 percent of the cases. Correspondingly, the 6th, 7th, 8th, and 9th stanines, moving from the center to the extreme upper end of the distribution in like increments, also encompass respectively, 17, 12, 7, and 4 percent of the cases. Examination of the chart on page 103 graphically illustrates these characteristics and allows direct comparisons to other scales. Note that a stanine is not a point on a scale like a percentile but a relatively broad interval. It is, therefore, insensitive to sizeable differences within a stanine interval and misleadingly sensitive to small differences on either side of the point separating adjacent stanine intervals. Nevertheless, stanine scores are coming into increasing use because of their simplicity and utility.

4. *Standard Scores*—The most powerful scores, statistically, are standard scores derived from the properties of the normal probability curve and preserving the absolute differences between scores, a feature percentile or stanine scores do not possess. Furthermore, they can be used in calculating averages and correlations yielding the same results as the original raw scores. Standard scores from a variety of tests also have the advantage of being directly comparable if the reference groups are equivalent. Their major disadvantages are two: if data are markedly skewed, they are inappropriate, and, because of their dependence on the standard deviation, they are difficult to explain to lay audiences.

a. *z-scores*—If a mean and standard deviation are computed for a given set of raw scores, each raw score can be expressed in terms of its distance from the mean in standard deviation units or *z-scores:*

$$z\text{-score} = \frac{\text{Raw Score} - \text{Mean}}{\text{Standard Deviation}} = \frac{X - M}{\sigma}$$

From the formula it is clear that z-scores at the mean have a value of zero, increasing in numerical size the farther they lie from the mean. Since 99.74 percent of all scores in a normal distribution fall between a range of three standard deviations above the mean and three standard deviations below the mean, z-scores greater than 3.00 are seldom reported though, theoretically, they have no limit. The z-score above the mean carries a plus sign; below the mean, a minus sign. The utility of z-scores comes from their relationship to properties of the normal curve of probability (see chart, page 103). Using a table for the area underneath a normal curve (see Table A, page 227), statements can be made about the proportion of cases above or below any z-score value or between any two z-score values.

b. *T-Scores*—Because z-scores have a mean of zero and involve decimals as well as plus and minus signs, they are awkward to interpret. *T*-scores get around this problem by arbitrarily setting a new mean equal to 50 and the standard deviation equal to 10. By understanding the properties of z-scores and the normal curve of probability, and making the simple conversion to *T*-scores, the advantages of both systems are combined (see chart, page 103).

c. *Other Standard Scores*—Many other scoring systems are based on properties of the normal probability curve. The College Entrance Examination Board (CEEB) simply multiplies the *T*-score system by 10, creating a mean of 500 and a standard deviation of 100. Tests of intelligence set the mean IQ at 100 and their standard deviations at 15, 16, or 20, depending on the test. Note that these differences in standard deviations further complicate comparisons of IQs between tests which differ in this respect.

5. *Grade Level Scores*[1]—Grade level scores are based on the relationship between scores on a test and the *average* performance of children at each of a series of grade levels. The average score for fourth graders in the norm group at the beginning of the fourth grade, for example, is assigned a grade level value of 4.0, for fifth graders, 5.0, and so forth. Each grade level is broken down further into ten substeps roughly equivalent to a ten-month school year, beginning, for example, in September for the fourth grade with 4.0 and ending in June with 4.9. Grade level scores are popular with educators and parents because they fit the framework of a pupil's progress from one level to the next in the school system. They have several serious shortcomings, however. They suggest an interval scale such that the growth of one grade level is an equivalent unit of growth throughout the system. This conclusion is seldom true, since progress at different grade levels depends heavily on the nature of the instructional program. It is a relationship supportable only when the instruction is continuous throughout the grades as in the case of mathematics and starts breaking down in an area such as reading after the primary grades when instruction, per se, ceases. From the eighth grade through high school, grade level scores are virtually meaningless since they are extrapolations from lower grade performance levels or represent subject matter taught in only one or two grades. Developmental characteristics peculiar to certain age levels that appear to be more often a function of maturational age rather than instruction further complicate the notion that a grade level is an equivalent unit of growth throughout the grades.

    The fact that gains slow down in the upper grades greatly compromises the interpretation of the performance of a child with superior ability, since he often exceeds the average of the highest grade covered by the norms. Superior children at lower grade levels often score two or more grade levels above their actual classroom placement; it is inaccurate, however, to assume they have mastery of a given subject at the higher grade level or that they could

---

1. The authors are indebted for many of these observations to Thorndike, R. L. and Hagen, E., *Measurement and Evaluation in Psychology and Education* (4th ed.), New York: Wiley, 1977.

work efficiently with the older children in that higher grade. Many bright children obtain high scores because they are faster and more accurate than the average for their own age and grade. To conclude that they have mastery of the subject at some advanced grade level is misleading. For instance, a child in the third grade, who might have a 6.5 grade level score in Arithmetic, most likely has *not* learned arithmetic as the average mid-year sixth grader knows it—to a large extent he is simply performing rapidly and efficiently with third grade arithmetic.

Another disadvantage arises when grade level scores in the lower ranges are interpreted too literally, suggesting that children "below grade level" are either poorly motivated (underachievers) or poorly taught. Grade level scores are normally distributed as are IQs, standard scores, and stanines. These other scores, along with percentile ranks, are less apt to raise unrealistic questions, since they do not remind us of grade placement, *per se*.

In general, grade level scores are most relevant in elementary schools where subject matter tends to be more often continuous. Beyond the sixth grade they progressively lose meaning. Furthermore, the same problems besetting grade level scores hold true for *age level scores*.

REFERENCE POPULATIONS—NORM GROUPS

Once a raw score is converted to some scale of measurement, usually in terms of a rank or deviation from the mean, the next question is, *To whom is he being compared?* Just to the other students in the classroom, as in the case of most teacher-made tests? To all other students at that age or grade level in the school or school district? To all other students at that age or grade level in the state or nation? Standardized tests report scores based on a norm group representing a defined population and until this comparison group is clearly known, a satisfactory interpretation of the score is not possible.

For many evaluation purposes, the selection of a norm group is crucial. The same raw score on the College Board Examination may represent, for example, the 90th percentile for typical four-year liberal arts colleges but only the 20th percentile for the highly selective Ivy League institutions. The appropriate norm group is even more critical where second languages and different socio-economic and subculture patterns are concerned. Another caution where age, grade, or class level norm groups are involved, is to be sure the points in time when the measurements were made are comparable. For example, were the local fourth graders tested at the same point during the year as the fourth grade norm group? Are the "freshmen" norms for entering freshmen, mid-year freshmen, or end-of-the-year freshmen?

Still another pitfall appears after all other considerations have been checked out, should the norm group have had different kinds or amounts of instruction in a given subject matter area. Some reading tests, for instance, are normed on populations whose average daily exposure to reading instruction is twice that of the local pupils; they may also differ as to the instructional emphasis or approach, one group receiving instruction more closely related to the test content than the other.

COMPARING NORM-REFERENCED WITH CRITERION-REFERENCES TESTS

Over the years, a controversy has arisen concerning the merits of norm-referenced tests in relation to those of criterion-referenced tests. As is often the case in such controversial matters, both types of tests have their advantages and limitations. Instead of addressing the concern of which form of measurement is better, a balanced viewpoint would ask this question: When is it appropriate to use one or the other type of measure? The answer is seldom straightforward or simple. It depends on (a) an adequate familiarity with the attributes of selected versions of both types of tests and (b) the requirements of the particular situation being assessed.

Typically, widely used norm-referenced and criterion-referenced tests are standardized. A standardized test is one that has been carefully constructed and field-tested as well as one that has carefully prepared and uniform directions for administration and scoring. Generally speaking, standardized tests are commercially produced.

A norm-referenced standardized test affords a comparison of the performance of each student to that of the norm group across a certain content coverage. Customarily, this content coverage tends to be general and broad, and the norm group is representative of students of a given age or grade level within a large geographical unit such as a county, state, or the nation. Norm-referenced tests vary in the degree to which they measure how much a student has learned. Nevertheless, they do emphasize reporting results in terms of where each student stands on the test in relation to the placement of students in the norm group. In standardized achievement tests of either a norm-referenced or criterion-referenced orientation, content validity is of supreme importance. Even in a norm-referenced test reflecting curricular objectives, content validity usually takes some precedence over the capability of the test to differentiate between high-performing and low-performing students. To provide a basis for the distribution of these two groups of differentially scoring students, the items of norm-referenced tests are selected, in part, such that students who pass any single item also tend to earn high scores on the total test, whereas students who fail on any single item are likely to earn low scores on the total test.

As a result of this practice, a score continuum ranging from high to low is created along which students can be spread and identified as showing different degrees of competence or capability. To afford a means of comparing the standings of students along the score continuum, percentile ranks (numbers indicating the percentages of students in the norm group who fall below given scores) are often employed, particularly to facilitate communication of the results of a testing experience. Sometimes, grade equivalents (numbers revealing the estimated grade level standing corresponding to given raw scores) are used. Researchers often prefer standard scores, which furnish a unit-free index revealing how many standard deviations above or below the mean a given raw score falls.

A criterion-referenced standardized test yields a comparison of each student's level of mastery to that of the total body of knowledge that the test has been designed to cover. Typically, this level of mastery is indicated by the percentage of items answered correctly among all possible items. The test is based on a criterion (or standard) of achievement that focuses solely on the mastering of content rather than on a determination of the rank ordering of students for evaluative purposes. For residents of California, a familiar example of a criterion-referenced test is the State of California Motor Vehicle Department's written examination for the driver's license. Test items are selected primarily to ensure content coverage irrespective of whether they prove to be easy or difficult. Many items that nearly everyone has answered correctly are retained, as this response behavior reflects a high level of mastery that is the ideal for the competence or proficiency standard desired as a consequence of a public school or private school training course. (It should be noted that such items are usually eliminated from norm-referenced tests, as they contribute nothing to the ranking of students.) The essential task in constructing sound criterion-referenced tests is the clear and specific definition of the content or subject matter to be covered by a particular instructional program in terms of comprehensive and measurable objectives. Scores on criterion-referenced tests are usually reported as "pass" or "fail" depending upon whether or not the criterion level has been attained.

It is possible for a standardized test to be both norm-referenced and criterion-referenced, although this circumstance is not common in most educational practice, as criterion-referenced tests are so specific that they have limited application. Moreover, it frequently occurs that the score distributions of criterion-referenced tests as well as the difficulty levels of a large proportion of the items provide a sufficiently wide range in resulting numerical values that traditional approaches of psychometric evaluation can still be employed.

In summary, a norm-referenced test indicates one's standing in the score distribution compared to that of students comprising a norm group (although it often provides additional information concerning which items in content areas have been answered correctly), and a criterion-referenced test reveals one's mastery level of a given body of knowledge anchored to specific curricular objectives. Both types of tests require a careful definition of the curricular or content objectives to be covered, comparable skills in writing items, and seasoned judgment in interpretation and use of scores for evaluation purposes.

The table that is placed on the adjacent page is an attempt to summarize some typical generalizable similarities and differences in the types of attributes or characteristics associated with norm-referenced and criterion-referenced tests. However, as norm-referenced tests often have criterion-referenced characteristics—a circumstance showing an increasingly evident trend—and as criterion-referenced tests for some groups can become norm-referenced for the same or other groups, each attribute needs to be examined carefully in light of possible unique or joint relevancies.[1]

---

1. The authors are indebted for much of this material to W. A. Mehrens and R. L. Ebel who expressed their ideas about criterion-referenced and norm-referenced tests in their article "Some Comments on Criterion-Referenced and Norm-Referenced Achievement Tests" that appeared in the periodical (newsletter) *NCME Measurement in Education,* Vol. 10, No. 1, Winter, 1979.

Attribute	Norm-Referenced Test (NRT)	Criterion-Referenced Test (CRT)
State of the Art	Highly developed; technically sound	Mixed & variable; technology developing
Developmental Cost	Major	Moderate to major
Consumer Cost	Relatively inexpensive	Relatively expensive
Utility	General purpose; long-lived	Situation-specific; short-lived
Content Validity & Coverage	Based on a specified content domain, appropriately sampled, and tending to have fewer items per objective. Tends to be general and broad.	Based on a specified content domain, appropriately sampled, and tending to have more items per objective. Tends to be specific and narrow.
Score Interpretation	In terms of a specified norm group (e.g., percentile ranks, grade equivalents)	In terms of a specified criterion of proficiency (e.g., percent mastery)
Item Development	Two main considerations: content validity and item discrimination	One main consideration: content validity
Standardized	Yes	Usually
Sensitivity to Instruction	Tends to be low to moderate, because of its general purpose nature	Tends to be high, when closely matched to a particular instructional situation
Reliability	High	Can be high, but sometimes hard to establish
Application	To assess the effectiveness of given instructional treatments in achieving general instructional objectives	To assess the effectiveness of given instructional treatments in achieving specific instructional objectives

References

Ebel, R. L. *Essentials of educational measurement.* Englewood Cliffs, N.J.: Prentice Hall, 1972.

Mehrens, W. A. and Ebel, R. L. Some comments on criterion-referenced and norm-referenced achievement tests. *NCME Measurement in Education,* (Winter) 1979, 10(1).

Mehrens, W. A. and Lehmann, I. J. *Measurement and evaluation in education and psychology* (2nd Ed.). New York: Holt, Rinehart, & Winston, 1978.

Millman, J. Criterion-referenced measurement. In W. J. Popham (Ed.). *Evaluation in education: Current applications.* Berkeley, CA: McCutchan Publishing Company, 1974 (Chapter 6).

Popham, W. J. *Criterion-referenced measurement.* Englewood Cliffs, N. J.: Prentice-Hall, 1978.

Popham, W. J. and Lindheim, E. The practical side of criterion-referenced test development. *NCME Measurement in Education,* (Spring) 1980, 10(4).

THE RELATIONSHIP BETWEEN TYPE OF TEST AND CLASSROOM INSTRUCTION

Figure 1, was designed (Baker and Hanson, 1978) to clarify the relationship between the type of test and its sensitivity to classroom instruction. The instruments available for assessment procedures are arrayed along a continuum of instructional influence, from most influenced to least influenced by classroom instruction. Further, the dotted lines around the three sets of boxes illustrate the "is happening–should be happening–planning to happen" concept as it is dealt with internally at the local district level. The types of tests represented within each set of dotted lines provide the most appropriate information for that particular level of educational responsibility. It is clear that the two most useful types of measurement instruments for making instruction-related decisions are the program-specific and domain-referenced measures.

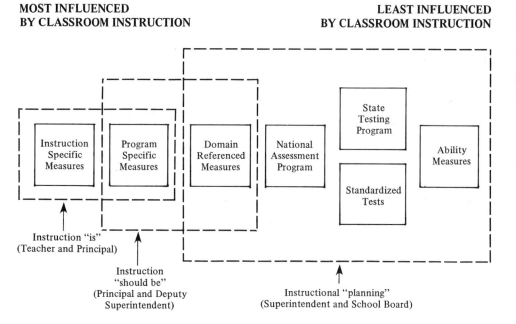

Figure 1: Influence of classroom instruction on test performance.

Baker, R. L., & Hanson, R. A. Information Requirements for Assessing the Effects of Formal Schooling, Los Alamitos, CA.: SWRL Educational Research & Development, 1978. (Reproduced with permission.)

STANDARD SCORE AND PERCENTILE RANK EQUIVALENTS
FOR NORMAL DISTRIBUTIONS OF SCORES

Standard Score		Approx. Percentile	Standard Score		Approx. Percentile	Standard Score		Approx. Percentile
z	T	Rank	z	T	Rank	z	T	Rank
-3.0	20	0.1	-0.9	41	18.4	1.2	62	88.5
-2.9	21	0.2	-0.8	42	21.2	1.3	63	90.3
-2.8	22	0.3	-0.7	43	24.2	1.4	64	91.9
-2.7	23	0.4	-0.6	44	27.4	1.5	65	93.3
-2.6	24	0.5	-0.5	45	30.8	1.6	66	94.5
-2.5	25	0.6	-0.4	46	34.5	1.7	67	95.5
-2.4	26	0.8	-0.3	47	38.2	1.8	68	96.4
-2.3	27	1.1	-0.2	48	42.1	1.9	69	97.1
-2.2	28	1.4	-0.1	49	46.0	2.0	70	97.7
-2.1	29	1.8	0.0	50	50.0	2.1	71	98.2
-2.0	30	2.3	0.1	51	54.0	2.2	72	98.6
-1.9	31	2.9	0.2	52	57.9	2.3	73	98.9
-1.8	32	3.6	0.3	53	61.8	2.4	74	99.2
-1.7	33	4.5	0.4	54	65.5	2.5	75	99.4
-1.6	34	5.5	0.5	55	69.2	2.6	76	99.5
-1.5	35	6.7	0.6	56	72.6	2.7	77	99.6
-1.4	36	8.0	0.7	57	75.8	2.8	78	99.7
-1.3	37	9.7	0.8	58	78.8	2.9	79	99.8
-1.2	38	11.5	0.9	59	81.6	3.0	80	99.9-
-1.1	39	13.6	1.0	60	84.1	3.1	81	99.9
-1.0	40	15.9	1.1	61	86.4	3.2	82	99.9+

Note: If one wishes to normalize a distribution of scores that may depart from normality, one first finds the percentile rank for a given raw score and then finds the approximate z or T score that corresponds to the percentile rank that was determined. This procedure is very common among test publishers who in having found a somewhat skewed distribution of scores wish to express the given raw scores in the form of standard score equivalents that can be conventionally interpreted for either research or dissemination purposes.

THE RASCH SCALING MODEL

The Rasch Model is a method of constructing tests. It provides a theory for (1) item analysis and selection, and (2) a measurement scale for reporting scores.

Essential Characteristics

The Rasch model states that the probability of a person answering correctly a test item is a function of two attributes or paramenters:

1. The *person* attribute — theoretically, any trait of interest in the measurement situation, but most often "ability," "achievement," and "aptitude." More specifically, it

is the amount of such a trait the person possesses to answer correctly a certain number of items like the ones on a given test.

2. The *item* attribute – in effect, the difficulty level, defined as that point on the ability scale where the person has a fifty percent chance of answering the item correctly.

As a result, the Rasch Model puts people and test items on the same scale. The estimation of these two attributes – person ability and item difficulty – is termed *calibration*. Item calibration involves the evaluation of the fit of the difficulty parameter. Test calibration requires the evaluation of the fit of the persons to the Rasch Model and the estimation of the ability parameter corresponding to each test score.

Underlying Assumptions

The fit of the items and persons to the Rasch Model depends on whether or not the following assumptions are met:

1. *Unidimensionality:* assumes that items can be arranged in order of difficulty along a single continuum such that the performance of a person on these items can be represented by a single score that is on the same continuum as the items. Implication: difficult items should be more often answered correctly by persons with high ability rather than by those with low ability.

2. *Equal Item Discrimination:* assumes that items represent equal units when summed to yield a total score.

3. *No Guessing:* assumes that no one correctly guesses an answer. Implication: when low ability persons guess correctly on difficult items the unidimensionality assumption is violated.

4. *Independence of Items:* assumes, for a person of a given ability, a response to one item is independent of a response to any other item; that is, a correct response to one item cannot depend on a correct response to any other item.

It is noteworthy that, although a great deal of research has focused on the effects of violating these assumptions, classical test theory makes these assumptions too – for example, when the test score equals the sum of all correct answers. Moreover, if the assumptions of the Rasch Model are met – specifically, the items and the persons fit the model – the estimates of ability and item difficulty are taken to be "specifically objective" or invariant. Implications: (1) for *items,* the estimates of item difficulty are independent of both particular persons and all other items in the calibration situation; (2) for *persons,* the estimates of their abilities are independent of both the particular items used in this determination and all other persons being measured. The invariance of item calibrations and person measurement has led to the concepts of "item-free," or "test-free," measurement and "person-free," or "sample-free," item calibration – concepts particularly appealing to test developers.

Implications for Test Development

Given the three basic components of test development – (1) content specification and item writing, (2) item analysis, and (3) test form assembly – the principal difference between the Rasch Model and traditional methods centers on item analysis. Traditional item analysis is based on two statistics: *item difficulty* (p) – the proportion of examinees correctly answering an item; and *item discrimination* (r) – the extent to which an item differentiates between high- and low-scoring students. The problem inherent in this procedure is that both item statistics vary from one group of examinees to another with the result that these statistics are sample-bound.

Rasch item statistics have the following attributes (at least theoretically) to overcome this limitation:

1. They are invariant from group to group — hence, sample free.
2. An estimate of the examinee's ability level can be made independent from the set of items on a particular test — hence, item-free person measurement.
3. Item difficulty and examinee's ability levels are referenced on the same scale.
4. The ability scale is equal-interval.

The Rasch model remains both a promising and perplexing method. The validity of its assumptions have been called into question and yet it continues to gain in use each year. Perhaps its two greatest drawbacks are the complex mathematical foundation which makes it extremely difficult to understand or to explain to non-technical audiences, and some emerging problems regarding the underlying assumptions and their empirical validations.

References

Demaline, R. *The Rasch Model and Title I Evaluation.* Portland, Oregon: Northwest Regional Educational Laboratory, March, 1979.

Journal of Educational Measurement, (Summer) 1977, 14(2). (Entire issue devoted to latent trait models.)

Lenke, J. M. The Rasch Model — An overview. Paper presented at the meeting of the Tenth Annual Large School Systems Invitational Conference on Measurement in Education (The Psychological Corporation), Houston, April 1978.

Rentz, R. R. and Rentz, C. C. Does the Rasch Model really work? *NCME Measurement in Education,* (Spring) 1979, 10(2).

THE DELPHI TECHNIQUE
Reaching Group Consensus Individually

When group consensus is desired, the traditional approach is a round table discussion of those concerned or their representatives. Disadvantages of this process are numerous: (1) the bandwagon effect of a majority opinion; (2) the power of a persuasive or prestigious individual to shape group opinion; (3) the vulnerability of group dynamics to manipulation; and (4) the unwillingness of individuals to abandon publicly stated positions.

The Delphi Technique (Helmer, 1967) was designed to generate group consensus while minimizing the foregoing disadvantages. In essence, it identifies the group members who will generate the consensus position but interacts with them individually to provide collective feedback of the emerging consensus to each member privately. Individuals then reconsider their initial positions in light of the group trends and make any adjustments felt to be appropriate. The final result is an informed consensus insulated from the forces of face-to-face group interaction.

Typical Sequence of Events

1. Identify the group members whose consensus opinions are sought. If the study goes beyond an intact group such that representatives must be selected, care must be taken to insure that all the various publics or positions are proportionately sampled.

2. *Questionnaire One.* Have each member generate a list of goals, concerns, or issues toward which consensus opinions are desired. Edit the results to a manageable summary of items presented in random order. Prepare the second questionnaire in an appropriate format for rating or ranking. (Note: if an established or acceptable listing of such items already exists, this first step can be bypassed.)

3. *Questionnaire Two.* Have each member rate or rank the resulting items.

4. *Questionnaire Three.* Present the results of Questionnaire Two in the form of Questionnaire Three, showing the preliminary level of group consensus to each item and repeating each member's earlier response. The respondent rates or ranks each item a second time, now aware of the preliminary group trend. For each item where the individual differs substantially from the group, and chooses to remain so on Questionnaire Three, the respondent should provide a brief reason or explanation.

5. *Questionnaire Four.* The results of Questionnaire Three are presented in the form of Questionnaire Four, showing the new level of group consensus for each item and repeating that member's latest rating or ranking, along with a listing by item of the major reasons members had for dissent from the prevailing group position. Each member rates or ranks each item for the third and final time, in light of the emerging pattern of group consensus and the reasons for dissent.

6. The results of Questionnaire Four are tabulated and presented as the final statement of group consensus.

References

Cyphert, F. R. and Gant, W. L. The Delphi Technique, *Phi Delta Kappan,* 1971, 42(5), 272-273.

Helmer, O. *Analysis of the future: The Delphi Technique.* Santa Monica, CA: Rand Corporation, 1967.

Rasp, A., Jr. Delphi: A decision-maker's dream. *Nation's Schools,* July 1973, 92(1), 29-32.

ITEM ANALYSIS[1]

Item analysis is a procedure to increase the reliability and validity of a test by separately evaluating each test item to determine whether or not that item *discriminates* in the same way the overall test is intended to discriminate. For example, given a test of academic aptitude or achievement, will students in the top half of the test score distribution also tend to get a particular item correct and students in the bottom half of this distribution tend to miss this same item? If so, such an item has favorable discriminating power and contributes to the overall reliability and validity of the test.

EXAMPLE A—*Steps in the Item Analysis of a True-False or Multiple Choice Aptitude or Achievement Test:*

1. Rank order the distribution of test scores from high to low.

2. Divide these ranked scores into two contrasting groups. The division point is arbitrary but common practice is to split the data in half, forming the Top and Bottom Halves; or, to increase the contrast, compare Upper and Lower Quarters. For ease of computation, use two groups of equal size.

3. Construct a four-fold table based on two pairs of categories. The first pair is simply the category *Wrong-Right* (for a specific test item); the second pair is the category *High-Scorers-Low Scorers* (depending on how the ranks were divided):

	Wrong	Right
High		
Low		

4. Calculate the chi square (χ^2) value of the resulting proportions using Computer Guide 10, p. 178.

5. If χ^2 is significant, it can be concluded that a dependable difference exists in the proportion of high and low scoring subjects who gave correct answers. Items that meet this criterion should be retained; items that fail to meet it should be discarded.

EXAMPLE B—*Steps in the Item Analysis of a Three-Choice Interest Inventory:*

Interest or personality inventories often attempt to discriminate between the preferences of two subgroups on a given series of items. For instance, if the following item is given to a group of art majors and physical education majors in four-year colleges, will it discriminate between them?

> I would enjoy browsing through old curio
> shops on weekends or vacations.   *A*   ?   *D**
> * *A*, Agree; ?, Undecided; *D*, Disagree.

---

1. See page 173 for a correlational approach to item analysis.

1. Divide the data into two groups: art majors and physical education majors.
2. Construct a 2 × 3 contingency table:

	Disagree	?	Agree
Art Majors			
P.E. Majors			

3. Calculate χ^2 using Computing Guide 12, p. 180.
4. If χ^2 is significant, it can be concluded that a dependable difference exists in the proportion of Art and P.E. majors who answered appropriately—presumably art majors tending to agree and P.E. majors tending to disagree.

SOME SOURCES OF INFORMATION ON TESTS AND MEASURES

Standard Tests and Measures:

1. Buros, Oscar K. (ed.) *The Eighth Mental Measurements Yearbook* (Vols. 1,2). Highland Park, New Jersey: Gryphon Press, 1978.
2. Buros, Oscar K. (ed.). *Tests in Print II,* Highland Park, New Jersey: Gryphon Press, 1974.
3. Buros, Oscar K. (ed.). *Reading Tests and Reviews.* Highland Park, New Jersey: Gryphon Press, 1968.
4. *Journal of Educational Measurement.* Quarterly Journal.
5. *Educational and Psychological Measurement.* Quarterly Journal.
6. *Review of Educational Research.* Every three years: *1968,* 1965, 1962, etc. Beginning in 1970, however, an unscheduled publication pattern replaces the cyclical one.
7. Miscellaneous test publishers' catalogs—most *current* source of information. See Buros for listing of publishers.
8. *Psychological Abstracts.*
9. *Educational Index.*
10. *ERIC* (Educational Resources Information Center): Nineteen clearing-houses, depending on the nature of the need. For general information regarding information retrieval resources, procedures, and publications, contact: USOE, 400 Maryland Avenue SW, Washington, D.C. 20202.
11. Thorndike, R. L., and Hagen, Elizabeth. *Measurement and Evaluation in Psychology and Education,* (4th ed.). New York: John Wiley and Sons, 1977.

Nonstandard Tests and Measures:

1. *Psychological Abstracts.*

2. *Educational Index.*

3. Webb, E. J., Campbell, D. T., Schwartz, R. D., and Sechrest, Lee. *Unobtrusive Measures: Nonreactive Research in the Social Sciences.* Chicago: Rand McNally, 1966.

4. Educational Testing Service, *Microfiche File,* Princeton, New Jersey. This is a comprehensive file of measures and instruments reported by researchers in the literature. It is important to state your measurement needs in clear and specific terms in order for ETS to match your request to an appropriate measure, if one exists.

5. Shaw, Marvin E. and Wright, Jack M. *Scales for the Measurement of Attitudes.* New York: McGraw-Hill Book Co., 1967. A review of the literature, with comprehensive exhibits and applications.

6. Oppenheim, A. N., *Questionnaire Design and Attitude Measurement.* New York: Basic Books, Inc., 1966.

7. *ERIC.* (See item 10, above.)

THREE TYPES OF VALIDITY[1]

	QUESTION	METHOD	COMMON USE	EXAMPLE
Content Validity	How well does the content of the test sample the kinds of things about which conclusions are to be drawn?	Logically conclude whether or not the test content comprises an adequate *definition* of what it claims to measure.	Achievement tests.	A test of school readiness is examined to see whether the content relates to knowledge and skills expected of first grade children following the kindergarten program.
Criterion-related Validity[2]	Does the test compare well with external variables considered to be direct measures of the characteristic or behavior in question?	Give the test and compare it with the criterion variable. The latter may be obtained concurrently or predicted, and then obtained in the future, depending on the recommended use of the original test.	Tests used in place of a more complicated procedure; or to select and classify persons.	Diagnosis of mental instability based on a card-sorting test compared with a more elaborate psychiatric examination; intelligence test scores used to predict future performance.
Construct Validity	To what extent do certain explanatory concepts or qualities account for performance on the test?	Based on the theory underlying the test, set up hypotheses regarding the behavior of persons with high or low scores. Test the hypothesis.	Tests used for description, or in scientific research.	A test of personality types is studied to see how well theoretical implications of the typologies account for actual results obtained.

Note: The term *"face validity"* often is used to indicate whether the instrument, on the face of it, appears to measure what it claims to measure. Will persons making use of this instrument, accept it as a valid measure in the everyday sense of the word? While face validity is not a rigorous concept, its importance never can be ignored on that basis. Its presence, in conjunction with the above categories of validity, reinforces overall acceptance. It also is true that face validity, in the absence of these other standards, can be dangerously misleading, just as its absence, when these other validities are, in fact, present, can lead to disbelieving and frustrating resistance among potential users.

1. Based on format originally developed by Lee J. Cronbach.
2. Formerly, Concurrent Validity and Predictive Validity.

VALIDITY[1,2]

Validity information indicates the degree to which the test is capable of achieving certain aims. Tests are used for several types of judgment, and for each type of judgment, a different type of investigation is required to establish validity. For purposes of describing the uses for three kinds of validity coefficients, we may distinguish three of the rather numerous aims of testing:

1. *The test user wishes to determine how an individual performs at present in a universe of situations that the test situation is claimed to represent.* For example, most achievement tests used in schools measure the student's performance on a sample of questions intended to represent a certain phase of educational achievement or certain education objectives.

2. *The test user wishes to forecast an individual's future standing or to estimate an individual's present standing on some variable of particular significance that is different from the test.* For example, an academic aptitude test may forecast grades, or a brief adjustment inventory may estimate what the outcome would be of a careful psychological examination.

3. *The test user wishes to infer the degree to which the individual possesses some hypothetical trait or quality (construct) presumed to be reflected in the test performance.* For example, he wants to know whether the individual stands high on some proposed abstract trait such as "intelligence" or "creativity" that cannot be observed directly. This may be done to learn something about the individual, or it may be done to study the test itself, to study its relationship to other tests, or to develop psychological theory.

Different types of tests are often used for each of the different aims, but this is not always the case. There is much overlap in types of tests and in the purposes for which they are used. Thus, a vocabulary test might be used as: (a) simply a measure of present vocabulary, the universe being all the words in the language; (b) a screening device to discriminate present or potential schizophrenics from organics; or (c) a means of making inferences about "intellectual capacity."

To determine how suitable a test is for each of these uses, it is necessary to gather the appropriate sort of validity information. The kind of information to be gathered depends on the aim or aims of testing rather than on the type of test. The three aspects of validity corresponding to the three aims of testing may be named content validity, criterion-related validity, and construct validity.

---

1. This material was taken from the *Standards for Educational and Psychological Tests and Manuals,* American Psychological association (Co-chairmen of joint committee, APA, AERA, NCME: John W. French and William B. Michael). Revised, 1966. Supplementary information with slightly different emphases about validity may now be found in a report by a new joint committee entitled *Standards for Educational and Psychological Tests,* published by the American Psychological Association in 1974 under the chairmanship of the late Frederick B. Davis.

2. While reliability coefficients are customarily greater than validity coefficients, validity is always the important question. Maximum possible validity $= \sqrt{\dfrac{\text{Reliability of Test}}{} \times \dfrac{\text{Reliability of Criterion}}{}}$

Content validity is demonstrated by showing how well the content of the test samples the class situations or subject matter about which conclusions are to be drawn. Content validity is especially important for achievement and proficiency measures and for measures of adjustment or social behavior based on observation in selected situations. The manual should justify the claim that the test content represents the assumed universe of tasks, conditions, or processes. A useful way of looking at this universe of tasks or items is to consider it to comprise a *definition* of the achievement to be measured by the test. In the case of an educational achievement test, the content of the test may be regarded as a definition of (or a sampling from a population of) one or more educational objectives. The aptitudes, skills, and knowledges required of the student for successful test performance must be precisely the types of aptitudes, skills, and knowledges that the school wishes to develop in the students and to evaluate in terms of test scores. Thus evaluating the content validity of a test for a particular purpose is the same as subjectively recognizing the adequacy of a definition. This process is actually quite similar to the subjective evaluation of the criterion itself. Unless, however, the aim of an achievement test is specifically to forecast or substitute for some criterion, its correlation with a criterion is *not* a useful evaluation of the test.

Criterion-related validity is demonstrated by comparing the test scores with one or more external variables considered to provide a direct measure of the characteristic or behavior in question. This comparison may take the form of an expectancy table or, most commonly, a correlation relating the test score to a criterion measure. Predictive uses of tests include long-range forecasts of one or more measures of academic achievement, prediction of vocational success, and prediction of reaction to therapy. On some occasions the criterion data are collected concurrently with the test; for example, when one wishes to know whether a testing procedure can take the place of more elaborate procedures for diagnosing personality disorders. A test that is related to one or more concurrent criteria will not necessarily predict status on the same criterion at some later date. Whether the criterion data should be collected concurrently with the testing or at a later time depends on whether the test is recommended for prediction or for assessment of present status.

Construct validity is evaluated by investigating what qualities a test measures, that is, by determining the degree to which certain explanatory concepts or constructs account for performance on the test. To examine construct validity requires a combination of logical and empirical attack. Essentially, studies of construct validity check on the theory underlying the test. The procedure involves three steps. First, the investigator inquires: From this theory, what hypotheses may we make regarding the behavior of persons with high or low scores? Second, he gathers data to test these hypotheses. Third, in light of the evidence, he makes an inference as to whether the theory is adequate to explain the data collected. If the theory fails to account for the data, he should revise the test interpretation, reformulate the theory, or reject the theory altogether. Fresh evidence would be required to demonstrate construct validity for the revised interpretation.

A simple procedure for investigating what a test measures is to correlate it with other tests. We would expect a valid test of numerical reasoning, for example, to correlate more highly with other numerical tests than with clerical perception tests. Another procedure is experimental. If it is hypothesized, for example, that form perception on a certain projective test indicates probable ability to function well under emotional stress, this inference may be checked by placing individuals in an experimental situation producing emotional stress and observing whether their behavior corresponds to the hypothesis.

Construct validity is ordinarily studied when the tester wishes to increase his understanding of the psychological qualities being measured by the test. A validity coefficient relating test to criterion, unless it is established in the context of some theory, yields no information about *why* the correlation is high or low, or about how one might improve the measurement. Construct validity is relevant when the tester accepts no existing measure as a definite criterion of the quality with which he is concerned (e.g., in measuring a postulated drive such as need for achievement), or when a test will be used in so many diverse decisions that no single criterion applies (e.g., in identifying the ability of Peace Corps trainees to adapt to new cultures). Here the traits or qualities underlying test performance are of central importance. It must be remembered, however, that, without a study of criterion-related validity, a test developed for diagnosis or prediction can be regarded only as experimental.

These three aspects of validity are only conceptually independent, and only rarely is just one of them important in a particular situation, A complete study of a test would normally involve information about all types of validity. A first step in the preparation of a predictive (*criterion-related*) instrument may be to consider what *constructs* are likely to provide a basis for selecting or devising an effective test. Sampling from a *content* universe may also be an early step in producing a test whose use for *prediction* is the ultimate concern. Even after satisfactory *prediction* has been established, information regarding *construct* validity may make the test more useful; it may, for example, provide a basis for identifying situations other than the validating situation where the test is appropriate as a predictor. To analyze *construct* validity, all the knowledge regarding validity would be brought to bear.

The three concepts of validity are pertinent to all kinds of tests. It is the intended use of the test rather than its nature that determines what kind of evidence is required.

Intelligence or scholastic aptitude tests most often use criterion-related validity to show how well they are able to predict academic success in school or college, but the nature of the aptitudes measured is often judged from the content of the items, and the place of the aptitude within the array of human abilities is deduced from correlations with other tests.

For achievement tests, content validity is usually of first importance. For example, a testing agency has a group of subject-matter specialists devise and select test items that they judge to cover the topics and mental processes relevant to the field represented by the test. Similarly, a teacher judges whether the final test in his course covers the kinds of situations about which he has been trying to teach his students certain principles or understandings. The teacher also judges content when he uses a published test, but he can appropriately investigate criterion-related validity by correlating this test with tests he has prepared or with other direct measures of his chief instructional objectives. When the same published achievement test is used for admissions testing, it may reasonably be checked against a later criterion of performance. In any theoretical discussion of what is being measured by the achievement test, a consideration of construct validity is required. Whether the score on a science achievement test, for example, reflects reading ability to a significant degree, and whether it measures understanding of scientific method rather than mere recall of facts are both questions about construct validity.

Development of a personality inventory will usually start with the assembly of items covering content the developer considers meaningful. Such inventories are then likely to be interpreted with the aid of theory; any such interpretation calls for evidence of construct validity. In addition, a personality inventory must have criterion-related validity, if, for example, it is to be used in screening military recruits who may be maladjusted.

Interest measures are usually intended to predict vocational or educational criteria, but many of them are also characterized by logical content and constructs. This makes it more likely that they can provide at least a rough prediction for the very many occupations and activities that exist and for which specific evidence of criterion-related validity has not been obtained.

For projective techniques, construct validity is the most important, although criterion-related validity using criteria collected either concurrently with the testing or afterwards may be pertinent if the instruments are to be used in making diagnostic classifications.

References

Cronbach, L. J. Test validation. In R. L. Thorndike (Ed.), *Educational measurement* (2nd ed.). Washington, D.C.: American Council on Education, 1971, pp. 443–507.

Guilford, J. P. and Fruchter, B. *Fundamental statistics in psychology and education* (6th ed.). New York: McGraw-Hill, 1978. (See Chapter 18 on validity.)

Guion, R. M. Recruiting, selection, and job placement. In M. D. Dunnette (Ed.), *Handbook of industrial and organizational psychology.* Chicago: Rand McNally, 1976. (Section IV, Chapter 18.)

Nunnally, J. C. *Psychometric theory* (2nd ed.). New York: McGraw-Hill, 1978. (See Chapter 3 on validity.)

RELIABILITY COEFFICIENTS

1. *Reliability* means the consistency between measurements in a series.
2. The *reliability coefficient* tells what proportion of the test variance is nonerror variance.
3. The *reliability coefficient* increases with the length of the test, a relationship which is much less pronounced for validity. (See Spearman-Brown formula, page 174).
4. The *reliability coefficient* increases with the spread or variance of scores.
5. A test may measure reliably at one level of performance and unreliably at another level. Items too difficult for some cause them to guess, yielding "reliable" but chance results; items too easy for others also provide "reliable" but nondiscriminatory information. The difficulty level of a test must be adjusted to the purposes of the testing.
6. Relationship between reliability and validity:
    a. For a test to predict a particular criterion, *predictive* (*criterion related*) *validity* is more important than reliability. When predictive validity is satisfactory, low reliability is not a serious problem (e.g., tests of creativity).
    b. Given two tests measuring the same thing, the test with the higher reliability will also have the higher *validity coefficient*.
    c. Rule for the limit reliability places on validity: The correlation between the test and independent criterion can never be higher than the square root of the product of the reliability of the test and the reliability of the criterion variable.
7. Types of reliability coefficients:
    a. *Coefficient of Stability* ("*test-retest*"): correlation between two successive measurements with the same test. Critical problem: optimizing the delay between the two

administrations to offset a spuriously high effect due to recall, if too short; or spuriously low effect due to the change in the make-up of the subject, if too long.

b. *Coefficient of Equivalence ("alternate forms")*: the successive administration of two parallel forms of the same test. (In terms of test theory, this is the most desirable index of test reliability, since it involves two different representative samples of items.)

c. *Coefficient of Internal Consistency ("split-half")*: a substitute for the "alternate forms" approach to reliability, dividing the items of the test independently into two equivalent halves. The Spearman-Brown formula (page 174) is usually applied to this result, to estimate the reliability of the complete test.

d. *Method of Rational Equivalence:* The Kuder-Richardson formulas 20 and 21 provide relatively conservative estimates of the coefficient of equivalence. Formula 21 (less accurate, but simple to compute):[1]

$$r_{KR21} = \frac{k}{k-1}\left(1 - \frac{M(k-M)}{ks^2}\right)$$

Where: items are scored 1 point if right and 0 points if wrong, M is the mean, k is the number of items, and s is the standard deviation.

RELIABILITY: POSSIBLE SOURCES OF VARIANCE IN A TEST SCORE[2]

I. Lasting and general characteristics of the individual

1. General skills (e.g., reading)

2. General ability to comprehend instructions, testwiseness, techniques of taking tests

3. Ability to solve problems of the general type presented in this test

4. Attitudes, emotional reactions or habits generally operating in situations like the test situation (e.g., self-confidence)

II. Lasting and specific characteristics of the individual

1. Knowledge and skills required by particular problems in the test

2. Attitudes, emotional reactions, or habits related to particular test stimuli (e.g., fear of high places brought to mind by an inquiry about such fears on a personality test)

---

1. For additional information on internal-consistency reliability, see Cronbach, L. J., *Essentials of Psychological Testing* (3rd ed.), New York, Harper & Brothers, 1971. Also consult Guilford, J. P. and Fruchter, B., *Fundamental Statistics in Psychology and Education* (6th ed.), New York, McGraw-Hill, 1978.

2. Source: After Thorndike, R. L., *Personnel Selection,* New York, Wiley, 1949, p. 73. Adapted for Cronbach, L. J., *Essentials of Psychological Testing* (erd ed.), New York, Harper & Brothers, 1970, p. 175.

III. Temporary and general characteristics of the individual (systematically affecting performance on various tests at a particular time)

1. Health, fatigue, and emotional strain

2. Motivation, rapport with examiner

3. E.g., effects of heat, light, and ventilation

4. Level of practice on skills required by tests of this type

5. Present attitudes, emotional reactions, or strength of habits (insofar as these are departures from the person's average or lasting characteristics—e.g., political attitudes during an election campaign)

IV. Temporary and specific characteristics of the individual

1. Changes in fatigue or motivation developed by this particular test (e.g., discouragement resulting from failure on a particular item)

2. Fluctuations in attention, coordination, or standards of judgment

3. Fluctuations in memory for particular facts

4. Level of practice on skills or knowledge required by this particular test (e.g., effects of special coaching)

5. E.g., temporary emotional states and strength of habits, related to particular test stimuli (e.g., a question calls to mind a recent bad dream)

6. Luck in the selection of answers by "guessing"

RELIABILITY[1]

Reliability refers to the accuracy (consistency and stability) of measurement by a test. Any direct measurement of such consistency obviously calls for a comparison between at least two measurements. (Whereas "accuracy" is a general expression, the terms "consistency" and "stability" are needed to describe, respectively, form-associated and time-associated reliability.) The two measurements may be obtained by *retesting* an individual with the identical test. Aside from practical limitations, retesting is not a theoretically desirable method of determining a reliability coefficient if, as usual, the items that constitute the test are only one of many sets (actual or hypothetical) that might equally well have been used to measure the particular ability or trait. Thus, there is ordinarily no reason to suppose that *one* set of (say) 50 vocabulary items is especially superior (or inferior) to another comparable (equivalent) set of 50. In this case it appears desirable to determine not only the degree of response variation by the subject from one occasion to the next (as is accomplished by the retest method), but also the extent of sampling fluctuation involved in selecting a given set of

---

1. This material was taken from the *Standards for Educational and Psychological Tests and Manuals,* American Psychological Association (Co-chairmen of joint committee, APA, AERA, NCME: John W. French and William B. Michael). Revised, 1966. Supplementary information with slightly different emphases about reliability may now be found in a report by a new joint committee entitled *Standards for Educational and Psychological Tests* published by the American Psychological Association in 1974 under the chairmanship of the late Frederick B. Davis.

50 items. These two objectives are accomplished most commonly by correlating scores on the original set of 50 items with scores by the same subjects on an independent but similar set of 50 items—an "alternate form" of the original 50. If the effect of content-sampling *alone* is sought (without the effects of response variability by the subject), or if it is not practical to undertake testing on two different occasions, a test of 100 items may be administered. Then the test may be divided into two sets of 50 odd-numbered items and 50 even-numbered items; the correlation between scores on the odd and the even sets is a "split-half" or "odd-even" correlation, from which a reliability (consistency) coefficient for the entire test of 100 items may be estimated by the Spearman-Brown formula (involving certain generally reasonable assumptions). Essentially the same type of estimated reliability coefficient may be obtained from item-analysis data through use of the Kuder-Richardson formulas (which involve various assumptions, some more reasonable and exact than others). It should be noted that despite the possible heterogeneity of content, the odd-even correlation between the sets of items may be quite high if the items are easy and if the test is administered with a short time limit. Such odd-even correlations are in a sense spurious, since they merely reflect the expected correlation between two sets of scores each of which is a measure of rate of work.

From the preceding discussion, it is clear that *different methods of determining the reliability coefficient take account of different sources of error.* Thus, from one testing to the other, the retest method is affected not only by response variability of the subjects but also by differences in administration (most likely if different persons administer the test on the two occasions). Reliability coefficients based on the single administration of a test ignore response variability and the particular administrative conditions: their effects on scores simply do not appear as errors of measurement. Hence, "reliability coefficient" is a generic term referring to various types of evidence; each type of evidence suggests a different meaning. It is essential that *the method used to derive any reliability coefficient should be clearly described.*

As a generic term reliability refers to many types of evidence, each of which describes the agreement or consistency to be expected among similar observations. Each type of evidence takes into account certain kinds of errors or inconsistencies and not others. The operation of measurement may be viewed as a sample of behavior; in a typical aptitude or achievement test the person is observed on a particular date as he responds to a particular set of questions or stimuli, and his responses are recorded and scored by a particular tester or system. The occasion is a sample from the period of time within which the same general inquiry would be pertinent; some sampling error is involved in selecting any one date of observation. The items that constitute the test are only one of many sets (actual or hypothetical) that might have been used to measure the same ability or trait. The choices of a particular test apparatus, test administrator, observer, or scorer, are also sampling operations. Each such act of sampling has some influence on the test score. It is valuable for the test user to know how much a particular score would be likely to change if any one of these conditions of measurement was altered.

There are various components that may contribute to inconsistency among observations: (a) response variation by the subject (due to changes in physiological efficiency, or in such psychological factors as motivation, effort, or mood): these may be especially important in inventories of personality; (b) variations in test content or the test situation (in "situational tests" which include interacting persons as part of the situation, this source of variation can be relatively large); (c) variations in administration (either through variations in physical factors, such as temperature, noise, or apparatus functioning, or in psychological factors, such as variation in the technique or skill of different test administrators or raters); and (d) variations in the process of observation. In addition to these errors of observation, scoring-error variance in test scores reflects variation in the process of scoring responses as well as mistakes in recording, transferring, or reading of scores.

The estimation of clearly labeled components of error variance is the most informative outcome of a reliability study, both for the test developer wishing to improve the reliability of his instrument and for the user desiring to interpret test scores with maximum understanding. The analysis of error variance calls for the use of an appropriate *experimental* design. There are many different multivariate designs that can be used in reliability studies; the choice of design for studying the particular test is to be determined by its intended interpretation and by the practical limitations upon experimentation. In general, where more information can be obtained at little increase in cost, the test developer should obtain and report that information.

Although estimation of clearly labeled components of error variance is the most informative outcome of a reliability study, this approach is not yet prominent in reports on tests. In the more familiar reliability study the investigator obtains two measures and correlates them, or derives a correlation coefficient by applying one of several formulas to part or item scores within a test. Such a correlation is often interpreted as a ratio of "true variance plus error variance." Many different coefficients, each involving its own definition of "true" and "error" variance, may be derived from a multivariate reliability experiment with the presence of controls for such factors as those of content, time, and mode of administration. Hence, any single correlation is subject to considerable misinterpretation unless the investigator makes clear just what sampling errors are considered to be error in the particular coefficient he reports. The correlation between two test forms presented on different days has a different significance from an internal-consistency coefficient, for example, because the latter allocates day-to-day fluctuations in a person's efficiency to the true rather than to the error portion of the score variance.

In the present set of *Standards*, the terminology by which the 1954 *Technical Recommendations* classified coefficients into several types (e.g., coefficient of equivalence) has been discarded. Such a terminological system breaks down as more adequate statistical analyses are applied and methods are more adequately described. Hence it is recommended that test authors work out suitable phrases to convey the meaning of whatever coefficients they report; as an example, the expression, "the stability of measurements by different test forms as determined over a 7-day interval," although lengthy, will be reasonably free from ambiguity.

References

Guilford, J. P. and Fruchter, B. *Fundamental statistics in psychology and education* (6th ed.). New York: McGraw-Hill, 1978. (See Chapter 17 on reliability)

Nunnally, J. C. *Psychometric theory* (2nd ed.). New York: McGraw-Hill, 1978. (See Chapter 7 on reliability)

Stanley, J. C. Reliability. In R. L. Thorndike (Ed.), *Educational measurement* (2nd ed.). Washington, D.C.: American Council on Education, 1971, pp. 356-442.

SURVEY DESIGN AND TECHNIQUES FOR SCHOOL RELATED USE

Purpose

Surveys are the most widely used technique in education and the behavioral sciences for the collection of data. They are a means of gathering information that describes the nature and extent of a specified set of data ranging from physical counts and frequencies to attitudes and opinions. This information, in turn, can be used to answer questions that have been raised, to solve problems that have been posed or observed, to assess needs and set goals, to determine whether or not specific objectives have been met, to establish baselines against which future comparisons can be made, to analyze trends across time, and generally, to describe what exists, in what amount, and in what context.

Characteristics

The guiding principles underlying surveys are that they should be:

1. Systematic — carefully planned and executed to insure appropriate content coverage and sound, efficient data collection.
2. Representative — closely reflecting the population of all possible cases or occurrences, either by including everyone or everything, or by using scientific sampling procedures.
3. Objective — insuring that the data are as observable and explicit as possible.
4. Quantifiable — yielding data that can be expressed in numerical terms.

Limitations

With the exception of surveys based on a search of records, surveys are dependent on direct communication with persons having characteristics, behaviors, attitudes, and other relevant information appropriate for a specific investigation. This makes them *reactive* in nature; that is, they directly involve the respondent in the assessment process by eliciting a reaction. Although direct interactions are often the most cost-effective, efficient, and credible means of collecting data, because the respondents are usually in the best position to speak for themselves and "tell it like it is," reactive methods run many risks of generating misleading information. Among these risks are the following:

1. Surveys only tap respondents who are accessible and cooperative.
2. Surveys often make the respondent feel special or unnatural and thus produce responses that are artificial or slanted.
3. Surveys arouse "response sets" such as acquiescence or a proneness to agree with positive statements or questions.
4. Surveys are vulnerable to over-rater or under-rater bias—the tendency for some respondents to give consistently high or low ratings.
5. In the case of interviews, biased reactions can be elicited because of characteristics of the interviewer or respondent, or the combination, that elicit an unduly favorable or unfavorable pattern of responses.

General Guidelines for Designing Surveys

1. Define the purpose and scope of the surveys in explicit terms—avoid "fishing expeditions" and rambling, redundant, ill-conceived approaches.

2. Avoid using an existing survey, if it was designed for a different purpose, population, or circumstance. Although they may serve as a point of departure, surveys usually have aims or situational factors that are specific to each application.

3. In designing questionnaires or interviews, one often finds it helpful to sit down with a group of potential respondents and explore what is meaningful or important to them, and how best to phrase questions to reflect their attitudes or opinions.

4. Field test instruments to spot ambiguous or redundant items and to arrive at a format leading to ease of data tabulation and analysis.

5. Examine the merits of using machine-scored answer sheets to facilitate tabulation and analysis.

6. As often as possible, use structured questions as opposed to unstructured and open-ended ones for uniformity of results and ease of analysis.

7. Do not ask questions out of idle curiosity—this approach will overtax the respondents. Avoid questions that are redundant or have obvious answers.

8. Avoid loaded or biased questions (usually by involving others in the wording process and by field testing) and be watchful of biased sampling.

9. Keep the final product as brief, simple, clear, and straightforward as possible. Complex instruments, while justified under special circumstances, generally will be resisted or rejected by most respondents, and cloud the analysis of the data.

10. Brainstorm the analysis needs to insure the clarity and comprehensiveness of the instrument.

11. Consider the necessary and sufficient characteristics of the respondent that must be collected at the time the survey is administered and on which the data analysis will be based: e.g., name, sex, address, age, race, occupation, education, and related background, life-history, and demographic factors. Be realistic and keep such characteristics to an absolute minimum, as they add to the length of the survey, the complexity of the analysis, and often invade the privacy of the respondent. Anonymous surveys are most common. Other information should be requested only if it is clearly needed. Often, a review of the literature will verify whether or not particular characteristics will yield useful information. Also, the more categories generated by the analysis matrix, the smaller will be the number of cases in any single cell; this instance may necessitate a larger sample size.

12. Finally, imagine various outcomes that might result from the survey, including surprising ones. This step helps to anticipate gaps or shortcomings in the approach, and may indicate the need for more background information about the respondents or additional questions. Nevertheless, this first step is not to open a floodgate; instead, it is aimed at catching crucial oversights that would otherwise subtract from the usefulness of the findings.

Types of Surveys

1. *Survey of Records.* These sources of data differ from those in the other survey types because they are nonreactive; i.e., they do not involve a direct response from people. Although this circumstance can be an advantage to the objectivity of the information, there are other problems with how and why records are kept that can offset this:

Advantages	Disadvantages
a. **Records are nonreactive.**	a. May involve confidential restrictions.
b. They are inexpensive.	b. Are often incomplete, inaccurate, and out-of-date.
c. Records often allow historical comparisons and trend analysis.	c. Changing rules for keeping records often makes year-to-year comparisons invalid.
d. If records are accurate and up-to-date, they provide an excellent baseline for comparisons.	d. Can be misleading unless knowledgeable person can explain how the records were compiled.
	e. Purpose of records usually is unrelated to purpose of surveys.
	f. Factual data only (no input on values or attitudes) are present.

2. *Mailed Questionnaires.* This appearance is the most commonly used survey method and often the most sterile or misleading, unless the following disadvantages are heeded and offset:

Advantages	Disadvantages
a. Are inexpensive.	a. Low response rate can occur, especially with less educated and older addressees inviting a nonrepresentative return.
b. Are wide-ranging.	
c. Can be well designed, simple and clear.	b. No assurance the questions were understood.
d. Are self-administering.	
e. Can be made anonymous.	c. No assurance addressee actually was the one who answered.

Note: Questionnaires should be carefully field tested to eliminate ambiguous or biased items and to improve format, both for ease of understanding and facility in analyzing results. Response rates can be improved with stamped return envelopes, follow-up reminders, advance contacts and publicity campaign, personalized letters of transmittal and, when a handful of questions with simple answers is sufficient, a preprinted return postcard can serve as the instrument.

3. *Telephone Surveys.* These are widely used in place of face-to-face interviews by professional pollsters for reasons under "advantages." In general, they tend to achieve similar results.

Advantages	Disadvantages
a. Is less costly than face-to-face interviews.	a. Unlisted telephones (as high as 25%; schools, however, tend to have telephone numbers available).
b. Can be conducted daytime or evenings.	b. Not everyone has a phone, particularly lower income homes.
c. Permits unlimited callbacks.	c. Can be viewed as intrusive into home privacy and can be confused with a disguised sales pitch.
d. Respondent is at ease in own home and tends to be more candid.	
e. Extended geographical coverage and WATS line availability makes feasible state or national samples, if appropriate.	d. Rules out many face-to-face advantages, including visual impressions of home environment.

4. *Group Interview.* Although the "interview" is normally a one-to-one relationship, for many purposes interviewing in groups is appropriate. Not only does it save time, but, if the behavior one is trying to understand takes place in a group interaction setting, the group interview will yield a better picture of this phenomenon.

Advantages	Disadvantages
a. Is more efficient and economical than one-to-one interviews.	a. May intimidate and suppress individual differences.
b. Results reflect group behavior and consensus.	b. Fosters conformity.
c. Reveals group interaction patterns.	c. Intensifies group loyalties and can rigidly polarize opinions.
d. As with brainstorming, can stimulate productivity of others.	d. Is vulnerable to manipulation by an influential and skillful member.

5. *Individual Interviews.* This approach is the conventional method of collecting data face-to-face. It not only can be helpful as the principal method, but also can be especially useful to explore a problem area about which insufficient information exists—for example, as a pilot study on which to base a more extensive questionnaire.

Advantages	Disadvantages
a. Is personalized.	a. Is expensive and time-consuming.
b. Permits in-depth, free responses.	b. May intimidate or annoy respondents with a racial, ethnic, or socio-economic background different from the interviewer.
c. Is flexible and adaptable.	
d. Allows impressions of respondent's gestures, tone of voice, home environment, etc.	c. Is open to overt manipulation or the subtle biases of the interviewer.
	d. Is vulnerable to personality conflicts.
	e. Requires skilled and trained interviewers.
	f. May be difficult to summarize findings.

Sampling Consideration

Whenever practical, especially if a survey touches on controversial matters or will lead to an important decision or conclusion, it is well to include all possible respondents. Otherwise, when this use of a total group is not feasible or sufficiently consequential, sampling is both appropriate and scientifically sound, as long as certain established procedures are followed. The key condition is that the sample must represent, in all important respects, the parent population. Many excellent references are available on the subject of sampling, for when there is a variety of approaches. In practice, the most common technique is to sample at random, such that each respondent in a population of respondents has an equal chance of being selected. There are two principal variations of this technique: (1) *simple random sampling:* e.g., a lottery-like drawing, taking every nth name in an alphabetical listing, or going to a table of random numbers; and (2) *stratified random sampling:* where various "strata" are designated, such as sex, age, socioeconomic levels, or grade levels in school, and predetermined proportions of respondents are then randomly selected from each stratum.

References

Borg, W. R. and Gall, M. D. *Educational research: An introduction* (3rd ed.). New York: Longman, 1979. (See Chapters 9 and 10)

Campbell, A. A. and Katona, G. The sample survey: A technique for social science research. In L. Festinger and D. Katz, (Eds.). *Research methods in the behavioral sciences,* New York: Dryden Press, 1953, pp. 15-55.

Webb, E. J., Campbell, D. T., Schwartz, R. D., and Sechrest, L. *Unobtrusive measures: Nonreactive research in the social sciences,* Chicago, Rand McNally, 1966. (See especially Chapter 1)

Weiss, C. H. Interviewing in evaluation research. In E. L. Struening and M. Guttentag (Eds.), *Handbook of evaluation research* (Vol. 1). Beverly Hills, Sage Publications, 1975, pp. 355-395.

Worthen, B. R. and Sanders, J. R. *Educational evaluation: Theory and practice.* Worthington, Ohio: Charles A. Jones Publishing Co., 1973. (See especially Table 4, pp. 286-287.)

THE MAILED QUESTIONNAIRE[1,2]

1. This is the single most widely used technique in education. It requires a careful, clear statement of the problem underlying the questionnaire. Otherwise, ambiguity and misinterpretation will invalidate the findings.

2. Constructing the questionnaire:

    a. Questionnaires tend to be planned poorly and overdone. To overcome "consumer resistance," they must be expertly designed and skillfully introduced and justified.

    b. State the reason for the questionnaire and explain how the information will be analyzed. Avoid wordiness and ambiguity.

    c. Objectivity is important. Lengthy subjective, open-ended answers are difficult for the respondent to write and for the investigator to evaluate. If the possible categories of responses can be anticipated, these should be offered as alternatives to an objective question. For example:

    > Do you have a systematic program for identifying gifted children in your school? YES _____ NO _____
    >
    > If yes, what means of identification do you use?
    > _____ a. Group intelligence test
    > _____ b. Individual intelligence test
    > _____ c. Achievement battery
    > _____ d. Aptitude battery
    > _____ e. Teacher ratings
    > _____ f. Other (specify) _____

    d. One of the best ways of developing good objective questions is to administer an open-ended form of the question to a small sample of subjects representative of the population in which you are interested. These more lengthy answers provide

---

1. Adapted from Borg, Walter R., *Educational Research.* New York: David McKay Company, Inc., 1963, pp. 204–221. By permission.
2. See also: Oppenheim, A. N. *Questionnaire Design and Attitude Measurement.* New York: Basic Books, Inc., 1966.

the data from which objective-type answers are derived. (Note: if your topic does not lend itself to this treatment, perhaps you should consider the interview which is far more adaptable to open-ended questions.)

e. Questions should be asked in such a way that they minimize the evaluation task, eliminating unnecessary processing steps and interpretation problems.

f. Avoid questions that are threatening to the respondent, exposing him to criticism or placing him in an awkward position. (Sometimes counteracted by assurances of "anonymity.")

g. Avoid questions which evoke predictable response biases and obscure objective information.

h. Avoid leading questions.

i. Pretest the questionnaire (see page 135).

3. The letter of transmittal (see pages 136–137).

4. The follow-up letter. A few days after the deadline established in the letter of transmittal, a follow-up letter should be sent to the nonrespondents. It should assume the tone that the respondent had intended to return the questionnaire but had perhaps overlooked doing so. It should reaffirm the importance of the study and the value of the individual's contribution to this important study. The Research Division of the National Education Association reports the following results in the return rates of questionnaires:

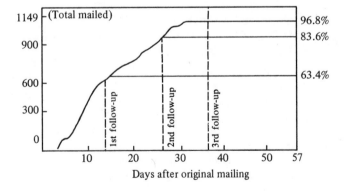

5. Nonresponding subjects—implications. In any questionnaire survey there will always be a percentage of nonresponding subjects, as evidenced in the above graph published by the NEA Research Division. The question must be asked, "How would the results have been changed if all subjects had returned the questionnaire?" Ordinarily, percentages under 20% can be reasonably ignored. Percentages over 20%, however, raise increasingly serious questions about the "hold-outs" and what they are withholding. For example, a common sampling bias arises when persons having a good program are more likely to respond than persons having a poor program. An effective correction technique is to select randomly a small sample of the nonrespondents and personally interview them to obtain the missing information. This will reveal any common trend among the nonrespondents that might prove important. The disadvantage of this technique is obvious—it is likely to be time-consuming, inconvenient, and expensive.

6. The effect of "anonymity." In order to encourage honest and frank answers, some surveys are designed to be returned anonymously. This is more likely to occur where the survey is getting at highly personal or controversial information. The disadvantage is that it usually conceals certain information about the respondent that might be of interest in the analysis, (e.g., sex, age, geographic location, organization, and position). Studies of common questionnaires returned either anonymously or with identification indicate that there is very little difference on most items. Adults tend to answer questions the same in either case.[1]

PRETESTING A QUESTIONNAIRE[1]

1. Select a sample of individuals who are representative of the population toward which the questionnaire is eventually intended.

2. Provide space on the trial questionnaire for the respondents to make reactions and suggested changes.

3. Administer the pretest under conditions comparable to those anticipated in the final study.

---

1. Adapted from Borg, Walter R., *Educational Research.* New York: David McKay Company, Inc., 1963, pp. 204–221. By permission.

4. Check the percent of responses as an estimate of what will occur in the final run; then, examine the returned trial questionnaires for trouble signs—items left blank or yielding no useful information, misinterpretations, and ambiguities. Check the comments for similar indications.

5. Analyse the results to assess the effectiveness of the trial questionnaire to yield the information desired.

6. Make appropriate additions, deletions, and modifications to the questionnaire. (For example, if answers to a particular question show sharp disagreements or raise further questions, additional clarifying questions may be necessary.)

7. Overall reaction of subjects to the questionnaires—what did they like, dislike, or want modified?

LETTER OF TRANSMITTAL[1]

1. Purpose: to elicit a maximum number of *returned* questionnaires.

2. General characteristics: a clear, brief, yet adequate statement of the purpose and value of the questionnaire.

3. Effectiveness:

   a. It must provide good reason for the subject to respond. It should involve him in a constructive and appealing way. His sense of professional responsibility, intellectual curiousity, and personal worth, are typical of response appeals.

   b. It should establish a reasonable, but firm, return date.

   c. An offer to send respondent a report of the findings is often effective, though it carries with it the ethical responsibility to honor such a pledge.

   d. If possible, use a letterhead and a signature that will lend prestige and official status to the letter of transmittal.

(Sample letter of Transmittal)[1]

WESTERN STATE UNIVERSITY
Anytown, California

College of Education
I. V. Tower, Dean

February 11, 1982

Mr. John A. Ford
Superintendent of Schools
Centercity, California

Dear Sir:

The attached questionnaire concerned with procedures used in selecting elementary school principals is part of a statewide study being carried on cooperatively by the the State Department of Public Instruction and Western State University. This project is concerned specifically with determining the present status of principal selection in our state. The results of this study will help to provide preliminary criteria to be used for developing better selection procedures and for improving the administrator training program at Western State University.

We are particularly desirous of obtaining your responses because your experience in principal selection will contribute significantly toward solving some of the problems we face in this important area of education. The enclosed questionnaire has been tested with a sampling of school administrators, and we have revised it in order to make it possible for us to obtain all necessary data while requiring a minimum of your time. The average time required for administrators trying out the questionnaire was $9\frac{1}{2}$ minutes.

It will be appreciated if you will complete the questionnaire prior to February 20 and return it in the stamped, special delivery envelope enclosed. Other phases of this research cannot be carried out until we complete analysis of the questionnaire data. We would welcome any comments that you may have concerning any aspect of principal selection not covered in the questionnaire. We will be pleased to send you a summary of questionnaire results if you desire. Thank you for your co-operation.

Sincerely yours,

I. V. Tower, Dean

Enc.
iv:ld

---

1. Adapted from Borg, Walter R., *Educational Research.* New York: David McKay Company, Inc., 1963, pp. 214–215. By permission.

THE RESEARCH INTERVIEW[1]

1. *Advantages* (over questionnaire):

    a. Permits greater depth.

    b. Permits probing to obtain more complete data.

    c. Makes it possible to establish and maintain rapport with respondent or at least determine when rapport has not been established.

    d. Provides a means of checking and assuring the effectiveness of communication between the respondent and the interviewer.

2. *Disadvantages:*

    Interviews are costly, time-consuming, and inconvenient. If the researcher takes advantage of the interview's adaptability, he introduces the problem of subjectivity and personal bias. Eagerness of the respondent to please the interviewer, a vague antagonism that sometimes arises between the interviewer and the respondent, and the tendency of the interviewer to seek out answers that support his preconceived notions all complicate this method. The thorough training required of the interviewer to offset these disadvantages becomes an additional burden, increasing the cost and time factors.

3. *Interview structure* (*Reliability increases with objectivity*):

    a. Unstructured interviews—The client-centered counseling technique of Carl Rogers illustrates the unstructured approach, giving the respondent broad freedom to express himself in his own way and in his own time. The interviewer may have a general or specific objective which he feels can best be met without imposing a structure on the respondent. Usually the information involved is of a highly personal and potentially threatening nature. Of the three interview structures, this one is the most vulnerable to subjective bias or errors of inexperience.

    b. Semistructured interviews—These are built around a core of structured questions from which the interviewer branches off to explore in depth. Again, accurate and complete information is desired with the additional opportunity to probe for underlying factors or relationships which are too complex or elusive to encompass in more straight-forward questions. Semistructured interviews require more training and skill both to probe at significant points and to avoid biasing tendencies.

    c. Structured interviews—The interviewer follows a well-defined structure resembling the format of an objective questionnaire, allowing clarification and elaboration within narrow limits. These tend to be factually oriented, aimed at specific information, and relatively brief. Structured interviews are suitable when accurate and complete information from all respondents is important and when the type of information sought fits readily into a structured inquiry.

---

1. Adapted from Borg, Walter R., *Educational Research.* New York: David McKay Company, Inc., 1963, pp. 221–233. By permission.

4. *Planning an interview study:*

   a. Define the purpose of the study—its background, theoretical basis, general goals, possible applications of results, and reasons for using the interview method.

   b. Translate the general goals into *detailed* and *specific objectives* which can be fitted to the particular interview pattern you plan to follow, constructing questions yielding useful information.

   c. Develop a tentative guide to be used during the interview, exploiting the advantages of the interview technique.

   d. Develop a satisfactory method of coding and/or recording responses. Generally, responses can be pre-categorized in a pilot study to anticipate the most frequent response patterns. Only responses falling outside these general categories would need to be written out. Tape recording of the interview may offer advantages, unless the nature of the interview is highly personal and produces guarded response. A generally poor technique is a written summary of information recorded during or following the interview. Because of the pace of an interview, the act of writing either slows the interview unnecessarily or causes the interviewer to be selective in the kind and amount of information he records, at the risk of introducing bias.

5. *Framing questions for the interview:*

   a. Questions must be framed in language that insures effective communication between the interviewer and the respondent. Omit all ambiguous vocabulary.

   b. Make certain respondent appreciates the purpose of each question he is asked. Avoid arousing any suspicion or resistance.

   c. Ascertain whether the population from which the respondents have been selected actually has the information sought by the interview and that the questions permit the reasonable recovery of this information.

   d. Avoid leading questions (questions which suggest a desirable or preferred answer).

   e. Insure that the frame of reference surrounding each question is clear so that each respondent hears the question in the same way, avoiding misinterpretations.

   f. Pretest the interview in a pilot study to eliminate weaknesses and experiment with alternative items or techniques.

6. *Overall fault of questionnaire/interview techniques:* their retrospective nature which introduces memory errors and contamination because of intervening events and biasing factors which increase with time. These should be checked out by comparing questionnaire/interview results against direct observations.[1]

---

1. Adapted from Borg, Walter R., *Educational Research.* New York: David McKay Company, Inc., 1963, pp. 221–233. By permission.

GUIDELINES FOR INTERVIEWS AND INTERVIEW SCHEDULES[1]

1. *Direct or Indirect?*—Most data-collection methods in behavioral research are direct or moderately indirect. Highly indirect means are rarely used. The direct approach is most efficient and effective for the purposes. The indirect approach is more useful where anxiety of conformity pressures are apt to conceal true response tendencies.

2. Interview techniques are especially appropriate for children.

3. Main shortcoming of the interview technique: time-consuming and expensive.

4. Three main purposes of the interview:
    a. An exploratory device to help identify variables and relations, to suggest hypotheses, and to guide other phases of the research.
    b. A main instrument in research.
    c. A supplement to other methods: to follow up unexpected results, to validate other methods, and to go deeper into the motivations of respondents and their reasons for responding as they do.

5. Usefulness of the interview depends upon the following considerations:
    a. Can data for the research be obtained in an easier or better way? In other words, how suitable is the interview technique for any given problem and relevant information required.
    b. To insure reliability, interviewers must be trained and questions must be pretested and revised to eliminate ambiguities and inadequate wording.
    c. To insure validity, it is essential to eliminate interviewer bias; questions must be tested for hidden biases.

6. *Structured or Unstructured?* (standardized or unstandardized)—which format to use depends upon the nature of the problem. Where straight-forward, factual information is involved, a structured approach is most efficient. Where highly complex or elusive questions are being raised, the unstructured approach is more fruitful.

7. Three types of schedule items:
    a. Fixed-alternative (closed) items. E.g., opinion polls (Do you, or don't you . . .?) *Advantages:* greater uniformity and reliability; easy to code responses and manipulate data. *Disadvantages:* superficial, artificial; furthermore, its forced-choice nature may irritate or threaten respondents.
    b. Open-ended items. *Advantages:* gives respondent a frame-of-reference with which to react, without placing any constraint on the reaction. Allows flexibility, depth, clarification, and probing. Enables interviewer to assess respondent's degree of sophistication and knowledge, encourages cooperation and establishment of

---

1. Adapted from Kerlinger, Fred N., *Foundations of Behavioral Research* (2nd ed.). New York: Holt, Rinehart, and Winston, 1973.

rapport. Allows unexpected responses which may reveal significant information not anticipated by the research design. *Disadvantages:* more time-consuming, more interviewer skill required, more subject to biasing influences, more difficult to record responses accurately and sufficiently.

   c. Scale items (respondent indicates his answer as a position along some scale). *Advantages:* objectivity; uniformity; reliability; easier to code responses and manipulate data; also, adds dimension of degree not reflected in the fixed-alternative item. *Disadvantages:* still tends to be somewhat artificial; the scale positions may irritate respondents. Also, scales are subject to the "over-rater set" and the "under-rater set"—the respondents who are unrealistically but consistently biased in being favorably or unfavorably disposed in their ratings.

8.   Criteria for question-writing:

   a.   Is the question related to the research problem and objective?

   b.   Is the type of question the right and appropriate one?

   c.   Is the item clear and unambiguous?

   d.   Is the question in any way leading?

   e.   Does the question demand knowledge and information that the respondent does not have?

   f.   Does the question demand personal or sensitive information that the respondent may resist?

   g.   Is the question loaded with social desirability?

9.   The self-administered instrument (e.g., mailed questionnaire):

   a.   *Advantages:*

      (1) When using well-constructed and pretested closed-type items, allows greater uniformity of response and greater reliability.

      (2) Allows anonymity (if desired), encouraging frankness and honesty if highly personal or threatening information is involved.

      (3) Can be distributed to a large number of persons with relative ease; e.g., it can be mailed.

      (4) Economical.

   b.   *Disadvantages:* (These tend to outweigh the aavantages.)

      (1) Low percentage of returns, raising serious questions about the nature of the nonrespondents and sampling bias.

      (2) Does not insure the uniformity of interpretation of each question.

      (3) If closed-type items are used, see item 7a, opposite page.

      (4) If open-ended items are used, respondent may object to writing out answers and resistances may be created that reduce the number of participants in the sample; or he may give a superficial and misleading answer to save time and vent his annoyance.[1]

---

1.   Adapted from Kerlinger, Fred N., *Foundations of Behavioral Research* (2nd ed.). New York: Holt, Rinehart, and Winston, 1973.

ATTITUDE SCALING[1]

General—All *methods of observation* are inferential, varying in the degree of objectivity they possess. Objective methods of observation prescribe the rules for the assignment of the same numerals to a given object by all raters or judges. In variance terms, observer variance is at a minimum.

A *scale*, essentially, is a measuring device allowing the assignment of symbols or numbers to individuals, or their behaviors, by rule. Such an assignment indicates the individual's possession of a corresponding amount of whatever the scale is claimed to measure.

TYPES OF ATTITUDE SCALES

Likert-type or Summated Rating Scales—These contain a set of items, all of which are considered approximately equal in attitude or value loading. The subject responds with varying *degrees of intensity* on a scale ranging between extremes such as agree-disagree, like-dislike or accept-reject. The scores of the position responses for each of the separate scales are summed, or summed and averaged, to yield an individual's attitude score.

Summated rating scales seem to be the most useful in behavioral research. They are easier to develop and yield about the same information as the more laboriously constructed equal-appearing interval scale. The main advantage of a summated scale lies in the greater variance obtained. The disadvantage, as with all scales, is the vulnerability of this variance to biasing response sets (e.g., the over-rater or the under-rater. See page 86).

1.	Capital punishment is a necessary penalty	SA	A	U	D	SD*
2.	Most pupils can handle an independent study program		SA	A	D	SD
3.	"School". . . . . . . Like ___: ___: ___: ___: ___: ___: ___ Dislike**						

   * *Strongly Agree — Agree — Undecided — Disagree — Strongly Disagree*
      The scale can be expanded to seven, or more, positions, although five positions are most common. Item 2 illustrates a forced choice achieved by eliminating the Undecided category.
  ** Adapted from the semantic differential technique. See pages 144-148.

Thurstone-type or Equal-appearing Interval Scales—These not only place the individual somewhere along an agreement continuum for a given attitude but also scale the attitude items themselves. Each item is assigned a *scale value* indicating the strength of attitude for an agreement response to the item. The items in the scale are assumed to be differentially ordered, rather than equal. It is more difficult to construct than the summated scale and yields similar results.

---

1. The third type of scale (Guttman or Cumulative) is also appropriate for cognitive scaling (measuring aptitudes or achievement).

1.	This district treats its teachers better than any other district.	(10.2)***
2.	Doing it all over again, I'd still teach for this district.	(8.5)
3.	The teachers and the district take equal advantage of each other	(5.0)
4.	If you don't have "pull" around here, you're dead.	(2.3)

*** This is the scaled value for the item. The person taking this test simply checks the items with which he agrees; the points corresponding to those items are totaled and then divided by the number of answered items to yield an average scaled value.

Steps in the construction of an equal-appearing interval scale:

a. Collect a series of short, concise statements reflecting attitudes of all shades toward a particular object or event.

b. Have a group of judges, working individually, sort these statements into a series of eleven piles, *A* through *K*, according to their relative degree of favorableness to unfavorableness.

c. For each item, plot the distribution of scaled values (1–11) assigned by the various judges, locating the *median* of this distribution (its *scaled value*).

d. Eliminate items whose *Q* value (semi-interquartile range, see page 158) is excessively large, indicating a major discrepancy among the judges.

e. Check for irrelevance by presenting the remaining items to a group of respondents, asking them to mark those statements with which they agreed. Items with poor internal consistency, statistically, are then eliminated.

f. Select from those items remaining the statements whose scale values are equally spaced along the attitude continuum ("equal-appearing interval").

Guttman-type or Cumulative Scales—These consist of a relatively small set of homogeneous items that are supposedly unidimensional, measuring one, and only one, attribute. Such scales get their name from the cumulative relation between items and the total scores of individuals. Items can be ordered in difficulty, complexity, or value-loading (from low to high) so that to answer correctly or approve the last implies success or approval on all the preceding ones; or, to miss or disapprove a middle item implies failure or disapproval on all the subsequent items. When the scale is cumulative and we know a subject's total score, we can predict his answering pattern.

Cumulative scales have limited application. They are appropriate where a single clear-cut attribute or stimulus dimension is involved. A well constructed scale may yield reliable measures of a number of psychological variables: cognitive complexity, tolerance, conformity, group identification, acceptance of authority, or permissiveness. Furthermore, these scales may be particularly useful with children because of their simplicity and brevity. They also may be adapted as a rating device for an observer rather than a subject.

I want to ask you some questions about a man known to have been a convicted criminal and to have served time in a state penitentiary.*

1. Would you object to such a person living in your community?
2. Would you object to him working where you are employed?
3. Would you object to inviting him into your home socially?
4. Would you object to his marrying a member of your family?

* Answering "Yes" to item 1 predicts "Yes" answers to items 2, 3, and 4; a "No" answer to item 4 predicts "No" answers to items 3, 2, and 1; a "No" answer to item 1 but "Yes" to item 2 predicts "Yes" answers for items 3 and 4.

1. What is 3×5?
2. What is 7×9?
3. What is 4×23?
4. What is 15% of 160?

The four multiplication problems at the left illustrate achievement items ordered according to difficulty or complexity level with similar implications if an item is passed or failed.

EXHIBITS AND REFERENCES

For a comprehensive reference with over 200 exhibits, see: Shaw, M. E. and Wright, J. M., *Scales For The Measurement of Attitudes*, New York: McGraw-Hill Book Co., 1967.

For a guide to the construction of attitude scales, see: Edwards, A., *Techniques Of Attitude Scale Construction*, New York: Appleton-Century-Crofts, 1957.

THE SEMANTIC DIFFERENTIAL

The semantic differential is a method for measuring the meaning of concepts. In practice, it has had two applications: (1) to measure objectively the *semantic properties* of words and concepts in a tri-dimensional semantic space; and, more commonly and simply, (2) as an *attitude scale,* restricting its focus to the *affective domain* (see page 211) or the *evaluative dimension* (see below).

A semantic differential scale has three elements: (1) the *concept* to be evaluated in terms of its semantic or attitudinal properties, (2) the *polar adjective pair* anchoring the scale, and (3) a series of *undefined scale positions* which, for practical purposes, is not less than five or more than nine steps, with seven steps as the optimal number in the experience of Osgood, its originator.

Osgood, et al.,[1] wanted a method of objectively measuring the semantic properties of words and concepts and factor analyzed 76 pairs of polar adjectives (opposite in meaning). They found three principal factors accounting for most of the semantic loadings:

1. Evaluative (e.g., "good-bad")
2. Potency (e.g., "hard-soft")
3. Activity (e.g., "fast-slow")

Pairs of these polar adjectives are then selected according to the purposes of the research and then arranged at opposite ends of a series of seven-point scales. The concept to be rated is then presented at the top of the combined scale. For example:

School

good	____:____:____:____:____:____:____	bad
slow	____:____:____:____:____:____:____	fast
large	____:____:____:____:____:____:____	small
ugly	____:____:____:____:____:____:____	beautiful
active	____:____:____:____:____:____:____	passive
light	____:____:____:____:____:____:____	heavy
clean	____:____:____:____:____:____:____	dirty
weak	____:____:____:____:____:____:____	strong
sharp	____:____:____:____:____:____:____	dull
delicate	____:____:____:____:____:____:____	rugged
dark	____:____:____:____:____:____:____	bright
rounded	____:____:____:____:____:____:____	angular

The subject is instructed to rate the concept "school" according to how he perceives it or feels towards it at the moment by placing an "X" somewhere along each of the seven-point scales anchored by the polar adjective pairs. In the above example, the resulting twelve individual scale responses can be converted to numerical quantities (scale positions 1–negative, weak, inactive—through 7–positive, strong, active) and treated statistically.

Steps in scale construction:

1. Select the concepts or other stimuli to be rated. These should be relevant to the research problem and sensitive to differences or similarities among the comparison groups.

2. Select the polar adjective pairs with which to anchor the various scales. Where attitudes are concerned, adjective pairs with high evaluative loadings are often appropriate, although the selection of polar adjectives on simply their "face value" for a given situation is acceptable. (See page 147 for sample lists of polar adjective pairs.) The *relevance* of adjective pairs to evaluate particular concepts can only

---

1. Osgood, C. E., Suci, G. J., and Tannenbaum, P. H., *The Measurement of Meaning*, Urbana, Illinois: University of Illinois Press, 1957.

be verified empirically. Apparently "irrelevant" pairs can yield significant information and apparently "relevant" pairs can prove disappointing.

3. Arrange the polar adjective pairs so that the favorable, potent, or active end of the scale is randomly placed in a right or left position to avoid position habits in the response pattern.

Analysis and evaluation of scaled data:

The semantic differential yields a large amount of data with a minimum of effort. By converting the scale positions to numerical values, various statistical assessments can be made:

good ___7___ : ___6___ : ___5___ : ___4___ : ___3___ : ___2___ : ___1___ bad

In variance terms, there are three main sources of variance: *concepts, scales,* and *subjects.* Thus, the scores can be analyzed for differences between concepts, between scales, between subjects, or any combination thereof. Some data analysis options are:

1. Compute a *t* test or a Median test of the significance of a difference between group means or medians for individual scales or for all scales summed.

2. *Profile analysis,* using the sign test. By plotting the profiles of mean (or median) response patterns between comparison groups down a set of scales, similarities or differences in the profiles can be observed. If there are consistently greater means for one group than for another (such that their profiles tend to stand apart), the statistical probability of such a consistent difference can be tested by referring to a Binomial Probability Table. An example of this analysis, along with a binomial probability table, appears on page 148.

3. *Distance-cluster analysis of semantic space.* Given Osgood's three axes of semantic space (evaluative, potency, activity), it is possible to derive a measure of distance along each axis for each concept. The *D* statistic used for this purpose, along with its application, is described by Osgood, Suci, and Tannenbaum in their book, THE MEASUREMENT OF MEANING (see footnote, opposite page).

4. For additional information on analysis techniques see, Kerlinger, F. N., *Foundations of Behavioral Research,* New York: Holt, Rinehart and Winston, Inc., 1965, pp. 564–580; Nunnally, J., "The Analysis of Profile Data," *Psychological Bulletin,* 1962, 59, pp. 311–319; and Snider, J. G., and Osgood, C. E. (Eds.), *Semantic Differential Technique,* Chicago: Aldine, 1969.

Note: a principal limitation inherent in this or any other scale which depends on a subjective judgment is *interpretation:* even though statistically significant differences between groups can be established, it is difficult to pin down either the theoretical or utilitarian meaning of this difference.

POLAR ADJECTIVE PAIRS

Excerpts from Osgood's Factor Analyzed List[1,2] Other Suggested Listings

		Factor Loading: Evaluative Potency Activity		
Evaluative				
1. good	bad	1.00	.00	.00
2. complete	incomplete	.32	.05	.05
3. sociable	unsociable	.42	−.19	.18
4. kind	cruel	.52	−.28	.00
5. clean	dirty	.45	−.26	.02
6. light	dark	.38	−.30	.01
7. graceful	awkward	.38	−.23	.05
8. pleasurable	painful	.37	−.25	.07
9. beautiful	ugly	.52	−.29	−.02
10. successful	unsuccessful	.51	.08	.29
11. important	unimportant	.38	.04	.31
12. true	false	.50	−.03	.01
13. positive	negative	.48	.00	.07
14. wise	foolish	.57	.06	.11
15. interesting	boring	.40	−.09	.22
Potency				
16. hard	soft	−.24	.97	.00
17. strong	weak	.30	.40	.10
18. severe	lenient	−.25	.43	.04
19. constrained	free	−.16	.21	−.04
20. constricted	spacious	−.16	.26	.04
21. heavy	light	−.20	.48	−.02
22. serious	humorous	.01	.23	.09
23. large	small	.09	.21	−.05
24. masculine	feminine	−.14	.47	.03
Activity				
25. active	passive	.17	.12	.98
26. excitable	calm	−.15	.03	.26
27. hot	cold	.12	.09	.26
28. fast	slow	.01	.26	.35
29. complex	simple	.17	.05	.25

Understandability[3]

predictable-unpredictable
understandable-mysterious
familiar-strange
simple-complicated
clear-confusing

Miscellaneous
(situational)

traditional-progressive
permissive-restrictive
authoritarian-democratic
structured-unstructured
formal-informal
accepting-rejecting
flexible-rigid
original-stereotyped
systematic-unsystematic
responsible-irresponsible
easy-difficult
happy-sad
empty-full
work-fun
open-closed
rich-poor
fresh-stale
near-far
relaxed-tense
genuine-false
deep-shallow
thick-thin
tender-tough
bright-dull
approach-avoid
pleasure-pain

1. Osgood, C. E., Suci, G. J., and Tannenbaum, P. H., *The Measurement of Meaning*, Urbana, Illinois: University of Illinois Press, 1957.
2. Jenkins, J. J., Russell, W. A., and Suci, G. J., An Atlas of Semantic Profiles for 360 words, *The American Journal of Psychology*, 1958, 71, pp. 688–699.
3. Nunnally, J., *Popular Conceptions of Mental Health*, New York: Holt, Rinehart, and Winston, Inc., 1961, Chapter 4.
4. Snider, J. G. and Osgood, C. E. (Eds.), *Semantic Differential Technique*, Chicago: Aldine, 1969.

Profile comparison of Mean responses of eighth grade achievers and nonachievers to the concept '*School;*'

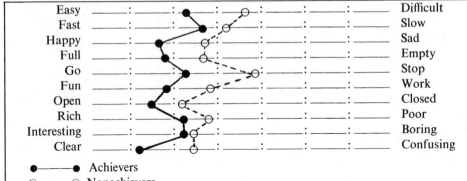

●——————● Achievers
○— — — —○ Nonachievers

The Sign Test of the Profile Pattern: The probability that all of the response means of the *Achiever* group would consistently fall to one side of all of the response means of the *Nonachiever* group (no cross-over patterns) is $P = .001$; an occurrence of 9 out of 10 is $P = .011$; an occurrence of 8 out of 10 is $P = .055$. See the table below to confirm these observations.

Table of one-tailed probabilities associated with values as small as observed values of x in the binomial test (*double* all entries for two-tailed tests):[1,2]

N \ x	0	1	2	3	4	5	6	7	8	9	10	11	12	13	14	15
5	031	188	500	812	969	*										
6	016	109	344	656	891	984	*									
7	008	062	227	500	773	938	992	*								
8	004	035	145	363	637	855	965	996	*							
9	002	020	090	254	500	746	910	980	998	*						
10	001	011	055	172	377	623	828	945	989	999	*					
11		006	033	113	274	500	726	887	967	994	*	*				
12		003	019	073	194	387	613	806	927	981	997	*	*			
13		002	011	046	133	291	500	709	867	954	989	998	*	*		
14		001	006	029	090	212	395	605	788	910	971	994	999	*	*	
15			004	018	059	151	304	500	696	849	941	982	996	*	*	*
16			002	011	038	105	227	402	598	773	895	962	989	998	*	*
17			001	006	025	072	166	315	500	685	834	928	975	994	999	*
18			001	004	015	048	119	240	407	593	760	881	952	985	996	999
19				002	010	032	084	180	324	500	676	820	916	968	990	998
20				001	006	021	058	132	252	412	588	748	868	942	979	994
21				001	004	013	039	095	192	332	500	668	808	905	961	987
22					002	008	026	067	143	262	416	584	738	857	933	974
23					001	005	017	047	105	202	339	500	661	798	895	953
24					001	003	011	032	076	154	271	419	581	729	846	924
25						002	007	022	054	115	212	345	500	655	788	885

* 1.0 or approximately 1.0

Where N = number of observations; x = number of exceptions (for example, out of twelve scales ($N = 12$), if ten are more favorable for a given group but two are less favorable, then $x = 2$.)

1. From *Nonparametric Statistics,* by S. S. Siegel. Copyright, New York: McGraw-Hill, 1956, (p. 250). Used by permission of McGraw-Hill Book Co.
2. For a discussion of one-tailed and two-tailed tests, see page

KINDS OF TESTS AND MEASUREMENTS COMMONLY USED

Purpose	Typical Examples
A. Cognitive Assessment	
1. Aptitude	Standardized, norm-referenced scholastic aptitude and intelligence tests
2. Achievement	Standardized: (a) norm-referenced tests—both general achievement batteries and specific content area tests; and (b) criterion-referenced tests—specific to a given content area
	Nonstandardized: Grade Point Averages, awards, honors
B. Affective Assessment	
1. Preferences/interests	Inventories, rating scales, adjective checklists,
2. Attitudes/beliefs	Q-Sort devices, sociometric methods, projective
3. Emotional/social attributes	instruments, questionnaires, interviews, opinion polls, unobtrusive measures
C. Perceptual-Motor Assessment	
1. Aptitude	Miscellaneous aptitude tests and batteries
2. Skills	Specific performance-based tests (e.g., typing proficiency, telephone repair proficiency, etc.)
D. Personality/Character Assessment	Miscellaneous instruments and projective devices
E. Behavior/Conduct Assessment	Miscellaneous observation techniques and self-report instruments
F. Environmental/Physical Assessment	Demographic and socioeconomic indicators, physical facility and materials inventories, staffing and miscellaneous resources

THE ROLE OF MEASUREMENT IN PROGRAM EVALUATION: SOME PERSPECTIVES

The Tyranny of the Instrument. An instrument, whether it is a test, scale, observation procedure, questionnaire, or interview schedule, only measures what it measures — nothing more, nothing less. One should take a long look at any instrument, once it is in place in an evaluation design, to be clear regarding what it can and cannot register. Beware of the "naming fallacy"* — giving a name to a test or other instrument such as "intelligence," "motivation," "attitude" and thereby maintaining that is what it measures. For example, on close inspection, many so-called achievement tests are sensitive to a very narrow range of content actually covered in instruction. Classroom activities outside this range, however meritorious and worthwhile, will contribute little to the measured outcome. The issue raised is the validity of the instrument. It should be a key consideration in its selection in the first place. Nevertheless, the restrictions inherent in any instrument should be kept in the forefront of attention in designing and evaluating any program.

The Law of Consequences. Program design traditionally sets objectives, plans strategies and activities to achieve these objectives, and then assesses progress toward their attainment. If satisfactory movement toward the objectives is not achieved, the program is then appropriately modified. An entirely new perspective emerges if, instead, one attends to *consequences.* Rather than looking for progress in terms of the objectives, one looks for effects, whatever their source, intended or not. The evaluator asks: What consequences do I observe; what goes with what; under what conditions; and with what outcomes? Not far removed from serendipity, the observer keeps an open mind and looks for effects, planned or not, that yield information of value to understanding and improving programs. The boldest approach to gain this stance is Michael Scriven's *goal-free* evaluation strategy** where the evaluator intentionally is shielded from the stated purposes and objectives of the program — the better not to see what is expected, but what is, in fact, happening. Such an unbiased perspective is likely to uncover unforeseen consequences and relationships that, in the long run, could have major significance.

The Backwards Approach. The straight-forward conduct of program evaluation is, first, to determine the objectives, and then to select or develop appropriate measures by which their attainment will be assessed. Beginning with an existing measurement because it is conveniently available or has apparent face validity, strictly speaking, is putting the cart before the horse. Nevertheless, there are occasions when it is either impractical or ineffective to follow this sequence. This event happens when the outcome measure is so well established that to depart from it would challenge the credibility of the evaluation or when the complexity or subjectivity of the variables underlying the objectives makes the identification of a given measurement procedure arbitrary across a range of defensible options. It is also true that for the majority of measurement situations, the options are often few in number. An example of the first instance would be the use of a publisher's norm-referenced achievement battery to evaluate a school's instructional program. An example of the second instance would be the use of pupil attendance records as an unobtrusive measure of attitudes toward school. In settings where credibility and practicality have, in effect, predetermined the outcome measures, it is the better part of wisdom to begin at the end — that is, with the outcome measures themselves and work backwards to setting program objectives that aim at these measures.

*Brigham, C. C., Intelligence tests of immigrant groups, *Psychological Review,* 1930, *37,* 158—165.
**Scriven, Michael, Goal-free evaluation. In E. House (Ed.), *School Evaluation.* Berkely, California: Mc-Cutchan, 1970.

MULTIPLE CRITERION MEASURES FOR EVALUATION
OF SCHOOL PROGRAMS[1]

I. *Indicators of Status or Change in Cognitive and Affective Behaviors of Students in Terms of Standardized Measures and Scales.*

1. Standardized achievement and ability tests, the scores on which allow inferences to be made regarding the extent to which cognitive objectives concerned with knowledge, comprehension, understanding, skills, and applications have been attained.

2. Standardized self inventories designed to yield measures of adjustment, appreciations, attitudes, interests, and temperament from which inferences can be formulated concerning the possession of psychological traits (such as defensiveness, rigidity, aggressiveness, cooperativeness, hostility, and anxiety).

3. Standardized rating scales and check lists for judging the quality of products in visual arts, crafts, shop activities, penmanship, creative writing, exhibits for competitive events, cooking, typing, letter writing, fashion design, and other activities.

II. *Indicators of Status or Change in Cognitive and Affective Behaviors of Students by Informal or Semiformal Teacher-made Instruments or Devices.*

1. Incomplete sentence technique: categorization of types of responses, enumeration of their frequencies, or rating of their psychological appropriateness relative to specific criteria.

2. Interviews: frequencies and measurable levels of responses to formal and informal questions raised in a face-to-face interrogation.

3. Peer nominations: frequencies of selection or of assignment to leadership roles for which the sociogram technique may be particularly suitable.

4. Questionnaires: frequencies of responses to items in an objective format and numbers of responses to categorized dimensions developed from the content analysis of responses to open-ended questions.

5. Self-concept perceptions: measures of current status and indices of congruence between real self and ideal self—often determined from use of the semantic differential or *Q*-sort techniques.

6. Self-evaluation measures: student's own reports on his perceived or desired level of achievement, on his perceptions of his personal and social adjustment, and on his future academic and vocational plans.

7. Teacher-devised projective devices such as casting characters in the class play, role playing, and picture interpretation based on an informal scoring model that usually embodies the determination of frequencies of the occurrence of specific behaviors, or ratings of their intensity or quality.

---

1. Metfessel, Newton S., and Michael, William B., "A Paradigm Involving Multiple Criterion Measures for the Evaluation of the Effectiveness of School Programs," *Educational and Psychological Measurement*, 1967. 27, 931–943.

METFESSEL and MICHAEL: MULTIPLE CRITERION MEASURES, cont'd.

    8. Teacher-made achievement tests (objective and essay), the scores on which allow inferences regarding the extent to which specific instructional objectives have been attained.

    9. Teacher-made rating scales and check lists for observation of classroom behaviors; performance levels of speech, music, and art; manifestation of creative endeavors, personal and social adjustment, physical well being.

    10. Teacher-modified forms (preferably with consultant aid) of the semantic differential scale.

III. *Indicators of Status or Change in Student Behavior Other than Those Measured by Tests, Inventories, and Observation Scales in Relation to the Task of Evaluating Objectives of School Programs.*

    1. Absences: full-day, half-day, part-day and other selective indices pertaining to frequency and duration of lack of attendance.

    2. Anecdotal records: critical incidents noted including frequencies of behaviors judged to be highly undesirable or highly deserving of commendation.

    3. Appointments: frequencies with which they are kept or broken.

    4. Articles and stories: numbers and types published in school newspapers, magazines, journals, or proceedings of student organizations.

    5. Assignments: numbers and types completed with some sort of quality rating or mark attached.

    6. Attendance: frequency and duration when attendance is required or considered optional (as in club meetings, special events, or off-campus activities).

    7. Autobiographical data: behaviors reported that could be classified and subsequently assigned judgmental values concerning their appropriateness relative to specific objectives concerned with human development.

    8. Awards, citations, honors, and related indicators of distinctive or creative performance: frequency of occurrence or judgments of merit in terms of scaled values.

    9. Books: numbers checked out of library, numbers renewed, numbers reported read when reading is required or when voluntary.

    10. Case histories: critical incidents and other passages reflecting quantifiable categories of behavior.

    11. Changes in program or in teacher as requested by student: frequency of occurrence.

    12. Choices expressed or carried out: vocational, avocational, and educational (especially in relation to their judged appropriateness to known physical, intellectual, emotional, social, aesthetic, interest, and other factors).

    13. Citations: commendatory in both formal and informal media of communication such as in the newspaper, television, school assembly, classroom, bulletin board, or elsewhere (see Awards).

METFESSEL and MICHAEL: MULTIPLE CRITERION MEASURES, cont'd

14. "Contacts": frequency or duration of direct or indirect communications between persons observed and one or more significant others with specific reference to increase or decrease in frequency or to duration relative to selected time intervals.

15. Disciplinary actions taken: frequency and type.

16. Dropouts: numbers of students leaving school before completion of program of studies.

17. Elected positions: numbers and types held in class, student body, or out-of-school social groups.

18. Extracurricular activities: frequency or duration of participation in observable behaviors amenable to classification such as taking part in athletic events, charity drives, cultural activities, and numerous service-related avocational endeavors.

19. Grade placement: the success or lack of success in being promoted or retained; number of times accelerated or skipped.

20. Grade point average: including numbers of recommended units of course work in academic as well as in noncollege preparatory programs.

21. Grouping: frequency and/or duration of moves from one instructional group to another within a given class grade.

22. Homework assignments: punctuality of completion, quantifiable judgments of quality such as class marks.

23. Leisure activities: numbers and types of; times spent in; awards and prizes received in participation.

24. Library card: possessed or not possessed; renewed or not renewed.

25. Load: numbers of units or courses carried by students.

26. Peer group participation: frequency and duration of activity in what are judged to be socially acceptable and socially undesirable behaviors.

27. Performance: awards, citations received; extra credit assignments and associated points earned; numbers of books or other learning materials taken out of the library, products exhibited at competitive events.

28. Recommendations: numbers of and judged levels of favorableness.

29. Recidivism by students: incidents (presence or absence or frequency of occurrence) of a given student's returning to a probationary status, to a detention facility, or to observable behavior patterns judged to be socially undesirable (intoxicated state, dope addiction, hostile acts including arrests, sexual deviation).

30. Referrals: by teacher to counselor, psychologist, or administrator for disciplinary action, for special aid in overcoming learning difficulties, for behavior disorders, for health defects, or for part-time employment activities.

31. Referrals: by student himself (presence, absence, or frequency).

32. Service points: numbers earned.

METFESSEL and MICHAEL: MULTIPLE CRITERION MEASURES, cont'd.

33. Skills: demonstration of new or increased competencies such as those found in physical education, crafts, homemaking, and the arts that are not measured in a highly valid fashion by available tests and scales.

34. Social mobility: numbers of times student has moved from one neighborhood to another and/or frequency with which parents have changed jobs.

35. Tape recordings: critical incidents contained and other analyzable events amenable to classification and enumeration.

36. Tardiness: frequency of.

37. Transiency: incidents of.

38. Transfers: numbers of students entering school from another school (horizontal move).

39. Withdrawal: numbers of students withdrawing from school or from a special program (see Dropouts).

IV. *Indicators of Status or Change in Cognitive and Affective Behaviors of Teachers and Other School Personnel in Relation to the Evaluation of School Programs.*

1. Articles: frequency and types of articles and written documents prepared by teachers for publication or distribution.

2. Attendance: frequency of, at professional meetings or at inservice training programs, institutes, summer schools, colleges and universities (for advanced training) from which inferences can be drawn regarding the professional person's desire to improve his competence.

3. Elective offices: numbers and types of appointments held in professional and social organizations.

4. Grade point average: earned in postgraduate courses.

5. Load carried by teacher: teacher-pupil or counselor-pupil ratio.

6. Mail: frequency of positive and negative statements in written correspondence about teachers, counselors, administrators, and other personnel.

7. Memberships including elective positions held in professional and community organizations: frequency and duration of association.

8. Model congruence index: determination of how well the actions of professional personnel in a program approximate certain operationally-stated judgmental criteria concerning the qualities of a meritorious program.

9. Moonlighting: frequency of outside jobs and time spent in these activities by teachers or other school personnel.

10. Nominations by peers, students, administrators or parents for outstanding service and/or professional competencies: frequency of.

METFESSEL and MICHAEL: MULTIPLE CRITERION MEASURES, cont'd.

11. Rating scales and check lists (e.g., graphic rating scales or the semantic differential) of operationally-stated dimensions of teachers' behaviors in the classroom or of administrators' behaviors in the school setting from which observers may formulate inferences regarding changes of behavior that reflect what are judged to be desirable gains in professional competence, skills, attitudes, adjustment, interests, and work efficiency; the perceptions of various members of the total school community (parents, teachers, administrators, counselors, students, and classified employees) of the behaviors of other members may also be obtained and compared.

12. Records and reporting procedures practiced by administrators, counselors and teachers: judgments of adequacy by outside consultants.

13. Termination: frequency of voluntary or involuntary resignation or dismissals of school personnel.

14. Transfers: frequency of requests of teachers to move from one school to another.

V. *Indicators of Community Behaviors in Relation to the Evaluation of School Programs.*

1. Alumni participation: numbers of visitations, extent of involvement in PTA activities, amount of support of a tangible (financial) or a service nature to a continuing school program or activity.

2. Attendance at special school events, at meetings of the board of education, or at other group activities by parents: frequency of.

3. Conferences of parent-teacher, parent-counselor, parent-administrator sought by parents: frequency of request.

4. Conferences of the same type sought and initiated by school personnel: frequency of requests and record of appointments kept by parents.

5. Interview responses amenable to classification and quantification.

6. Letters (mail): frequency of requests for information, materials, and servicing.

7. Letters: frequency of praiseworthy or critical comments about school programs and services and about personnel participating in them.

8. Participant analysis of alumni: determination of locale of graduates, occupation, affiliation with particular institutions, or outside agencies.

9. Parental response to letters and report cards upon written or oral request by school personnel: frequency of compliance by parents.

10. Telephone calls from parents, alumni, and from personnel in communications media (e.g., newspaper reports): frequency, duration, and quantifiable judgments about statements monitored from telephone conversations.

11. Transportation requests: frequency of.

The book of nature is written in the mathematical language. Without its help it is impossible to comprehend a single word of it.

Galileo

CHAPTER FIVE

STATISTICAL TECHNIQUES AND THE ANALYSIS OF DATA

Good planning in research or evaluation studies anticipates the problem of the analysis of the data. Appropriate statistical techniques are foreseen and the manner of their application is specified. Many excellent texts exist detailing approaches to this task. The purpose of this section is to summarize briefly the more generally used techniques and to provide guidelines regarding the use of statistical techniques.

OVERVIEW OF STATISTICAL METHODS

A. Numbers and Their Use
1. Nominal Scale—in place of a name (to identify).
2. Ordinal Scale—to indicate order (to rank).
3. Interval Scale—to indicate equal intervals (to add and subtract).
4. Ratio Scale—to indicate ratio (to multiply and divide).

B. Central Tendency ("Averages")
1. Mean
2. Median
3. Mode

C. Distribution (Spread)
1. Standard Deviation and Variance
2. Semi-interquartile Range $\left(\dfrac{Q_3 - Q_1}{2} \right)$
3. Range $\left(\dfrac{\text{Range}}{6} \cong \text{one standard deviation when } N \cong 100) \right)$

D. Comparisons and Relationships between Numbers
1. *Simple Correlation*—measures the degree of relationship between two variables. May be positive (direct) or negative (indirect or inverse).
2. *Partial Correlation*—involves the relationship between two variables in a situation where three or more variables are present, holding one or more variables constant and allowing the others to vary.
3. *Multiple Correlation*—involves the correlation between a dependent variable (or a criterion variable) and an optimally weighted combination of two or more independent (predictor) variables.
4. *Factor Analysis*—a technique for analyzing patterns of intercorrelation among many variables, isolating the dimensions to account for these patterns of correlation and, in a well-designed study, to allow inferences concerning the psychological nature of the construct represented by the dimension.
5. *$\bar{z}$-Ratio* or *t-Ratio*—test the (null) hypothesis that two samples come from two populations with the same mean and differ only because of sampling error. ($\bar{z}$ applies to **populations** with or without equal variances; *t* assumes the population variances are equal.)
6. *Analysis of Variance*—tests one or more (null) hypotheses that the means of all groups sampled come from populations with equal means and differ only because of sampling error. (*F* test: the technique used in Analysis of Variance which compares the Between-group variance to the Within-group variance.)
7. *Chi-square*—a measure of squared deviations between observed and theoretical numbers in terms of frequencies in categories or cells of a table, determining whether such deviations are due to sampling error or some interdependence or correlation among the frequencies. It involves a comparison of frequencies of two or more responding groups. Very useful in tables involving frequencies of Yes-No answers.

MEASURES OF CENTRAL TENDENCY AND VARIABILITY[1]

A. When to Use the Three Averages:

1. Compute the arithmetic *mean* when:

   a. The greatest reliability is wanted. It usually varies less from sample to sample drawn from the same population.

   b. Other computations, as finding measures of variability, are to follow.

   c. The distribution is symmetrical about the center, and especially when it is approximately normal.

   d. We wish to know the "center of gravity" of a sample.

2. Compute the *median* when:

   a. There is not sufficient time to compute the mean.

   b. Distributions are markedly skewed. This includes the case in which one or more extreme measurements are at one side of the distribution.

   c. We are interested in whether cases fall within the upper or lower halves of the distribution and not particularly in how far from the central point.

   d. An incomplete distribution is given.

3. Compute the *mode* when:

   a. The quickest estimate of central value is wanted.

   b. A rough estimate of central value will do.

   c. We wish to know what is the most typical case.

B. When to use the three measures of dispersion:

1. Use the *range* when:

   a. The quickest possible index of dispersion is wanted.
   $$\frac{\text{Range}}{6} \cong \text{one standard deviation when } N \geqslant 100$$

   b. Information is wanted concerning extreme scores.

2. Use the *semi-interquartile range, Q,* (see preceding page) when:

   a. The median is the only statistic of central value reported.

   b. The distribution is truncated or incomplete at either end.

   c. There are a few very extreme scores or there is an extreme skewing.

   d. We want to know the actual score limits of the middle 50 percent of the cases.

3. Use the *standard deviation* when:

   a. Greatest dependability of the value is wanted.

   b. Further computations that depend upon it are likely to be needed.

   c. Interpretations related to the normal distribution curve are desired.

   (Note: The standard deviation has a number of useful relationships to the normal curve and to other statistical concepts.)

---

1. From *Fundamental Statistics in Psychology and Education* (4th ed.), J. P. Guilford, Copyright: McGraw-Hill Book Company, New York, 1965. Used with permission of McGraw-Hill Book Company.

FREQUENCY DISTRIBUTION

1. The frequency distribution is a table in which all score units are listed in one column and the number of individuals receiving each score appear as *frequencies* in the second column:

Simple Frequency Distributions—	Grouped Frequency Distributions—
When the score range is small (no more than 20 score units), these can be listed in simple rank order from highest to lowest in column one and the frequencies entered in column two:	When the score range is large (more than 20 score units), these are grouped into a hierarchy of *class intervals* of equal width in column one and the corresponding frequencies in column two:

Score	f
15	1
14	0
13	3
12	2
11	6
10	5
9	2
8	4
7	1
6	2
	$N = \overline{26}$

Class Interval	f	Cum. f[1]
42–44	3	120
39–41	11	117
36–38	8	106
33–35	23	98
30–32	35	75
27–29	14	40
24–26	10	26
21–23	9	16
18–20	6	7
15–17	1	1
	$N = \overline{120}$	

2. Rules for constructing *class intervals* in a *grouped frequency distribution:*
    a. In general, there should be *between 10 and 20 class intervals* based on the *optimal number* that will efficiently summarize the data without distorting its shape. Too few compress the data, concealing meaningful changes in its shape; too many stretch out the data creating unnecessary gaps.
    b. The *width of the class interval* is a function of the range of the raw scores and the number of class intervals desired. In the above example, if the raw score range was $49 - 17 = 32$ and the researcher wanted about 10 class intervals, then: $32 \div 10 = 3.20$. Rounded to the nearest whole number, a class interval width of 3 is obtained.
    c. In general, when the *width of the class interval* is less than 10 score units, odd number widths (1, 3, 5, 7, 9) are more convenient since the midpoint of the interval will be a whole number. For interval sizes of 10 and above, multiples of 5 (10, 15, 20, etc.) are recommended.
    d. *"Real"* versus *"Apparent" limits* for the class interval. In statistical calculations based on grouped data (e.g., see Computing Guide 3, page 167), it is necessary to use the real limit (rather than the apparent limit) of a given class interval. For example, in the above grouped frequency distribution the interval 36–38 has apparent lower and upper limits of 36 and 38. Strictly speaking, however, the real lower and upper limits of the interval 36–38 are 35.5 and 38.5.

---

1. "Cumulative frequency"—necessary for the construction of a cumulative frequency curve or ogive (see opposite page).

GRAPHIC REPRESENTATIONS OF DATA–(Examples based on data from preceding page)

A. HISTOGRAM OR BAR GRAPH:

B. FREQUENCY POLYGON:

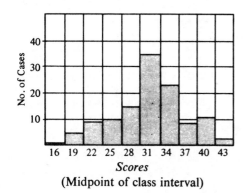

Scores
(Midpoint of class interval)

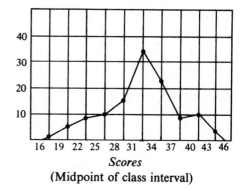

Scores
(Midpoint of class interval)

1. Histograms or bar graphs and frequency polygons are very similar, both being constructed from frequency distributions.

2. The *scores* are plotted along the horizontal baseline, also called the abscissa or X axis. The *frequencies* (number or percent of cases) are plotted along the vertical axis, also called the ordinate or Y axis.

    a. *For the histogram or bar graph,* the width of each bar corresponds to the *real limits* of the width of each class interval (see opposite page). In the above example, this fact holds true although the midpoints of each class interval are presented for clearer reading. The height of each bar corresponds to the frequency or percent of cases in that interval.

    b. *For the frequency polygon,* the points are plotted directly over the *midpoints* of each class interval.

    c. For good graphic proportions, the vertical axis should be roughly two-thirds the length of the horizontal axis.

C. CUMULATIVE FREQUENCY CURVE:

1. Cumulative frequency curves represent the graphing of a cumulative distribution and plotted according to procedures similar to the frequency polygon.

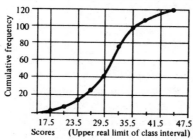

2. Using the X and Y axes noted above, points are plotted directly above the *upper real limit* of each interval (see preceding page). This is necessary because the cumu-

lative frequency represents the number of percent of cases that have scores equal to or below the value at that particular upper limit.

3. Cumulative frequency curves are useful when we are primarily interested in determining the position of an individual in a group, rather than the general form of the group performance as in the case of the histogram or frequency polygon.

SCATTER DIAGRAMS, SCATTERGRAMS, OR SCATTER PLOTS

The Graphic Representation of Correlation

1. Using $\frac{1}{4}$-inch graph paper, lay out X (horizontal) and Y (vertical) axes representing two correlated variables.
2. On the X axis, or baseline, low scores begin on the left and increase toward the right of the graph. On the Y axis, or vertical, low scores begin at the bottom and increase toward the top of the graph.
3. For each individual, locate the intersection of the X and Y axes equivalent to his scores on the X and Y variables, respectively. Mark this intersection with a dot and repeat the operations for all individuals in the study.

EXAMPLES:

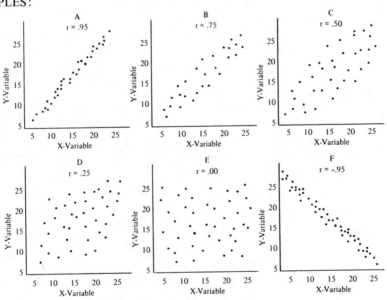

INTERPRETATION: These examples can be interpreted according to the following general principals, given the conditions in steps 1, 2, and 3 above:

1. The slope of the regression line, if it *rises* when moving across the graph from left to right, indicates a *positive correlation* (Example A). If it falls when moving from left to right, this indicates a *negative correlation* (Example F).
2. When all the dots appear to lie very close to the regression line (Example A), the correlation is very high, approaching .90 to 1.00.

3. When the dots scatter around the regression line forming an ellipse midway between a straight line and a full circle (Example C), the correlation is moderate, approaching .50.
4. When the dots scatter around the entire graph more or less equally dispersed in all directions and resembling a full circle (Example E), the correlation is very low, approaching zero.

THE ANALYSIS OF CROSSBREAKS[1]

1. The crossbreak is one of the most useful graphic displays in data analysis. It can be used with nearly any kind of data and has the graphic power of pointing up similarities and differences in sharp contrast.

    In its most elementary form, it appears as the familiar 2 × 2 contingency table:

	Nonachievers	Achievers
Middle Class	8	22
Lower Class	19	11

2. *Application*—to any data that can be dichotomized into classes or groups. The entries are usually in the form of *frequencies* or *percentages* for their respective variables.

3. *Purpose:*

    a. To facilitate the study and analysis of relations by arranging data into tabular frequencies which clearly display trends and patterns in the relationship.

    b. To facilitate statistical analyses such as the *chi square* test (see Computing Guide 10, page 178) and indices of association such as the *phi coefficient* (see Guilford, J. P., *Fundamental Statistics in Psychology and Education* (4th ed.), New York: Mc-Graw-Hill, 1965, pp. 333–338).

    c. To study and test a relationship between two variables while controlling for the effects of a third variable, unmasking "spurious" relationships.. In other words, it allows us to observe and control for differences in degree of relationships at different levels of a control variable.

    d. To clarify and spell out research problems and the relationships between particular variables in both the problem formulation and data analysis phases of research. Crossbreaks make visible what goes with what in the research design and quickly expose misconceptions or design inadequacies which can be corrected.

4. *Kinds of crossbreaks*—While the 2 × 2 table is the simplest and most common example of a crossbreak, more complex crossbreaks are frequently used: 2 × 3, 3 × 3, 3 × 4,

---

1. For an extended dicsussion on this topic, see Kerlinger, F. N., *Foundations of Behavioral Research*, (2nd ed.), New York: Holt, Rinehart and Winston, 1973, Chapter 10.

etc. While there is no theoretical limit to the complexity of these contingency tables, for practical purposes tables in excess of 5 × 5 tend to be unclear, difficult to analyze or interpret, and are rarely reported.

5. *Relationship between crossbreaks and chi square*—Because the chi square test is applied to data in the form of crossbreaks, see pages 177-181 for additional discussion on the use of crossbreaks.

COMPUTING GUIDE 1.
Determining Percentile Equivalents Graphically.[1]

1.	Begin with the raw scores (these are scores of 75 ninth-grade boys on Bennett Form AA).	37 43 27 44 27 27 26 31 35 42 50 35 43 36 26 50 47 36 26 32 32 38 36 21 24 40 39 35 38 36 38 21 17 26 35 22 18 50 30 38 50 16 45 8 34 26 34 28 41 27 39 41 30 23 33 22 31 36 40 54 24 22 8 33 42 41 41 31 34 36 32 20 22 34 41
2.	Identify the highest score and the lowest score. If there is a wide range, choose a class interval of 1, 2, 5, 10, 20, etc., and divide the range into classes of equal width. Fifteen or more classes are desirable.	Highest score = 54; lowest score = 8; range = 47. Class interval of 5 will be used. (A smaller interval, such as 2, would be preferable but would be inconvenient in this computing guide.)

Scores	Tallies	Frequency (f)	Cumulative Frequency	Cumulative Percent
50–54	///	5	75	100
45–49	//	2	70	93
40–44	/// /// //	12	68	90
35–39	/// /// /// //	17	56	75
30–34	/// /// ////	14	39	52
25–29	/// ///	10	25	33
20–24	/// ///	10	←15	20[b]
15–19	///	3	5[a]	7
10–14		0	2	3
5–9	//	2	2	3
			0	0
		$\overline{75}$ N		

3. Tally the number of cases with each score.

4. Write the number of tallies in the Frequency (f) column. Add this column to get N, the number of cases.

5. Begin at the bottom of the column and add frequencies one at a time to determine the cumulative frequency, the number of cases below each division point

a. 5 cases fall below 19.5; 15 below 24.5; etc.
b. 20 percent of the cases fall below 24.5; 20 is the cumulative percentage corresponding to a raw score of 24.5.

1. Cronbach, Lee J. *Essentials of Psychological Testing* (3rd ed.). New York: Harper & Row, 1970.

6. Divide the cumulative frequencies by N to determine cumulative percentages.

7. Plot cumulative percentage against score. (In practice, a large sheet of graph paper would be used.)

8. Draw the smooth curve which best fits the points plotted.

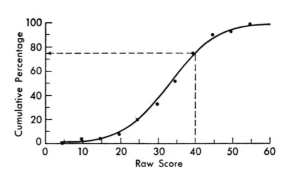

9. Determine the percentile equivalent of a score by reading from the curve. (The lines on the chart show how one finds that the percentile equivalent of a raw score of 40 is 74.)

Percentile Equivalents

Raw	%ile	Raw	%ile	Raw	%ile
12	2	24	17	36	60
13	2	25	20	37	64
14	3	26	22	38	67
15	3	27	26	39	71
16	4	28	29	40	74
17	5	29	33	41	77

COMPUTING GUIDE 2
Determining the Mean and Standard Deviation for Ungrouped Data.[1]

		X	d	d^2
1.	Arrange the raw scores in ascending order	16	5.5	30.25
		14	3.5	12.25
		12	1.5	2.25
		11	.5	.25
		10	−.5	.25
		10	−.5	.25
		9	−1.5	2.25
		9	−1.5	2.25
		8	−2.5	6.25
		6	−4.5	20.25
		$\Sigma X = 105$	$\Sigma d = 0.0$	$\Sigma d^2 = 76.50$

2. To find the mean, sum the raw scores and divide by N, the number of cases:

$$M = \frac{\Sigma X}{N} = \frac{105}{10} = 10.5$$

3. To find the standard deviation:

   a. Subtract the mean from each raw score, obtaining the deviation score, d

   $$X - M = d$$

   b. Square each deviation score, obtaining d^2.

   c. Sum the squared deviations, obtaining

   $$\Sigma d^2 = 76.50$$

   d. Obtain the standard deviation by extracting the square root of the sum of the squared deviations divided by N:

   $$\text{s.d.} = \sqrt{\frac{\Sigma d^2}{N}} = \sqrt{\frac{76.50}{10}} = 2.77$$

---

1. An alternative formula for computing Σd^2 follows where X is the raw score and N is the number of cases. It is useful when a hand calculator is available:

$$\Sigma d^2 = \frac{1}{N} [N\Sigma X^2 - (\Sigma X)^2]$$

and

$$\text{s.d.} = \frac{1}{N^2} [N\Sigma X^2 - (\Sigma X)^2]$$

COMPUTING GUIDE 3
Determining the Mean and Standard Deviation for Grouped Data.[1]

<table>
<tr><td>1.</td><td>Begin with the raw scores (these are scores of 75 ninth-grade boys on Bennett Form AA)</td><td colspan="11">37 43 27 44 27 27 26 31 35 42 50
35 43 36 26 50 47 36 26 32 32 38
36 21 24 40 39 35 38 36 38 21 17
26 35 22 18 50 30 38 50 16 45   8
34 26 34 28 41 27 39 41 30 23 33
22 31 36 40 54 24 22   8 33 42 41
41 31 34 36 32 20 22 34 41</td></tr>
</table>

2. Identify the highest score and the lowest score. If there is a wide range, choose a class interval of 1, 2, 5, 10, 20, etc., and divide the range into classes of equal width. Seven to fifteen classes are desirable.   Highest score = 54; lowest score = 8; range = 47. Class interval of 5 will be used. (A smaller interval, such as 2, would be preferable but would be inconvenient in this computing guide.) *Note:* The interval 50–54 is, in fact, 5 units wide: *50–51–52–53–54,* or strictly speaking, 49.5–54.5.

3. Tally the number of cases with each score.

4. Write the number of tallies in the Frequency (f) column. Add this column to get N, the number of cases.

5. Select any interval, usually near the middle of the distribution. Call this the arbitrary origin. (Here, the 30–34 interval is used.)

Scores	(f)	d	fd	fd^2
50–54 ||||/	5	4	20	80
45–49 //	2	3	6	18
40–44 |||| |||| //	12	2	24	48
35–39 |||| |||| |||| //	17	1	17	17
30–34 |||| |||| ////	14	0	0	0
25–29 |||| ||||	10	−1	−10	10
20–24 |||| ||||	10	−2	−20	40
15–19 ///	3	−3	−9	27
10–14	0	−4	−0	0
5– 9 //	2	−5	−10	50
	75		+18	290
	N		Σfd	Σfd^2

Determine the deviation (d) of each interval from the arbitrary origin.

6. Multiply in each row the entries in the *f* and *d* columns, and enter in the *fd* column.

7. Multiply the entries in the *d* and *fd* columns and enter in the *fd^2* column. Add the *fd* and *fd^2* columns. (Σ is a symbol meaning "sum of".)

8. Substitute in the following formulas:

$$c \text{ (correction)} = \frac{\Sigma fd}{N} \qquad c = \frac{18}{75} = .24$$

$$M \text{ (mean)} = A.O. + ic^* \qquad M = 32.0 + 5(0.24)$$
$$M = 32.0 + 1.20 = 33.20$$

$$\text{s.d.} = i\sqrt{\frac{\Sigma fd^2 - Nc^2}{N-1}} \qquad \text{s.d.} = 5\sqrt{\frac{290 - 75(0.24)^2}{74}} = 5\sqrt{\frac{285.7}{74}}$$

$$= 5\sqrt{3.86} = 5(1.96) = 9.80$$

*A.O. is the midpoint of the score-interval selected as arbitrary origin, and *i* is the width of the interval.

1. Cronbach, Lee J. *Essentials of Psychological Testing* (2nd ed.), New York: Harper & Brothers, 1960, p. 79.

APPROPRIATE CORRELATIONAL TECHNIQUES FOR DIFFERENT FORMS OF VARIABLES[1,2]

Technique	Symbol	Variable 1	Variable 2	Remarks
Product–moment correlation	r	Continuous	Continuous	The most stable technique
Rank–difference correlation (Rho)	ρ	Ranks	Ranks	Often used instead of product–moment when number of cases is under 30
Kendall's Tau	τ	Ranks	Ranks	Preferable to Rho for numbers under 10
Biserial correlation	r_{bis}	Artificial dichotomy	Continuous	Sometimes exceeds 1—has a larger standard error than r—commonly used in item analysis
Widespread biserial correlation	r_{wbis}	Widespread artificial dichotomy	Continuous	Used when you are especially interested in persons at the extremes on the dichotomized variable
Point–biserial Correlation	r_{pbis}	True dichotomy	Continuous	Yields a lower correlation than r and much lower than r_{bis}
Tetrachoric correlation	r_t	Artificial dichotomy	Artificial dichotomy	Used when both variables can be split at critical points
Phi coefficient	ϕ	True dichotomy	True dichotomy	Used in calculating interitem correlations on multiple choice or two choice items
Contingency coefficient	C	2 or more categories	2 or more categories	Comparable to r_t under certain conditions—closely related to chi-square

1. Borg, Walter R., *Educational Research: An Introduction*, David McKay Co., New York, 1963, p. 157. By permission.
2. Concerning the Variable 1 and Variable 2 categories in the above chart, a *continuous* variable is one representing an underlying continuum tending to be normally distributed. Examples include such variables as height, weight, and ability or achievement as measured by standardized tests. *Artificial dichotomies* can be

SELECTED SOURCES FOR ADDITIONAL COMPUTATIONAL AIDS AND
ACCOMPANYING INTERPRETIVE INFORMATION

The several computational or calculation aids that have been presented in this volume may be supplemented by those in other texts. The so-called cookbook approaches appear in many books, several of which also provide interpretive comments. Typically, step-by-step guidelines in outline form accompany the solution of a statistical or quantitatively oriented research problem in conjunction with summarized interpretive, evaluative, or qualifying information. A few helpful sources include the following:

Bernstein, A. L. *A handbook of statistics solutions for the behavioral sciences.* New York: Holt, Rinehart, and Winston, 1964.

Bruning, J. L. and Kintz, B. L. *Computational handbook of statistics* (2nd ed.). Glenview, Ill.: Scott, Foresman, 1977.

Dinham, S. M. *Exploring statistics: An introduction for psychology and education.* Monterey, California: Brooks/Cole, 1976.

Huck, S. W., Cormier, W. H., and Bounds, W. G., Jr. *Reading statistics and research.* New York: Harper and Row, 1974.

Linton, M., Gallo, P. S., Jr., and Logan, C. A. *The practical statistician: Simplified handbook of statistics.* Monterey, California: Books/Cole, 1975.

McCall, R. B. *Fundamental statistics for psychology* (3rd ed.). New York: Harcourt, Brace Jovanovich, 1980.

Siegel, S. *Nonparametric statistics for the behavioral sciences.* New York: McGraw-Hill, 1956.

Wilson, J. A. R., Robeck, M. C., and Michael, W. B. *Psychological foundations of learning and teaching* (2nd ed.). New York: McGraw-Hill, 1974 (Chapter 19).

---

constructed by arbitrarily dividing continuous variables into two groups, usually about the center of the data. Examples include such classifications as achiever-nonachiever, above average-below average, pass-fail, and warm-cold on an attitude scale. *True dichotomies* involve relatively clear-cut (though not necessarily absolute) differences, allowing the data to be categorized into two groups. Examples include such dichotomies as male-female, living-dead, teacher-nonteacher, dropout-nondropout, and smoker-nonsmoker. Other variables that can be treated *as if* they were true dichotomies for the purposes of computing, for example, a point-biserial correlation coefficient, include: color blind-noncolor blind, alcoholic-nonalcoholic, and right-wrong responses with respect to a particular test item in item analysis (see example, page 173.) The distributions underlying true dichotomies, if not absolute differences, tend to be bimodal and/or relatively discontinuous. For a more complete discussion of these problems, see the references cited above.

COMPUTING GUIDE 4. The Product-Moment Correlation Coefficient[1] (Pearson r)

1. Begin with the pairs of raw scores to be studied.

X	Y	X	Y	X	Y	X	Y	X	Y
24	35	27	38	26	39	29	35	30	42
25	39	28	37	30	39	24	38	28	37
24	39	29	36	32	40	17	24	30	39
25	36	19	34	30	42	29	38	26	37
31	43	28	37	25	38	29	38	26	39
22	38	27	32	32	43	27	36	23	37
30	43	25	38	26	37	30	39	20	29
24	35	30	41	24	36	26	40	25	38
25	40	31	41	21	32	25	33	15	31

2. Tabulate the points in a scatter diagram, entering one tally for each pair of scores. (The first pair [24–35] is tabulated in the cell above 24 on the X scale, and opposite 35 on the Y scale. This cell is outlined in the illustration.)

	f_y	d_y	$f_y d_y$	$f_y d_y^2$	$\Sigma f d_x$	$\Sigma f d_x d_y$
43	3	6	18	108	15	90
42	2	5	10	50	8	40
41	2	4	8	32	9	36
40	3	3	9	27	5	15
39	7	2	14	28	9	18
38	8	1	8	8	-2	-2
37	6	0			3	
36	4	-1	-4	4	1	-1
35	3	-2	-6	12	-1	2
34	1	-3	-3	9	-7	21
33	1	-4	-4	16	-1	4
32	2	-5	-10	50	-4	20
31	1	-6	-6	36	-11	66
30		-7				
29	1	-8	-8	64	-6	48
28		-9				
27		-10				
26		-11				
25		-12				
24	1	-13	-13	169	-9	117

(Scatter diagram, Y axis 43 down to 24, X axis 15 16 17 18 19 20 21 22 23 24 25 26 27 28 29 30 31 32.)

Totals: 13 613 ; 9 ; 473
N $\Sigma f_y d_y$ $\Sigma f_y d_y^2$ $\Sigma f d_x d_y$

f_x	1	1			1	1	1	1	1	5	7	5	3	3	4	7	2	2	[45]
d_x	-11	-10	-9	-8	-7	-6	-5	-4	-3	-2	-1	0	1	2	3	4	5	6	
$f_x d_x$	-11				-9		-7	-6	-5	-4	-3		-10	-7	3	6	12	28	10	12
$f_x d_x^2$	121				81		49	36	25	16	9		20	7	3	12	36	112	50	72

N = 45 $\Sigma f_x d_x$ = 9 $\Sigma f_x d_x^2$ = 649

---

1. Cronbach, Lee J., *Essentials of Psychological Testing* (2nd ed.). New York: Harper & Brothers, 1960, pp. 124–125.

3. Count the number of tallies in each column, and write it below the diagram in a row labeled f_x. Count the number in each row, and write it beside the diagram in a column labeled f_y.

4. Select an arbitrary origin for X and for Y, and determine the mean and standard deviation for each as in Computing Guide 3 (computation not shown).

$$
\begin{array}{ll}
A.O._x = 26.0 & A.O._y = 37.0 \\
c_x = \quad .20 & c_y = \quad .29 \\
M_x = 26.2 & M_y = 37.3 \\
s_x = \quad 3.83 & s_y = \quad 3.72
\end{array}
$$

5. In each cell of the scatter diagram, multiply the number of tallies by the value of d_x written below that column, and write the product in the cell. (In the outlined cell, for instance, there are two tallies, and d_x is -2; the product is -4.)

In each row, add the numbers written in the cells, and place in a column labeled $f_y d_x$.

Multiply each entry in this column by d_y and enter in a column labeled $fd_x d_y$.

Add the column $fd_x d_y$.

Substitute the numbers in the following formula:

$$
r_{xy} = \frac{\dfrac{\Sigma fd_x d_y}{N} - c_x \cdot c_y}{s_x \cdot s_y}
$$

$$
r_{xy} = \frac{\dfrac{473}{45} - .06}{3.83 \cdot 3.72}
$$

$$
r_{xy} = \frac{10.51 - .06}{14.24} = \frac{10.45}{14.24}
$$

$$
r_{xy} = .73
$$

Note: To determine the statistical significance of the obtained r, see Table D, page 230.

COMPUTING GUIDE 5
Rank–Difference Correlation[1] (Spearman rho)

	Example
1. Begin with the pairs of scores to be studied.	Man *A* ($x = 30$; $c = 25,000$)
	Man *A* has ranks 4, 6
2. Rank men from 1 to *N* (number of men) in each set of scores. (Note that the lowest man must have rank *N*, unless he ties with someone.)	$N = 10$ In case of tied scores, see footnote 2 below.
3. Subtract the rank in the right-hand column from the one in the left-hand column. This gives the difference D. (As a check, make sure that this column adds to zero.)	Man *A*: 4–6 $= -2$
4. Square each difference to get D^2.	Man A: $(-2)^2 = (-2)(-2)$ $= 4$
5. Sum this column to get ΣD^2.	
6. Apply the formula: $$\rho \text{ (rho)} = 1 - \frac{6(\Sigma D^2)}{N(N^2 - 1)}$$	$$\rho = 1 - \frac{6(36)}{10(100 - 1)}$$
7. To determine the statistical significance of this coefficient, see Table E, page 231. In this instance *r* is significant at the 5% level, but not significant at the 1% level.[3]	$= 1 - \dfrac{216}{990}$ $= 1 - .218$ $\rho = .782$

Man	Test	Scores Criterion (c)	Test	Ranks Criterion	Rank Differ- ence (*D*)	Squared Differ- ence (D^2)
A	30	$25,000	4	6	−2	4
B	34	38,000	2	2	0	0
C	32	30,000	3	4	−1	1
D	47	40,000	1	1	0	0
E	20	7,000	9	10	−1	1
F	24	10,000	7	9	−2	4
G	27	22,000	5	7	−2	4
H	25	35,000	6	3	3	9
I	22	28,000	8	5	3	9
J	16	12,000	10	8	2	4
					$\Sigma D = 0$	$\Sigma D^2 = 36$

1. Cronbach, Lee J., *Essentials of Psychological Testing,* (3rd ed.). New York: Harper & Row, 1970, p. 129.
2. In many sets of data, two or more scores will be tied. Simply assign the *mean* rank to all the tied scores based on the span of rank positions equal to the number of tied scores. E.g., if two scores are tied for ranks 7 and 8, both are ranked as 7.5 and will be flanked by ranks 6 and 9. If three scores are tied for ranks 10, 11, 12, all three are ranked as 11 and will be flanked by ranks 9 and 13; etc. In this way, the number of ranks are balanced for all cases of ties and the total number of ranks equals *N*.
3. Item 7 added to Cronbach's Computing Guide for this Handbook only.

COMPUTING GUIDE 6

The Point–biserial Correlation Coefficient for data where one variable is a true dichotomy and the other variable is continuously distributed.[1,2]

1.	Compute the standard deviation for the total set of scores on the continuous variable, designating this value as σ_t.	See Computer Guide 2 or 3.
2.	Divide the data into two subgroups based on the dichotomized variable and compute their respective means on the continuous variable. Designate the mean of the subgroup with the higher performance or ability as M_p and the mean of the subgroup with the lower performance or ability as M_q.	M_p = higher subgroup M_q = lower subgroup
3.	Determine the proportion of cases in each of the subgroups. Let p = proportion of cases in the higher subgroup and q = proportion of cases in the lower subgroup.	p = number of cases in the higher subgroup divided by the total number of cases in both subgroups. $q = 1.00 - p$
4.	Solve for r_{pbis}:	$r_{\text{pbis}} = \dfrac{M_p - M_q}{\sigma_t} \sqrt{pq}$

EXAMPLE: In the item-analysis of a particular test, it is useful to know the relationship between the response patterns of Right or Wrong on a specific test item and the performances on the overall test scores. Suppose those scoring Right on the item in question also score higher on their total test scores than the group whose answers to this item are Wrong. If we are given the following statistical information about these two groups, coded according to the above notations, a point-biserial correlation coefficient can be derived:

Given:

$\sigma_t = 12.4$
$M_p = 134.6$
$M_q = 125.8$
$N_p = 29$
$N_q = 31$

Then:

$$r_{\text{pbis}} = \frac{M_p - M_q}{\sigma_t} \sqrt{pq} = \frac{134.6 - 125.8}{12.4} \sqrt{(.483)(.517)} =$$

$$\frac{8.8}{12.4} \sqrt{.249711} = (.7097)(.4997) = .35$$

---

1. See discussion regarding continuous and dichotomous data in footnote no. 2, page 168-169.
2. A test of statistical significance for this correlation coefficient is equivalent to a t-test of the difference between the two means.

COMPUTING GUIDE 7   Use of the Spearman–Brown Formula to estimate reliability after a test is lengthened or shortened.[1]

1. Suppose that a test has a known reliability. The Spearman–Brown Formula, given at right, estimates the reliability of the score from a similar test n times as long with homogeneous content.	$$r_n = \frac{nr}{1 + (n-1)r}$$ where r is the original reliability; r_n is the reliability of the test n times as long
2. To predict the reliability of a test twice as long as the original test, substitute in the formula $n = 2$.	If r is .40, $r_2 = \dfrac{2(.40)}{1 + (1).40}$ $= \dfrac{.80}{1.40} = .57$
3. Suppose the original test is to be reduced to only half its original length. The reliability of the short test is estimated using $n = \frac{1}{2}$.	$r_{\frac{1}{2}} = \dfrac{\frac{1}{2}(.40)}{1 + (\frac{1}{2} - 1)(.40)}$ $= \dfrac{.20}{1 - \frac{1}{2}(.40)} = \dfrac{.20}{.80}$ $= .25$

The Spearman–Brown Formula permits us to estimate what reliability the test would have if it were lengthened or shortened. The formula assumes that when we change the length of the test, we do not change its nature. Extreme increases in test length, however, introduces boredom and may reduce reliability. Added items or added periods of observation may not confer the same behavior or ability as the original test.

Note: An increase in test length has a great effect on reliability but a much smaller effect on validity.

COMPUTING GUIDE 8

The $\bar{z}$-test,* or Critical Ratio, to determine a significant difference between two sample means.[2] (Large Samples)[3]

*Note: $\bar{z}$ assumes the two samples come from two populations with equal means but not necessarily equal variances.

1. Determine the means and standard deviations for *each* of the two samples in question.	See Computer Guide 2 or 3.
2. Determine the $\bar{z}$-ratio.	$$\bar{z} = \frac{M_1 - M_2}{\sqrt{\dfrac{\sigma_1{}^2}{N_1 - 1} + \dfrac{\sigma_2{}^2}{N_2 - 1}}}$$

1.   Cronbach, Lee J., *Essentials of Psychological Testing,* (2nd ed.). New York: Harper & Brothers, 1960, p. 76.
2.   See Mnemonic Table for Null Hypothesis, page 187.
3.   Although no hard and fast rule exists as a dividing line between large and small samples, in practice a sample size greater than 30 typically is considered large and one of 30 or less is considered small.

3. Enter Table A, page 227, to determine whether the $\bar{z}$-ratio indicates a significant difference between the two sample means.

$\bar{z}$ values at the .05 and .01 levels for one-tailed and two-tailed tests:[1],**

	One-tailed test	Two-tailed test
.05	≥ 1.65 or ≤ -1.65	≥ 1.96 or ≤ -1.96
.01	≥ 2.33 or ≤ -2.33	≥ 2.58 or ≤ -2.58

**Note: Concerning negative numbers, -1.70 is *less than* -1.65.

EXAMPLE: Achievement test scores for an experimental and control group.

Step	Experimental (Sample 1)	Control (Sample 2)
1	Given: $N_1 = 44$ $\quad M_1 = 78.09$ $\quad \sigma_1 = 17.44$	Given: $N_2 = 49$ $\quad M_2 = 68.14$ $\quad \sigma_2 = 18.03$

2.
$$\bar{z} = \frac{M_1 - M_2}{\sqrt{\dfrac{\sigma_1^2}{N_1 - 1} + \dfrac{\sigma_2^2}{N_2 - 1}}} = \frac{78.09 - 68.14}{\sqrt{\dfrac{(17.44)^2}{43} + \dfrac{(18.03)^2}{48}}}$$

$$= \frac{9.95}{\sqrt{\dfrac{304.15}{43} + \dfrac{325.08}{48}}} = \frac{9.95}{\sqrt{7.07 + 6.77}}$$

$$= \frac{9.95}{\sqrt{13.84}} = \frac{9.95}{3.72} = 2.67$$

3. Entering Table A, page 227, a $\bar{z}$ value of 2.67 corresponds to a point on the normal curve above which 0.38 percent of the area lies. Presuming a one-tailed test of significance for the research hypothesis that the mean ($\overline{M}_1$) of the experimental population is greater than the mean ($\overline{M}_2$) of the control population ($\overline{M}_1 - \overline{M}_2 > 0$), the null hypothesis that a difference between the first and second population means ($\overline{M}_1 - \overline{M}_2$) is negative or at most equal to zero can be rejected at the .01 level. The null hypothesis of no difference ($\overline{M}_1 - \overline{M}_2 = 0$) also would be rejected for a two-tailed test at the .01 level, had that been the case.

---

1. One-tailed tests predict a difference in only one direction, either plus (but not minus) or minus (but not plus); two-tailed tests predict a difference simultaneously in either direction. See pages 184-186 for further implications of hypothesis testing.

COMPUTING GUIDE 9

The *t*-test* to determine a significant difference between two sample means. (Satisfactory for Large Samples; particularly appropriate for Small Samples)[1]

1.	Determine the *means* and sum of squares, Σd^2, for each of the two samples in question.	See Computer Guide 2 or 3.
2.	Determine the *t*-ratio.	$$t = \frac{M_1 - M_2}{\sqrt{\left(\dfrac{\Sigma d^2{}_1 + \Sigma d^2{}_2}{N_1 + N_2 - 2}\right)\left(\dfrac{N_1 + N_2}{N_1 N_2}\right)}}$$
3.	Determine degrees of freedom, *df*.	$df = N_1 + N_2 - 2$
4.	Enter appropriate table to determine whether the *t*-ratio indicates a significant difference between the two sample means.	a. If *df* is greater than 30, use Table A, page 227, where the values at the .05 and .01 levels for one-tailed and two-tailed tests are;[2]

	One-tailed test	Two-tailed test
.05	≥ 1.65 or ≤ -1.65	≥ 1.96 or ≤ -1.96
.01	≥ 2.33 or ≤ -2.33	≥ 2.58 or ≤ -2.58

b. If *df* is 30 or less, Use Table B, page 228.

Note: t assumes the two samples come from two populations with equal means *and* equal variances. Concerning negative numbers, -1.70 is *less than* -1.65.

EXAMPLE: Two groups of children have been taught spelling using two teaching strategies: Method A or spaced practice and Method B or massed practice. The research hypothesis predicts that spaced practice is superior to massed practice, as measured by a selected spelling test.

Step	Method A—Spaced Practice	Method B—Massed Practice
1	Given: $N_1 = 10$ $M_1 = 25.5$ $\Sigma d^2{}_1 = 168.50$	Given: $N_2 = 10$ $M_2 = 22.0$ $\Sigma d^2{}_2 = 178.00$

2	$$t = \frac{M_1 - M_2}{\sqrt{\left(\dfrac{\Sigma d^2{}_1 + \Sigma d^2{}_2}{N_1 + N_2 - 2}\right)\left(\dfrac{N_1 + N_2}{N_1 N_2}\right)}} = \frac{25.5 - 22}{\sqrt{\left(\dfrac{168.50 + 178.00}{10 + 10 - 2}\right)\left(\dfrac{10 + 10}{(10)(10)}\right)}}$$
	$$t = \frac{3.5}{\sqrt{\left(\dfrac{346.50}{18}\right)\left(\dfrac{20}{100}\right)}} = \frac{3.5}{\sqrt{3.85}} = \frac{3.5}{1.96} = 1.786$$

3	Since *df* is $N_1 + N_2 - 2$, or 18, we enter Table B, page 228, finding that a *t*-value of plus 1.786 for a one-tailed test as predicted by the research hypothesis is significant at the .05 level.

---

1. In general the power of *t* is enhanced when the sample sizes and the variances underlying the two samples are equal, or nearly equal. Departures from these two conditions tend to compromise the use of *t*.
2. See footnote no. 1, page 175, regarding one-tailed and two-tailed tests.

CHI SQUARE

Chi square is a means of answering questions about data existing in the form of frequencies, rather than as scores or measurements along some scale. Typically, the question we want answered when we have such frequency data is *whether the frequencies observed in our sample deviate significantly from some theoretical or expected population frequencies.* The frequencies refer to the categories with which we have classified our data. Examples of the latter include such common classifications as male or female, yes or no, agree or disagree, pass or fail, or achiever or nonachiever.

If, for example, we want to know whether or not there is a significant difference in the proportions of students from either *higher* or *lower socio-economic* backgrounds who *complete high school* or who become *dropouts*, the chi square test would be the appropriate statistical tool to apply. We simply select an unbiased sample of students from the two defined populations (higher and lower socio-economic backgrounds), determine whether or not they completed high school or became dropouts (being careful to avoid contaminating factors which might bias our interpretation), and apply the chi square test. Classification patterns with more than two dimensions are possible with chi square. For example: high, average, or low achievers; freshmen, sophomores, juniors, or seniors; or the letter grade categories of A, B, C, D or F.

Restrictions on the Use of Chi Square:

1. Chi square can be used only with frequency data. (Note that data normally reported as scores along some scale of measurement such as IQ's, or achievement test scores can be categorized into frequency form; for example, high, average, and low scoring ranges.)

2. Chi square requires that the individual events or measures are independent of each other. In other words, each response must be free of any influence upon the nature of any other response in the set of responses being compared.

3. In general, no theoretical frequency should be smaller than 5.[1] (In this event, for 2 x 2 tables, use Fisher's Test of Exact Probability. See Siegel, S. *Nonparametric Statistics,* New York: McGraw-Hill, 1956, p. 94.)

4. There must be some logical or empirical basis for the way the data are categorized.

5. The sum of expected and the sum of observed frequencies must be the same.

6. The algebraic sum of the discrepancies between the observed and the corresponding expected frequencies will be zero.

---

1. The theoretical frequency for any cell is the product of the two marginal totals common to that cell divided by the total number of cases, N.

COMPUTING GUIDE 10
Chi Square for a 2 × 2 Table.[1]

<table>
<tr><td>1.</td><td colspan="2">Arrange data in a 2 × 2 table: (Note: Cells are assigned letter values to facilitate calculation.)</td></tr>
</table>

	B	A	A + B
	D	C	C + D

B + D   A + C $\underline{N}$

2. Compute chi square:

$$\chi^2 = \frac{N(AD - BC)^2}{(A+B)\ (C+D)\ (A+C)\ (B+D)}$$

3. Determine whether a one-tailed or two-tailed test is involved.

4. In Table C, page 229, chi square values for 1 degree of freedom (number of rows—1 times number of columns − 1) are listed both for one-tailed and two-tailed tests.   A chi square value as large as 3.84 is significant at the .05 level for a two-tailed test and at the .025 level for a one-tailed test.

EXAMPLE: A test of whether or not there is a significant difference between the proportions of girls or boys who prefer either listening to the radio or reading a book in their free time; equivalent to determining whether there is a relationship between sex membership and activity preference.

RADIO   BOOK

	RADIO	BOOK	
GIRLS	47 B	A 62	(62 + 47)
BOYS	58 D	C 39	(39 + 58)

(47 + 58)   (62 + 39) $\underline{206}$

$$\chi^2 = \frac{N(AD - BC)^2}{(A + B)(C + D)(A + C)(B + D)} = \frac{206[(62)(58) - (47)(39)]^2}{(109)(97)(101)(105)} = \frac{640,282,814}{112,126,665} = 5.71$$

From information given in Item 3, above, (or Table C, page 229), we conclude that there is a significant difference between boys and girls in their preference for listening to the radio or reading a book in their free time. This difference is significant at the 5% level but is not large enough to be significant at the 1% level.

1. Siegel uses a formula involving a *correction for continuity* for a 2 x 2 table *(df = 1)*. Optional, when $N > 100$; desirable when $N < 100$. See Siegel, S. S., *Nonparametric Statistics*, New York: McGraw-Hill, 1956, p. 107:

$$\chi^2 = \frac{N\left[(AD - BC) - \dfrac{N}{2}\right]^2}{(A + B)(C + D)(A + C)(B + D)}$$

COMPUTING GUIDE 11 Median Test for a difference between two medians.

Many times data are available that do not permit mathematical operations involved in calculating the mean and standard deviation. Typically, such data either are markedly skewed or represent an ordinal (rank-ordered) scale of measurement. In place of either a $\bar{z}$-test or t-test for a significance of the difference between two sample *means*, we use the median test which asks whether there is a significant difference between the *medians* of two samples.

The median test turns out to be nothing more than a *chi square* calculation using the median as a dividing point to form frequency categories. It is a procedure for testing whether it is probable that two independent groups (not necessarily the same size) have been drawn from populations with the same median.

1. Combine the two sets of ranks or scores from the two samples into a single rank-ordered distribution, determining the *new combined median*. Keep track of which of the two original samples each score represents.

2. Using the new combined median as the dividing point, cast these data into a 2 × 2 table:

	Group I	Group II
No. of scores above combined median:	B	A
No. of scores below combined median:	D	C

3. Follow the procedure for finding chi square for a 2 x 2 table given in Computing Guide 10, on the preceding page, using the formula in the footnote, corrected for continuity.

EXAMPLE: A counselor in a high school obtains two samples of percentile ranks and wants to know if they are significantly different:

Sample I: 17, 23, 23, 28, 31, 34, 37, 39, 42, 47, 56, 58, 61
Sample II: 23, 26, 35, 40, 43, 44, 44, 47, 52, 56, 59, 65, 70, 72, 77

Putting together the two sets of scores, the new combined median is 43.5. The resulting frequencies are cast into a 2 × 2 table and we obtain these results:

	Sample I	Sample II
No. of scores above combined median:	4 (B)	(A) 10
No. of scores below combined median:	9 (D)	(C) 5

Then:
$$= \frac{N\left[(AD - BC) - \dfrac{N}{2}\right]^2}{(A + B)(C + D)(A + C)(B + D)} = \frac{28[56]^2}{(14)(14)(15)(13)} = \frac{87,808}{38,220} = 2.297$$

According to Table C, page 229, a chi square value of 2.297, for one degree of freedom and a *two-tailed* test (since only a difference was sought), is *not* significant and the null hypothesis must be accepted.

---

1. When N for the sum of both samples is less than 30 (small sample), see Siegel, S. *Nonparametric statistics for the behavioral sciences,* New York: McGraw-Hill, 1956, pp. 111-112 and pp. 96-104, as the Fisher exact probability test may be necessary.

COMPUTING GUIDE 12 Chi Square for Categories Exceeding a 2 × 2 Table

1. Arrange data in an appropriate table format (e.g., 2 × 3, 3 × 3, 3 × 4, 4 × 4, etc.) based on categories used in your study.   See EXAMPLE below.

2. Apply the chi square formula:

$$\chi^2 = \Sigma \frac{(O - E)^2}{E}$$

3. Determine degrees of freedom: df = number of columns (k) − 1 *times* number of rows (r) − 1.

4. Enter Table C, page 229, for appropriate df to determine significance.   See EXAMPLE below.

EXAMPLE:[1] Is there a significant relationship between the responses of persons with membership in one of four groups representing different socioeconomic levels and their responses to the question, "Is your family more prosperous (better off) today than two years ago, less prosperous, or the same?" Group A is the highest socioeconomic level; Group D, the lowest.

Group	More	Same	Less	Uncertain	Total
A	115 (120)	245 (229.5)	125 (131)	15 (19.5)	500
B	375 (360)	690 (688.5)	375 (393)	60 (58.5)	1500
C	460 (480)	920 (918)	540 (524)	80 (78)	2000
D	250 (240)	440 (459)	270 (262)	40 (39)	1000
Column Total	1200	2295	1310	195	5000

O	E	$O-E$	$(O-E)^2$	$\dfrac{(O-E)^2}{E}$
115	120	−5	25	.208
375	360	15	225	.625
460	480	−20	400	.833
250	240	10	100	.417
245	229.5	15.5	240.25	1.047
690	688.5	1.5	2.25	.003
920	918	2	4	.004
440	459	−19	361	.786
125	131	−6	36	.275
375	393	−18	324	.824
540	524	16	256	.489
270	262	8	64	.244
15	19.5	−4.5	20.25	1.038
60	58.5	1.5	2.25	.038
80	78	2	4	.051
40	39	1	1	.026

$$\chi^2 = 6.908$$

---

1. Data taken from Spence, J. T., Underwood, B. J., Duncan, C. P., and Cotton, J. W. *Elementary statistics.* New York: Appleton-Century-Crofts, 1968, p. 204.

COMPUTING GUIDE 12 (cont'd.)

Computational steps:

1. Arrange data for *observed frequencies* in 4 × 4 table format (four groups—A, B, C, and D; four types of responses—"more," "same," "less," "uncertain").

2. Compute values for the *expected frequencies* (in parentheses) by multiplying the *column total* times the *row total*, for each cell in the table and dividing this product by N. For example, in the first cell in row A with an observed frequency of 115:

$$\frac{(1200)(500)}{5000} = 120$$

3. In each cell subtract the theoretical frequency from the observed frequency to obtain the deviation: $O - E$.

4. Square the deviation: $(O - E)^2$

5. Divide each squared deviation by the theoretical frequency of each cell:

$$\frac{(O - E)^2}{E}$$

6. Determine chi square by summing the resulting quotients:

$$\chi^2 = \Sigma \frac{(O - E)^2}{E} = 6.908$$

7. Determine degrees of freedom (df): number of columns $-$ 1, times number of rows $-$ 1, equals 9.

8. Enter Table C, page 229, for 9 df to determine whether a chi square value as large as 6.908 is statistically significant. Since a chi square value of at least 16.92 must be obtained to be significant at even the 5% level of significance, we accept the null hypothesis of no relationship and conclude that whatever differences appear to exist in the data, they are probably due to chance. In other words, the observed differences in the sample data are not statistically significant and may be attributed to chance.

ANALYSIS OF VARIANCE

The $\bar{z}$-test or t-test (Computer Guides 8 and 9) answer the question, Is the difference between *two* sample means statistically significant? Typically, one mean represents an experimental group receiving some treatment condition and the other mean represents a control group. Many research problems in education, however, involve more than two groups and yield more than two means. For example, we may want to study the effects of two methods of teaching in relationship to two levels of intelligence upon achievement test scores—a 2×2 design involving four group means:

	Low IQ	High IQ
Method A	M_2	M_1
Method B	M_4	M_3

Or, consider the more complex investigation of three teaching strategies in conjunction with three age levels of children compared to the child's sex—a $3 \times 3 \times 2$ design involving 18 group means. The advantages of these factorial designs are important: they yield information about the *main effects* of particular variables by themselves (e.g., the effect of method alone, intelligence alone, or age level alone) and they also yield information about *interactions* between variables (e.g., method *and* intelligence, or method *and* age level).[1]

The task of *pairing up* all relevant combinations of two sample means and computing individual $\bar{z}$ or t-tests soon becomes oppresive. Furthermore, if none of these tests happens to be statistically significant, a great deal of effort is spent in this determination. Also, when dealing with a large number of such individual tests, *chance alone* allows 5% of the differences between pairs of sample means to reach the .05 level of significance. A single composite test to compare all sample means simultaneously and to tell us whether or not a statistically significant difference exists somewhere in the data overcomes these disadvantages. It has the additional advantage of a more accurate estimate of the population variance since it could base this estimate on all the sample data taken together, rather than just two samples, as in the case of the $\bar{z}$ or t-test. Carrying out either of these tests after an F-test can be a hazardous undertaking; correct procedures are described in most of the works in statistics and in experimental design cited near the end of this chapter.

Analysis of variance is the statistical tool having these characteristics. It answers the question, Is the variability *between* groups large enough in comparison with the variability *within* groups to justify the inference that the means of the populations from which the different groups were sampled are not all the same? In other words, if the variability between groups means is large enough, we can conclude they probably come from different populations and that there is a statistically significant difference present in the data. The particular statistical test yielding the answer is the F-ratio:

$$F = \frac{\text{Between Group Variance}}{\text{Within Group Variance}}$$

While *analysis of variance* is the first step in the analysis of these more complex designs, it is only a preliminary and exploratory tool. If a significant F-ratio is obtained, the researcher only knows that somewhere in his data something other than chance is probably operating. He next must attempt to isolate the presence, nature, and extent of this non-

---

1. See "FACTORIAL DESIGNS," pp. 76-79; and "ANALYSIS OF CROSSBREAKS," pp. 163-164.

chance influence. In many instances he will then proceed with either $\bar{z}$ or t-tests, now that he has established the worth of such an effort, although the hazards referenced previously should be investigated. These individual tests also are strengthened by a more accurate estimate of the population variance gained in the analysis of variance calculation.

Underlying assumptions—Guilford (see "References" below) notes four principal assumptions underlying analysis of variance as a parametric technique:

1. The contributions to variance in the total sample must be additive.
2. The observations within sets must be mutually independent.
3. The variances within experimentally homogeneous sets must be approximately equal.
4. The variations within experimentally homogeneous sets should be from normally distributed populations.

The general strategy to follow in meeting these assumptions is (1) random sampling within sets and (2) use of a good metric scale. To the extent that the above assumptions are compromised, the F-ratio tends to be less significant than it appears.

Some sources of information on analysis of variance—Analysis of variance is a complex tool with many limitations, applications, and variations in form. Since it cannot realistically be reduced to a series of Checklists or Computer Guides, the investigator must consult the standard texts on this subject (see below) and, if possible, seek expert assistance in its application.

ANALYSIS OF COVARIANCE

Many times in studies of the type suitable for analysis of variance, there will be initial differences between groups on pretest criteria that arise either by chance or, more likely, because of the inability of the educational researcher to select subjects at random. This includes sets of data that are not independent, involving correlated means. *Analysis of covariance* adjusts for initial differences between groups and for the correlation between means. In effect, it permits the comparison of groups on one variable when information is available on another variable correlated with it, or on several such variables. It is generally preferable to *matching* subjects for the same purpose. Random assignment is recommended.

ANALYSIS OF VARIANCE AND COVARIANCE AND COMPUTER PROGRAMS

Because of the speed and capacity of computers and the availability of computer programs, many research data using analysis of variance and/or covariance are processed in this way. The investigator should make use of data processing facilities in his community. If operational programs are available, the cost is very nominal.

MULTIVARIATE STATISTICAL PROCEDURES

During the past fifteen years large-scale advances have been made in treating statistically large numbers of independent and dependent variables in a variety of contexts. In particular, multiple regression techniques, simple and multiple discriminant function analyses, canonical correlation methods, and factor analytic approaches have been widely applied largely because of the increased capabilities of electronic computers. An overview section on these multivariate procedures is included near the end of this chapter along with a substantial number of relevant references that the reader may consult.

HYPOTHESIS TESTING AND STATISTICAL SIGNIFICANCE

1. *The Research Hypothesis and the Null Hypothesis*

   a. The *research hypothesis* states the expectations of the researcher in positive terms. It identifies the variables or conditions which, in causal relationship, will be advanced to account for the results and is often derived from a theory.

   b. The *null hypothesis*—the hypothesis of "no relationship or difference"—is the one actually tested statistically. It is an arbitrary convention hypothesizing that any relation or difference in the findings is due to chance or sampling error and puts this supposition to a probability test. Theoretically, it is an hypothesis set up for possible *rejection* and though the degree of relationship or margin of difference need not be zero, it frequently is.

2. *Stating the Null Hypothesis*—four alternatives, using the example of the difference between two sample means:[1]

   a. There is no difference between the means of the two populations from which the two samples were drawn at random.

   b. The two means in the two populations from which the samples were respectively drawn at random are equal.

   c. The mean of the sampling distribution of differences between an infinite number of pairs of means of randomly drawn samples equals zero.

   d. Any difference between two sample means drawn randomly from their respective populations is due to sampling error—that is, such differences can readily be attributed to chance.

3. *Accepting or Rejecting the Null Hypothesis—What it Means*

   Testing the null hypothesis results in one of two outcomes:

   a. *Accepting (failing to reject)* the null hypothesis as true, in which case it is concluded that any differences in the results are:

   (1) not statistically significant, therefore are probably

   (2) due to sampling error or chance.

   b. *Rejecting* the null hypothesis as false, in which case it is concluded that the differences in the results are:

   (1) statistically significant, therefore are probably

   (2) due to some determining factor or condition, other than chance.

   Accepting the null hypothesis also means that the corresponding research hypothesis is not supported or disconfirmed. Rejecting the null hypothesis also means the corresponding research hypothesis has survived a test of disconfirmation and, in that sense, is supported. More precisely, the differences in the data reasonably cannot be

---

1. Adapted from notes for a seminar presented by William B. Michael. This material is essentially the same as that appearing in Wilson, J. A. R., Robeck, M. C., and Michael, W. B., *Psychological foundations of learning and teaching* (2nd ed.), New York: McGraw-Hill, 1974, pp.

attributed to chance and the causal factors stated in the research hypothesis may possibly explain the difference, but not necessarily so as long as there are *plausible rival hypotheses* also to account for the data. Obviously, the more tests of disconfirmation a given research hypothesis can survive, the stronger is the evidence in its support.

4. *Accepting or Rejecting the Null Hypothesis—Two Types of Errors*

   a. *Type I (Alpha) Error*—to reject the null hypothesis of no differences when it is true. In other words, to conclude falsely that a difference exists in the data when in fact it does not. Since such an error is particularly embarrassing to the scientist (saying something exists when it does not), he tends to avoid risking this error and chooses a conservative level of significance which minimizes it.

   b. *Type II (Beta) Error*—to accept the null hypothesis of no differences when it is false. In other words, to conclude falsely that a difference does not exist in the data when in fact it does.

   c. *The decision between risks*—Whether to run the risk of a Type I or Type II error, since the probability of one increases as the other decreases, is a question of utility. Which is preferable in a given situation: (1) a Type I *fine screen* designed to eliminate chance differences at the expense of throwing away some genuine differences in the process? or (2) a Type II *coarse screen* that lets through some of the unwanted chance differences to insure that most of the genuine differences are kept? When the consequences of mistaking a chance difference for a genuine difference are too costly and the risk of such an error must be minimized, a conservative level of significance is set, avoiding the Type I error. When, on the other hand, there is a search for all promising leads and no genuine prospect can be overlooked, a liberal level of significance is selected, avoiding the Type II error. *Note: To avoid the probability of either error, increase the sample size, N.*

5. *Rejecting the Null Hypothesis and Theory-Building*[1]
   The task of theory-building and data analysis is to *reject* inadequate hypotheses. Experimental findings never confirm or prove a theory. Rather, the successful theory is tested and escapes being disconfirmed and the more tests of this nature it survives, the stronger it stands. Strictly speaking, the null hypothesis can never be accepted— it can only be rejected or fail to be rejected.

6. *One-tailed and Two-tailed Tests of the Null Hypotheses*
   When a particular research hypothesis simply predicts that a *difference* will exist in the data and allows this difference to be in *either direction* (larger or smaller), it is a two tailed test of its null hypothesis counterpart, since the difference can fall in either tail of this sampling distribution. If, on the other hand, the research hypothesis predicts the direction of the difference (*either* larger *or* smaller), it is a one-tailed test of the corresponding null hypothesis.

---

1. Based on a discussion by D. T. Campbell and J. C. Stanley. *Experimental and Quasi-experimental Designs for Research.* Chicago: Rand McNally, 1966.

7. *The Power of a Statistical Test*

The power of a statistical test is defined as the probability of rejecting the null hypothesis of no differences when it is actually *false*. In other words, differences really do exist, and the null hypothesis ought to be rejected:

$$\text{Power} = 1 - \text{probability of Type II error}$$

The power of a statistical test is a function of:

a. The underlying assumptions of the test: parametric tests make stronger assumptions than nonparametric tests.

b. Whether the test is one-tailed (often more powerful in a certain region of admissable alternative hypotheses of interest) or two-tailed (less powerful in that same region).

c. Sample size N: as N increases, power usually increases. *Power efficiency* refers to the increase in sample size necessary to make test X as powerful as a second test Y.

8. *Level of Significance and Replication*[1]

While the conventional level for rejecting the null hypothesis is $p = .05$ or $.01$ (5 percent and 1 percent, respectively), significance levels of 10 to 20 percent are tolerable in preliminary investigations, *with replication*. Note: If two successive findings are each significant at the 10 percent level, this is roughly equivalent to a single finding at the 1 percent level since the two kinds of outcomes are about equally probable. Moreover, replication provides empirically stronger evidence than a single occurrence and justifies the more liberal test of the null hypothesis, avoiding the Type II error.[2]

9. *Statistical Significance versus Practical Significance*

In the researcher's zeal to obtain statistically significant findings, he often overlooks the more relevant question: Is it educationally significant? Is the difference large enough to be practical? Are the gains important enough to be worth the cost and effort to obtain them? This question gets at the trade off factor in educational decision-making and involves the problem of accountability in cost effectiveness economics. Even when these practical matters are settled or in the background, there are valuable considerations of social and psychological nature that frequently override a choice based solely on statistical significance.

---

1. Based on notes taken at a Field Studies Workshop given by staff members of the Far West Regional Laboratory, Berkeley, California, 1968.
2. For another consideration of this problem, see Guilford, J. P. *Fundamental Statistics in Psychology and Education,* (4th ed.). New York: McGraw-Hill, 1965, pp. 248-250.

Mnemonic Table for Null Hypothesis: Two-tailed Test of Significance of Differences between Means for Large-sample Approach

z-Value (Critical Ratio)	Associated Probability Value (P)	Acceptance or Rejection of Null Hypothesis	Conclusion regarding Null Hypothesis (NH)	Conclusion regarding Statistical Significance	Conclusion regarding Research Hypothesis (RH)*	Tail-area Picture relative to z Value
$z < 1.96$ (z less than 1.96)	$P > .05$ (P greater than .05)	Accepted (tenable)	The NH is supported. It is not unreasonable to believe that the two samples come from two populations with equal means.	Not significant (NS). The difference between the two means is statistically not significant.	RH not supported	Less than 95% — Large tail area (relatively low confidence level—less than 95%)
$1.96 \leq z < 2.576$ (z greater than, or at least equal to, 1.96, but less than 2.576)	$.01 < P \leq .05$ (P less than, or at most equal to .05, but greater than .01)	Rejected at .05 level, but accepted at .01 level (untenable at .05 level but tenable at .01 level)	The NH is probably not supported. It is reasonable to believe that the two samples come from two populations with different means.	Significant at .05 level, but not at .01 level (S). The difference between the two means is statistically significant at .05 level (but not at .01 level)	RH supported	Between 95 and 99% — Small tail area (relatively high confidence level—between 95 and 99%)
$z \geq 2.576$ (z greater than, or at least equal to, 2.576)	$P \leq .01$ (P less than, or at most equal to, .01)	Rejected at .01 level as well as at .05 level (untenable at both .05 and .01 levels)	The NH is very probably not supported. It is very reasonable to believe that the two samples come from two populations with different means.	Very significant at or beyond .01 level (as well as at .05 level) (VS). The difference between the two means is statistically significant at or beyond .01 level—very significant.	RH very strongly supported	At least 99% — Very small tail area (relatively very high confidence level—at least 99%)

* If research hypothesis is positively stated.

From *Psychological foundations of learning and teaching* by Wilson, J.A.R., Robeck, M.C., and Michael, W.B. Copyright © 1969 by McGraw-Hill, Inc., p. 556. Used with permission of McGraw-Hill Book Co.

THE SEARCH FOR PROMISING PRACTICES:
AVOIDING THE TYPE II ERROR[1]

Traditional research as a form of educational inquiry stresses principles of rigorous design in order to maximize both internal and external validity (particularly internal validity). Customarily, conservative standards of statistical significance are employed relative to which the probability for the rejection of the null hypothesis is set at or below .05. The logic of this approach has been to avoid the Type I error—namely concluding that a treatment makes a difference between the means of one or more experimental groups and a comparison group when, in fact, it does not or that an association exists between two variables when indeed it does not.

On the other hand, such a rigorous approach may tend to be counterproductive in an educational setting in which learning outcomes can be the result of many complex factors acting independently and jointly in addition to the one under investigation. In educational and psychological research, differences between the means of groups or the magnitudes of correlation coefficients obtained are likely to be low at best. This circumstance is further compounded when the sample sizes are quite small, as is often the case in research with human subjects. The risk that the researcher now faces is likely to be one associated with Type II error—concluding that the treatment has not yielded a difference or observable effect when, in fact, it has or that two variables are not related when indeed they are.

A pragmatic solution to this dilemma has been proposed by N. L. Gage, Professor of Education and Psychology at Stanford University. In its most rudimentary form, the solution ignores standards of meticulous design and statistical significance on the grounds that neither design rigor nor statistical significance is *necessarily* crucial. Specifically, research on any variable when it actually is of consequence usually will yield outcomes suggestive of genuine effects or relationships with or without elegant designs or statistical precision. In any given study by itself such an implied assumption would not be warranted. By examining several investigations concerned with a common treatment variable—especially when each study differs from the other in terms of particular design weaknesses—one can simply count the number of times relative to which the results are favorable. If there is a preponderance of findings in the anticipated or hypothesized direction, the effect of the independent variable in question would be supported. This level of support would be reinforced by the fact that the common treatment variable had yielded results holding across nearly all studies, whereas support for each of the rival hypotheses challenging the effect of the common treatment variable arises from particular design weaknesses and varies from one study to another. It follows that if one has to shift from one criticism to a different one to call the common treatment variable into question as each of several studies is being examined that circumstance in itself indirectly supports the possible influence of the common treatment variable.

Consistent with this orientation of evaluating the probable impact of a treatment variable is use of a statistical significance test such as the nonparametric sign test (based on applying the binomial distribution) that would indicate in a set of experiments how many times the results favored the common treatment variable. For example, if in 18 investigations in which the outcome was registered as being present or absent in relation to the occurrence of a com-

1. Based on an article by: Gage, N.L. The yield of research on Teaching. *Phi Delta Kappan*, 1978, 59, 229-235.

mon treatment variable the researcher noted an anticipated effect 13 times, he could infer that the probability of that number of so-called favorable events was less than .05 provided that the various research studies could be assumed to be independent of one another.

Expanding upon this approach, Gage has offered a second procedure which makes use of somewhat complex techniques. This procedure requires the investigator to take into account both the sample sizes and the magnitudes of the statistical significance levels associated with the reported differences or with observable relationships in a given set of studies. The result of this process can afford even a stronger means than that provided by the first approach in concluding that a selected treatment variable has, in fact, registered an effect when viewed across several independent studies. The reader who wishes to pursue these points at greater length will find the article by Gage that has been cited in the footnote to be of considerable interest.

SAMPLING

1. When we *sample*, we are drawing from some *population* of possible cases.

2. The sample will deviate from the true nature of the defined population by a certain amount due to chance variations in drawing the sample's few cases from the population's many possible cases. This is called *sampling error* and is distinguished from non-chance variations due to *determining factors* (e.g., biased sampling procedures, effects of independent variables, research conditions, and other causal agents or circumstances).

3. The problem that sampling error presents to sampling statistics occurs in two important settings:
    a. *When we wish to generalize from a sample to a particular population.* In doing so, we must estimate the size of the sampling error. If it is sufficiently small, we reasonably can conclude that any difference between the sample mean and the estimated population mean is due to chance—therefore, the sample is representative of the population and allows generalizations about that population. If it is too large to assign to chance variations, we must conclude that the sample is not representative of the defined population and we should avoid generalizations.
        EXAMPLE: In a consumer survey, a researcher draws a sample of consumer opinions about alternative packaging procedures for a new product, from which he makes inferences about the *population* of all possible consumers.
    b. *When we wish to determine whether two or more samples were drawn from the same, or different populations.* Instead of making generalizations from a single sample to some population, we now are asking if two or more samples are sufficiently different to rule out chance and point to some determining (causative) agent or condition; or, if they are sufficiently similar to attribute any differences to chance alone. We are asking, in other words, is there a systematic (nonchance) difference between the two samples, supporting the conclusion that each represents a different population?
        EXAMPLE: A research psychologist investigates the effect of a drug on the maze-learning behavior of rats using two samples of rats, an experimental group

receiving the drug and a control group not receiving the drug.

Typically, in setting 3a we hope to attribute differences to chance so that we can generalize about the population. In setting 3b, however, we hope to rule out chance so that we can attribute differences to determining factors and causal relationships.

4.   *Two Modes of Sampling from a Population of Possible Cases:*

    a. *Random sampling*—Selecting cases or subjects in such a way that all have an equal probability of being included and the selection of one case has no influence on the selection of any other case. Drawing names from a hat, taking every tenth name from an alphabetical listing, or entering a table of random numbers are typical methods of sampling at random.

    b. *Stratified random sampling*—When there are two or more ways of classifying the data—sex, age, educational level, intelligence level, socioeconomic status, or ethnic membership—and it is important to insure that each category is *proportionately represented* in the sample, the population is subdivided into the appropriate strata and then a predetermined quota of cases is drawn *at random* from each substratum.

5.   *Small or Large Samples?*

Between the economy and convenience of small samples and the reliability and representativeness of large samples lies a trade off point balancing practical considerations against statistical power and generalizability.

Some of the merits of small samples are listed on page 96. In addition, small samples are more appropriate for in depth case studies or where complex techniques of eliciting or evaluating behavior are involved, such as psychodrama, role playing, intensive counseling or interviewing procedures, or projective instruments.

Nevertheless, it remains true that the larger the sample, the smaller the sampling error and, other things being equal, it is preferable to increase the sample size wherever practical. Large samples, moreover, often are essential when the following factors are present:[1]

    a. *When a large number of uncontrolled variables are interacting unpredictably* and it is desirable to minimize their separate effects by sampling from a large variety of situations representing different amounts and combinations of these variables. The result is to mix them together randomly, cancelling out chance imbalances. Example: a study involving two teaching methods sampling equally from twenty teachers, rather than two. This minimizes the possible source of interaction between one of the methods and a highly effective teacher, where the difference is more attributable to this one teacher than to the method.

    b. *When the total sample is to be divided into several subsamples* and these subsample categories are the actual units of comparison. Obviously, it is the size of the subsample that is critical in estimating the sampling error, not the size of the total sample. Example: when studying the interaction between a given curriculum

1.   Adapted from Borg, Walter R., *Educational Research: An Introduction,* New York: David McKay Company, 1963, pp. 171–174.

innovation and such organismic variables as age, grade level, sex, socioeconomic status, ethnic membership, and the school attended, breaking down the overall sample into smaller comparison groups based on these classifications.

c. *When the population is made up of a wide range of variables and characteristics* and a small sample would run a high risk of missing or misrepresenting many of these differences. Example: a census study to determine the nature of a city, state, or national population.

d. *When differences in the results are expected to be small* and it is important to insure against losing these differences in the "noise" background of the inevitable error variance. Example: a school district wants to evaluate the effect of a new lighting system on student attitude and achievement. Assuming that the lighting change is a minor improvement, it would be unrealistic to anticipate large increments of gain on the student variables and the district would be satisfied to demonstrate any gain at all.

6. *Pitfall in Sampling: The Volunteer*—Many studies, knowingly or unknowingly, build in a *volunteer* factor in the selection of participants. Questionnaire or interview studies depending on the voluntary cooperation of the respondent or a research investigation permitting some teachers to select themselves into one or more of the treatment groups illustrate this problem. The pitfall is the likelihood that volunteers differ from nonvolunteers, compromising the interpretation and generalizability of the results. See page 61, item 6 and page 62, item 1, for relationship to internal and external validity, respectively.

ESTIMATING SAMPLE SIZE REQUIRED FOR MAKING INFERENCES ABOUT MAGNITUDES OF POPULATION PROPORTIONS

When one is preparing to select a sample from a population of known size (finite population), how large must the sample be before reliable inferences can be made about the proportion of individuals in the population who would be responding in a designated manner? If one assumes that the population proportion P of individuals answering "yes" or "agree" is .50 and that the proportion Q, or 1-P in the population replying "no" or "disagree" is also .50, it is possible to determine how large a sample size S would be needed when the sample is randomly chosen from a population of size N so that the probability would be .95 that the sample proportion p would fall within .05 (5 percentage points) of the population proportion P. In other words, in randomly drawing 100 samples all of the same size S, 95 out of 100 would yield a proportion p within .05 units of the true population proportion P. It should be mentioned that the selection of a value of .50 for P is a conservative approach that will tend to overestimate the size of the interval within which a designated probability of occurrence of sample proportions would fall if P is less than .50 or greater than .50.

In the table that follows this discussion, entries for the required sample size S are provided in a column immediately to the right of that portraying corresponding finite populations of given size N. These values for S are those that would be necessary to provide the outcome discussed in the previous paragraph. As an illustration, the sample size S of 278 cases would be needed from a finite population with N equal to 1,000 cases so that there would be a 95 percent level of confidence that the sample proportion p would be within an amount of .05 of the population value of .50 for P. It should be emphasized that all samples are assumed to have been drawn at *random*. Moreover, if P differed slightly from .50, a somewhat smaller sample could be used than that specified in the table.

In their 1970 article in *Educational and Psychological Measurement* (which has been referred to in the footnote at the bottom of the table to follow) Krejcie and Morgan have provided the following formula for estimating the sample size S needed relative to (a) population of a known size, (N), (b) a specified confidence level (e.g., .95) associated with a chi square statistic for one degree of freedom, and (c) the designated degree of accuracy as reflected by the amount of sampling error d that can be tolerated. (Thus, for the tabular entries d was set at .05—a value equivalent to $\pm$ 1.96 times the standard error of the proportion $\sigma_{\overline{p}}$. The formula is as follows:

$$ S = \frac{X^2\ NP\ (1 - P)}{d^2\ (N - 1) + X^2 P\ (1 - P)}\ , \text{in which} $$

S = required sample size

N = the given population size

P = population proportion that for table construction has been assumed to be .50, as this magnitude yields the maximum possible sample size required

d = the degree of accuracy as reflected by the amount of error that can be tolerated in the fluctuation of a sample proportion p about the population proportion P—the value for d being .05 in the calculations for entries in the table, a quantity equal to $\pm$ 1.96 $\sigma_{\overline{p}}$.

X^2 = table value of chi square for one degree of freedom relative to the desired level of confidence, which was 3.841 for the .95 confidence level represented by entries in the table

TABLE FOR DETERMINING NEEDED SIZE S OF A RANDOMLY CHOSEN SAMPLE FROM A GIVEN FINITE POPULATION OF N CASES SUCH THAT THE SAMPLE PROPORTION p WILL BE WITHIN ± .05 OF THE POPULATION PROPORTION P WITH A 95 PERCENT LEVEL OF CONFIDENCE[1]

N	S	N	S	N	S
10	10	220	140	1200	291
15	14	230	144	1300	297
20	19	240	148	1400	302
25	24	250	152	1500	306
30	28	260	155	1600	310
35	32	270	159	1700	313
40	36	280	162	1800	317
45	40	290	165	1900	320
50	44	300	169	2000	322
55	48	320	175	2200	327
60	52	340	181	2400	331
65	56	360	186	2600	335
70	59	380	191	2800	338
75	63	400	196	3000	341
80	66	420	201	3500	346
85	70	440	205	4000	351
90	73	460	210	4500	354
95	76	480	214	5000	357
100	80	500	217	6000	361
110	86	550	226	7000	364
120	92	600	234	8000	367
130	97	650	242	9000	368
140	103	700	248	10000	370
150	108	750	254	15000	375
160	113	800	260	20000	377
170	118	850	265	30000	379
180	123	900	269	40000	380
190	127	950	274	50000	381
200	132	1000	278	75000	382
210	136	1100	285	100000	384

Note: N is population size; S is sample size.

1. Krejcie, R. V. and Morgan, D. W. Determining sample size for research activities, *Educational and Psychological Measurement,* 1970, 30, 607–610.

WAYS OF INTERPRETING CORRELATION COEFFICIENTS

1. In its simplest form, a correlation coefficient is a number indicating the degree of relationship between two variables. It measures to what extent variations in one go with variations in the other:

    1.00 A perfect positive correlation: changes in one variable are accompanied by equivalent changes in the *same* direction in the other variable, without exception.

     .00 No correlation: changes in one variable have no relationship, or are randomly related, to changes in the other variable.

    −1.00 A perfect negative correlation: changes in one variable are accompanied by equivalent changes in the *opposite* direction in the other variable, without exception.

2. A correlation coefficient requires two sets of measurements on the same groups of individuals, or on matched pairs of individuals, and cannot be computed on one person alone.

3. *Coefficient of Determination, r^2*

    The correlation coefficient, r, is a measure of the strength of relationship between two variables. It does not represent a percentage of the determinants they have in common unless it is squared and becomes an estimate of variance called the coefficient of determination. When the latter is multiplied by 100, it indicates the percentage of variance held in common by the two variables, X and Y, assuming linear regression. It answers the question, How much of the variance in Y is accounted for, associated with, or determined by the variance in X? The following table summarizes the relationship between r and r^2, expressing the latter as a percentage to the nearest whole unit ($100r^2$ and rounded):

r	Percent of Variance $100r^2$	r	Percent of Variance: $100r^2$
.00	0%	.55	30%
.05	0	.60	36
.10	1	.65	42
.15	2	.70	49
.20	4	.75	56
.25	6	.80	64
.30	9	.85	72
.35	12	.90	81
.40	16	.95	90
.45	20	.98	96
.50	25	.99	98

The implications of this table can be illustrated by the relationship between grade point average (GPA) and intelligence (IQ) which, in the general population, fluctuates about an r of .50. This suggests that, in variance terms, 25 percent of factors accounting for GPA can be attributed to factors also accounting for IQ; therefore 75 percent of the determinants of GPA are independent of the IQ. Furthermore, an r of .7071 is necessary before 50 percent of the underlying variance is held in common between two measures.

4.   The practical significance of a correlation coefficient in making accurate predictions is revealed in the following table by Thorndike and Hagen:[1]

ACCURACY OF PREDICTION FOR DIFFERENT VALUES OF THE CORRELATION COEFFICIENT
(1000 cases in each row or column)

	$r = .00$					$r = .60$			
	Quarter on Criterion					*Quarter on Criterion*			
Quarter on Predictor	*4th*	*3rd*	*2nd*	*1st*	Quarter on Predictor	*4th*	*3rd*	*2nd*	*1st*
1st	250	250	250	250	1st	45	141	277	537
2nd	250	250	250	250	2nd	141	264	318	277
3rd	250	250	250	250	3rd	277	318	264	141
4th	250	250	250	250	4th	537	277	141	45
	$r = .40$					$r = .70$			
	Quarter on Criterion					*Quarter on Criterion*			
Quarter on Predictor	*4th*	*3rd*	*2nd*	*1st*	Quarter on Predictor	*4th*	*3rd*	*2nd*	*1st*
1st	104	191	277	428	1st	22	107	270	601
2nd	191	255	277	277	2nd	107	270	353	270
3rd	277	277	255	191	3rd	270	353	270	107
4th	428	277	191	104	4th	601	270	107	22
	$r = .50$					$r = .80$			
	Quarter on Criterion					*Quarter on Criterion*			
Quarter on Predictor	*4th*	*3rd*	*2nd*	*1st*	Quarter on Predictor	*4th*	*3rd*	*2nd*	*1st*
1st	73	168	279	480	1st	6	66	253	675
2nd	168	258	295	279	2nd	66	271	410	253
3rd	279	295	258	168	3rd	253	410	271	66
4th	480	279	168	73	4th	675	253	66	6

From this table a number of conclusions can be reached. For instance, if the correlation between a Predictor and a Criterion happens to be .50, then out of the 1000 cases falling in the fourth, or lowest, quarter on the Criterion, on the Predictor only 73 (7.3 percent) scored in the first quarter, 168 (16.8 percent) scored in the second quarter, 279 (27.9 percent) scored in the third quarter, and 480 (48.0 percent) scored in the fourth quarter.

It is also clear that the higher the correlation, the fewer the errors in prediction. The diagonal entries represent cases that fall in the same quarter on both Predictor and Criterion. Note that the further out from the diagonal, the greater the discrepancy between the two variables; also, the higher the correlation, the fewer the discrepancies when moving out from the respective diagonals.

---

1.   Thorndike, R. L., and Hagen, E. *Measurement and Evaluation in Psychology and Education* (3rd ed.). New York: Wiley, 1969, p. 173. By permission.

5. The size of *r* increases directly with the variability of the measurements. The more variable the measurements, the higher the correlation coefficient, other things being equal. The problem of *restriction of range* is illustrated by the finding that, when dealing with the normal range of variability in the general population, there is an *r* of about .50 between IQ and achievement. When this range is restricted, as among students qualifying for graduate school, this correlation approaches zero.

6. *Correlation and Causation*

Science is ultimately concerned with identifying cause-and-effect relationships. Since such relationships are always correlated, there is a strong tendency to reverse the process and infer cause-and-effect status between two or more variables based on an established correlation coefficient. The danger is clear: *correlation does not necessarily imply causation*. Two variables simply may be correlated with a third variable, as in the case of a positive correlation between water temperature and the incidence of drownings along the coast of California. It is incorrect to conclude that warm ocean water is more dangerous and the explanation lies in the obvious fact that more people go swimming when the water is warm, an activity increasing the exposure factor.

A perusal of research on teaching convinces one that the causal interpretation of correlational data is overdone rather than underdone and that plausible rival hypotheses are often overlooked. Furthermore, to establish the temporal antecedent-consequent nature of a causal relationship, observations extended in time, if not experimental intrusion of the treatment variable, are essential. For example, where teacher and pupil behavior are correlated, we would almost never consider the viewpoint that the pupil behavior was *causing* the teacher behavior, but the other way round. The causal interpretation of a simple or a partial correlation depends upon both the presence of a compatible plausible causal hypothesis and the absence of plausible rival hypotheses to explain the correlation upon other grounds.[1]

7. *Nonlinear or Curvilinear Relationships*

The standard assumption underlying most correlation coefficients is that the relationship between the two variables is linear: as one increases or decreases, so does the other, forming a straight-line regression function. Certain relationships, however, are not this consistent. Chronological age and achievement, for example, increase rapidly in childhood and youth; then level off in the twenties, typically declining with advancing years, creating a U-shaped regression line. A linear correlation study between these two variables using a large age span (age 5 to 65) would probably yield an *r* of zero. In fact, there is a sizeable relationship that simply changes rate and direction with age. Another example would be the relationship between IQ and job performance requiring average ability. Job performance will generally increase between an IQ range of 90 to 110; beyond these limits performance falls off due either to lack of aptitude for lower scores or boredom and lack of challenge for higher scores. Such a relationship is described as *curvilinear*, since high Criterion ratings only occur within an optimum range on the Predictor and decreases in both directions beyond this range:

The simplest procedure for detecting nonlinear trends in correlation data is to construct a scatter diagram (see page 162), inspecting the shape of the plots for bends and curves in the regression line departing from a straight-line function. For a statistical test of

---

1. Adapted from Campbell, D. T. and Stanley, J. C. *Experimental and Quasi-experimental Designs for Research*. Chicago: Rand McNally, 1966.

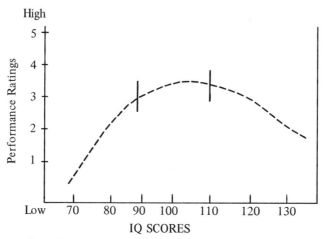

linearity-nonlinearity and the most commonly used correlation technique for nonlinear data, the *correlation ratio*, see first entry in item eight, below.

8. *Special Correlation Problems and Methods*[1]
    Nonlinear regression. The most widely used statistical test to assess the curvature in a regression line is the *F* test of linearity. The statistical method to determine a correlation coefficient with nonlinear data is the *correlation ratio*.

    Data where both sets vary along a continuous scale of measurement but one set is arbitrarily dichotomized. Example: a correlation study between IQ and a pass-fail outcome of a driver's license examination. Use the *biserial correlation method*.

    Data where one set varies along a continuous scale of measurement but the other set is a true dichotomy. Example: a correlation study between achievement test scores and the dichotomy, male-female. Use the *point-biserial correlation method*.

    Data where both sets vary along a continuous scale of measurement but both are arbitrarily dichotomized. Example: a correlation study between achievement test scores and IQ levels when both variables are dichotomized about their respective medians. Use the *tetrachoric correlation method*.

    Data where both sets are true dichotomies. Example: a correlation study between residential status (resident-nonresident) and marital status (married-single). Use the *phi coefficient correlation method*.

9. *Other Special Correlation Problems and Methods*
    For problems involving more than two variables, such as partial correlation, multiple correlation, and factor analysis, consult Guilford[1] or other advanced treatments of correlation methodology.

10. *Two Final Precautions*
    A major weakness of the correlation method is its encouragement of the *"shotgun" approach* to research, devouring all data in sight indiscriminately. Such data are extremely difficult to interpret and mostly useless. Also, the *reliability* of a correlation coefficient varies directly with the sample size.

1. Guilford, J. P. *Fundamental statistics in psychology and education* (4th ed.). New York: McGraw-Hill, 1965, Chapter 14.

THE PROBLEM OF HITS AND MISSES IN PREDICTIVE VALIDITY:[1]

Many decisions ask for a prediction of success or failure on some future behavior called the *Criterion Variable*, basing the prediction on a *Predictor Variable:* for example, selecting college applicants by predicting their future grade point average (criterion variable) basing the prediction on scores obtained on the College Board Examination (predictor variable).

Since the correlation coefficient between these two variables is imperfect, some of the predictions will be correct (hits) and others will be incorrect (misses). The hits include those correctly predicted to be either successful (*True Positives*) or unsuccessful (*True Negatives*). The misses include those wrongly predicted to be successful (*False Positives*)—those who passed the examination but were unsuccessful in college; and those wrongly predicted to be unsuccessful (*False Negatives*)—those who scored too low on the examination to qualify for admission yet would have succeeded if given the opportunity.

Consider the following Fourfold Table superimposed on a correlation surface (scattergram) representing the distribution of scores between the Predictor Variable and the Criterion Variable:

PREDICTOR VARIABLE—Test Score

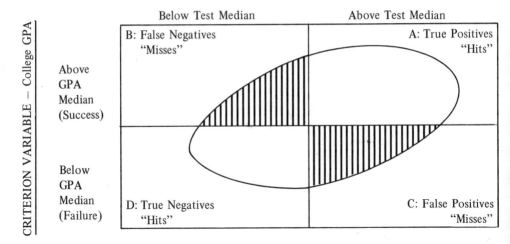

The symbols *A*, *B*, *D*, and *C* stand for the numbers of individuals in the first, second, third, and fourth quadrants, respectively. The following statements can then be made:

Let $H = \dfrac{A + D}{N}$ = the proportion of individuals in the total population of size N who are correctly placed (hits).

Let $E = \dfrac{A + D}{N} - .5000$ = the proportion of correctly placed individuals in excess of the chance proportion of .50 which is associated with an r of zero.

---

1. Adapted from Michael, William B., An interpretation of the coefficients of predictive validity and of determination in terms of the proportions of correct inclusions or exclusions in cells of a fourfold table. *Educational and Psychological Measurement*, 1966, 26, pp. 419–425.

$$\text{Let } I = \frac{100\left(\dfrac{A + D}{N}\right) - .5000}{.5000} = \text{the percentage of improvement in correct placements relative to the proportion of .50 for an } r \text{ of zero.}$$

Note: When r is negative, similar definitions are formed using $B + C$ in place of $A + D$.

Three Indices Explaining Predictive Validity for Various Values in r and r^2 when a Correlation Surface is Subdivided at the Median in Both the Predictor and Criterion Variables

r	r^2	H	E	I
.00	.0000	.5000	.0000	0.00
.05	.0025	.5159	.0159	3.18
.10	.0100	.5319	.0319	6.38
.15	.0225	.5479	.0479	9.59
.20	.0400	.5641	.0641	12.82
.25	.0625	.5804	.0804	16.09
.30	.0900	.5970	.0970	19.40
.35	.1225	.6138	.1138	22.76
.40	.1600	.6310	.1310	26.20
.45	.2025	.6486	.1486	29.72
.50	.2500	.6667	.1667	33.33
.55	.3025	.6854	.1854	37.07
.60	.3600	.7048	.2048	40.97
.65	.4225	.7252	.2252	45.05
.70	.4900	.7468	.2468	49.36
.75	.5625	.7699	.2699	53.99
.80	.6400	.7952	.2952	59.03
.85	.7225	.8234	.3234	64.68
.90	.8100	.8564	.3464	71.29
.95	.9025	.8989	.3989	79.78
1.00	1.0000	1.0000	.5000	100.00

Using the above table, the relationships between the indices H, E, and I to both r and r^2 are quickly ascertained. For example, when $r = .60$ and $r^2 = .36$, the Proportion of Correct Placements, H, is .7048, meaning that about 7 out of 10 individuals are being correctly predicted on the criterion. The Proportion of Incorrect Placements, $1 - H$, would be .2952 (the proportion of misses). The index E has a value of .2048, reflecting the proportion in the total population accurately placed in excess of the chance proportion of .5000 when $r = $ zero. This corresponds to an improvement index I of 40.97 percent in correct placements over that obtainable by chance when $r = $ zero.

Note that when $r = .71$, r^2 is nearly .50 and H approaches .75—an improvement of about 50 percent of correct placements over chance. Since .71 is close to the upper limit of predictive validities in most selection programs, in a situation using *median splits* where chance allows 2 out of 4 correct placements, the Predictor Variable would yield 3 out of 4 correct placements. With smaller selection ratios (.10 to .25)[1], this yield will increase to as much as 4 out of 5, or higher.

---

1. "Selection ratio" indicates the proportion of individuals in an applicant group who are chosen because they fall above a certain cutting score.

MULTIVARIATE STATISTICAL PROCEDURES

As indicated previously on page 183, multivariate statistical methods have been receiving increasing attention in light of substantial advances in electronic computer capabilities. Although this volume is an introductory one, an extremely brief overview of four widely employed multivariate techniques is presented. The interested reader can find additional information of varying levels of complexity in the following section of references dealing with multivariate statistical procedures (at the very end of this chapter).

Multiple Regression Analysis

In multiple regression analysis two important objectives are (a) to determine the degree of relationship given by an index number known as the multiple correlation coefficient between a customarily continuous criterion measure (dependent variable) and an optimally weighted combination of two or more predictor (independent) variables that are usually continuous and (b) to predict the standing of individuals in a sample on the criterion variable from scores earned in a weighted linear combination of predictor variables along with an indication of an expected margin of error. Occasional instances do arise in which the criterion variable is dichotomous or trichotomous rather than strictly continuous. Numerous procedures are available for selection of predictor variables to maximize the degree of relationship between the criterion measure and a weighted composite of predictors and correspondingly to minimize the errors of prediction. Typically, the most efficient prediction and highest degree of multiple correlation occurs when each predictor variable shows a modest to high correlation with the criterion measure, but a low or preferably zero correlation with every other predictor. The multiple correlation coefficient obtained for a given sample is likely to be inflated in value as a function of favorable sampling errors that entered into the selection of the predictors. Hence it is important that the regression equation or prediction equation derived from one sample be applied to another to ascertain how much shrinkage in the multiple correlation has occurred. Known as a cross-validation procedure, the observed scores in the criterion measure for the new sample are correlated with the predicted scores of the new sample as derived from the regression equation obtained from the first sample.

Multiple regression techniques have been widely employed in the selection of personnel in business and industry and in the civil and military services of the nation. Multiple regression techniques have been particularly effective in decision making concerning which of several measures should be included in a test battery for selection of personnel. The multiple correlation coefficient is an indicator of the validity of a battery or combination of tests—a validity coefficient that typically exceeds the value of the zero-order coefficient associated with a single predictor.

Discriminant Function Analysis

Whereas multiple regression analysis is often employed for selection purposes, discriminant analysis is used primarily to classify individuals into two or more categories such as occupational groups, college majors, or personality types. A simple discriminant analysis is concerned with the prediction of membership in one of two categories of a dependent variable from scores on two or more predictor variables, and a multiple discriminant analysis is directed toward prediction of membership in one of three or more categories in a dependent variable from scores on a similar composite of two or more predictor variables. In the instance of a dichotomous criterion measure to which values of one or zero could be assigned, the simple discriminant analysis equation will register weights proportional to those found for the multiple regression equation and thus will afford a comparable solution in the prediction process. Accuracy of prediction in discriminant analysis is often evaluated in terms of the frequencies of correct and incorrect placements in the criterion categories as predicted in relation to the actual frequencies of placement in the same categories. As in multiple regression analysis, it is important to carry out cross-validation procedures, as once again, predictor variables are often chosen for inclusion in the discriminant equation on the basis of patterns of correlation coefficients that have been distorted by sampling error.

Canonical Analysis

Representing in effect an extension of multiple regression analysis, a canonical analysis permits the estimation of the maximum degree of association (canonical correlation) between a linear set or weighted combination of two or more criterion variables with a corresponding linear set or weighted combination of two or more predictor variables. Typically, both criterion and predictor measures are continuous. The canonical solution provides (a) first a choice of an initial pair of dimensions (a linear combination of variables)—one from the group of criterion measures and the other from the group of predictor variables—that affords the highest possible degree of association or correlation and (b) the progressive selection of remaining pairs of dimensions until non-chance or reliable variance in scores has been almost entirely extracted. However, never more dimensions can be identified than the number of variables in the smaller set of criterion or predictor measures. The successive canonical correlations between each criterion set and predictor set do not necessarily show a progressive diminution in value. As implied earlier, each canonical coefficient portrays the maximum possible amount of association between two canonical variates within a given pair of dimensions. In short, the weights assigned to members of the predictor composite (a canonical variate for the set of independent variables) yields the most nearly correct potential prediction of standing on the optimally but differently weighted members of the criterion composite (a canonical variate for the group of dependent variables).

It has been the writers' experience that canonical correlations and associated analyses do not provide for nearly so meaningful psychological interpretability of behavioral data as do alternative multivariate methodologies such as those found in multiple regression analysis, simple or multiple discriminant analysis, or factor analysis. However, it is possible to square the canonical correlation coefficient to identify what proportion of variance is shared by the pair of extracted dimensions.

This squaring of a correlation coefficient in the instance of multiple regression analysis furnishes a means of ascertaining what proportion of variance in the criterion measure is accounted for by the composite of optimally weighted predictor variables. Moreover, a technique known as commonality analysis applied to multiple regression data permits an identification of what porportion of variance each independent variable contributes by itself and in combination with other predictor variables to the variance in the criterion measure. This approach has been described at length and illustrated in the 1973 text by Kerlinger and Pedhazur that is cited in the references at the conclusion of this chapter.

Factor Analysis

Factor analysis is a statistical procedure that affords an explanation of how the variance common to several intercorrelated measures can be accounted for in terms of a small number of dimensions with which the variables are correlated. In addition to describing a parsimonious structure in the covariation present among many variables in terms of a relatively small number of common factors, the technique provides a means for testing of hypotheses regarding anticipated structures and for generating new hypotheses to account for unanticipated dimensions that may emerge.

The correlation of a variable (typically a test) with a statistically isolated dimension is called a factor loading for that variable. Customarily, at least three (test) variables must register correlations or loadings on a factor so that it can be given a psychologically meaningful interpretation. It is not uncommon to find clusters or groupings of variables that will yield modest to high correlations on just one factor or possibly two factors, but virtually zero loadings with other dimensions. Once the factor solution has been found that is psychologically interpretable, an improved understanding of the constructs represented by the variables often results.

As a rule, one can identify about one third as many dimensions as there are correlated variables. From the loadings that these variables display on the factor dimensions, it is possible to reproduce rather closely the initial matrix of correlations among all the variables.

It should also be pointed out that the factor dimensions may or may not be correlated with one another. Many factor analysts prefer to work (for reasons of simplicity of interpretation and of mathematical computations) with independent factor dimensions that are said to be orthogonal to one another. The presence of correlated dimensions is said to be associated with an oblique solution. Test variables also register loadings on oblique factors, although the magnitudes of these loadings will differ from those found in the orthogonal solution. In summary it may be mentioned that three kinds of potential correlations exist: (a) correlations among pairs of the initial variables (typically tests), (b) correlations between each test and a factor dimension (orthogonal or oblique), and (c) correlations among the dimensions themselves (correlations which are zero in the orthogonal case). Mathematical procedures exist for determining these correlations from raw score data that can be entered into gigantic electronic computers for processing. Despite the existence of relatively objective statistical procedures, the output may be difficult to interpret psychologically particularly in the absence of a careful design for the selection of variables (within a well defined and carefully delineated test domain) that are congruent with the constructs of at least a rudimentary theory or model.

The meaningful use of factor analysis depends upon a considerable amount of training and psychological insight. The references set forth in the concluding section of this chapter should be helpful to the interested reader who wishes to expand his horizons in a challenging and useful methodology.

General References in Statistics

Dinham, S. M. *Exploring statistics: An introduction for psychology and education.* Monterey, Calif.: Brooks/Cole, 1976.

Dixon, W. J. and Massey, F. J., Jr. *Introduction to statistical analysis* (3rd ed.). New York: McGraw-Hill, 1969.

Ferguson, G. A. *Statistical analysis in psychology and education* (4th ed.). New York: McGraw-Hill, 1976.

Glass, G. V. and Stanley, J. C. *Statistical methods in education and psychology.* Englewood Cliffs, N. J.: Prentice Hall, 1970.

Guilford, J. P. and Fruchter, B. *Fundamental statistics in psychology and education* (6th ed.). New York: McGraw-Hill, 1978.

Hays, W. L. *Statistics* (3rd ed.). New York: Holt, Rinehart and Winston, 1981.

Hinkle, D. E., Wiersma, W., and Jurs, S. G. *Applied statistics for the behavioral sciences.* Chicago: Rand McNally, 1979.

Hopkins, K. D. and Glass, G. V. *Basic statistics for the behavioral sciences.* Englewood Cliffs, N. J.: Prentice Hall, 1978.

McCall, R. B. *Fundamental statistics for psychology* (3rd ed.). New York: Harcourt Brace Jovanovich, 1980.

McNemar, Q. *Psychological statistics* (5th ed.). New York: Wiley, 1975.

Minium, E. W. *Statistical reasoning in psychology and education* (2nd ed.). New York: Wiley, 1978.

Roscoe, J. T. *Fundamental research statistics for the behavioral sciences* (2nd ed.). New York: Holt, Rinehart, and Winston, 1975.

Runyon, R. P. and Haber, A. *Fundamentals of behavioral statistics* (4th ed.). Reading, Mass.: Addison-Wesley, 1980.

Shavelson, R. J. *Statistical reasoning for the behavioral sciences.* Boston: Allyn and Bacon, 1981.

Siegel, S. *Nonparametric statistics for the behavioral sciences.* New York: McGraw-Hill, 1956.

Walker, H. M. and Lev, J. *Elementary statistical methods* (3rd ed.). New York: Holt, Rinehart and Winston, 1969.

Walker, H. M. and Lev, J. *Statistical inference.* New York: Holt, 1953. (Cited for historical importance.)

Weinberg, G. H. and Schumaker, J. A. *Statistics: An intuitive approach* (3rd ed.). Monterey, Calif.: Brooks/Cole, 1974.

Experimental Design

Campbell, D. T. and Stanley, J. C. *Experimental and quasi-experimental designs for research.* Chicago: Rand McNally, 1966.

Cook, T. D. and Campbell, D. T. The design and conduct of quasi-experiments and true experiments in field settings. In M. D. Dunnette (ed.), *Handbook of industrial and organizational psychology.* Chicago: Rand McNally, 1976.

Cook, T. D. and Campbell, D. T. *Quasi-experimentation: Design and analysis issues for field settings.* Chicago: Rand McNally, 1979.

Edwards, A. L. *Experimental design in psychological research* (4th ed.). New York: Holt, Rinehart and Winston, 1972.

Kirk, R. E. *Experimental`design: Procedures for the behavioral sciences.* Belmont, Calif.: Wadsworth, 1968.

Winer, B. J. *Statistical principles in experimental design* (2nd ed.). New York: McGraw-Hill, 1971.

Multivariate Statistical Procedures

Bentler, P. M. Multivariate analysis with latent variables: Casual modeling. In M. R. Rosenzweig and L. W. Porter (eds.), *Annual review of psychology* (Vol. 31). Palo Alto, Calif.: Annual Reviews, 1980. (A very basic article with excellent bibliography.)

Bock, R. D. *Multivariate statistical methods in behavioral research.* New York: McGraw-Hill, 1975. (An advanced book requiring considerable statistical sophistication.)

Cohen, J. and Cohen, P. *Applied multiple regression/correlation analysis for the behavioral sciences.* Hillsdale, N. J.: Erlbaum, 1975. (Intermediate difficulty level.)

Cooley, W. W. and Lohnes, P. R. *Multivariate data analysis.* New York: Wiley, 1971. (Combines general theoretical principles with many computer programs.)

Ezekiel, M. and Fox, K. A. *Methods of correlation and regression analysis: Linear and curvilinear.* New York: Wiley, 1965.

Gorsuch, R. L. *Factor analysis.* Philadelphia: Saunders, 1974.

Guertin, W. H. and Bailey, J. P. *Introduction to modern factor analysis.* Ann Arbor, Mich.: Edwards, 1970. (Elementary text.)

Harman, H. H. *Modern factor analysis* (2nd ed.). Chicago: University of Chicago Press, 1967. (Authoritative but relatively difficult text.)

Joreskog, K. G. and Sorbom, D. *LISREL IV: Analysis of linear structural relationships by the method of maximum likelihood (user's guide).* Chicago: National Educational Resources, 1978. (A very basic document affording information for computer programs in causal modeling and confirmatory factor analysis.)

Kerlinger, F. N. and Pedhazur, E. J. *Multiple regression in behavioral research.* New York: Holt, Rinehart and Winston, 1973. (A basic text in multiple regression analysis and in associated topics in multivariate analysis that is extremely clearly written with a minimum of mathematical notation.)

Lindeman, R. H., Merenda, P. F., and Gold, R. Z. *Introduction to bivariate and multivariate analysis.* Glenview, Ill.: Scott, Foresman, 1980. (A well written text that provides a most favorable balance between a verbalized psychological interpretation of multivariate methods of data analysis and mathematical notation.)

Merrifield, P. R. Factor analysis in educational research. In F. N. Kerlinger (ed.), *Review of Research in Education* (Vol. 2). Itasca, Ill.: F. E. Peacock, 1974.

Michael, W. B. Prediction methods. In H. F. Mitzel, J. H. Best, and W. Rabinowitz (eds.). *Encyclopedia of Educational Research* (5th ed.). Toronto: MacMillan, 1982.

Nie, N. H., Hull, C. H., Jenkins, J. G., Steinbrenner, K., and Bent, D. H. *SPSS: Statistical package for the social sciences* (2nd ed.). New York: McGraw-Hill, 1975. (Basic computer programs.)

Nunnally, J. C. *Psychometric theory* (2nd ed.). New York: McGraw-Hill, 1978. (Chapters 5, 10, 11, and 12.) (Intermediate difficulty level.)

Rummel, R. J. *Applied factor analysis.* Evanston, Ill.: Northwestern University Press, 1970. (Relatively easy text to read.)

Tatsuoka, M. M. *Multivariate analysis: Techniques for educational and psychological research.* New York: Wiley, 1971.

Thorndike, R. M. *Correlational procedures for research.* New York: Gardner Press, 1978. (Very clearly written with superb diagrams.)

Timm, N. H. *Multivariate analysis with applications in education and psychology.* Monterey, Calif.: Brooks/Cole, 1975.

Van de Geer, J. P. *Introduction to multivariate analysis for the social sciences.* San Francisco: W. H. Freeman, 1971.

Weiss, D. J. Multivariate procedures. In M. D. Dunnette (ed.), *Handbook of industrial and organizational psychology.* Chicago: Rand McNally, 1976. (An excellent overview of multivariate methods.)

"When I use a word," Humpty Dumpty said,
"it means just what I choose it to mean—neither more nor less."
"The question is," said Alice, "whether you can make words mean so many different
things."
"The question is," said Humpty Dumpty,
"which is to be the master—that's all."

Lewis Carroll
THROUGH THE LOOKING GLASS

CHAPTER SIX

STATING COGNITIVE AND AFFECTIVE OBJECTIVES

WRITING BEHAVIORAL OBJECTIVES

Educational *objectives* typically are the offspring of parent goal statements. Educational *goals* are broadly philosophical, global, relatively timeless and nonmeasurable. For example:

○ To prepare students for a life of responsible citizenship

○ To provide students with the basic competencies to survive

○ To enable students to develop a wholesome self-concept

As these statements stand, they lack tangible substance. They can only be evaluated subjectively in terms of impressions or opinions. To assess whether or not the goals have been attained it is necessary to spell out each goal into a set of clear, concrete, measurable objectives. In contrast to goals, *behavioral objectives* are highly specific, discretely quantifiable, and time-bound. They can be operationally defined in terms of the learner activities or performance characteristics that will be visible and manifest when the objective has been reached.

In his pioneering work in this area Mager (1962) specified three necessary elements in a behavioral objective: (1) a statement of the *observable behavior* which will be expected of the student in demonstrating mastery, (2) a description of the *conditions* or the learning task with its constraints under which the student demonstrates his competence, and (3) a specification of a *criterion* level of performance. Kibler, Barker, and Miles (1970) added two elements to behavioral objectives: (4) the *product* or result of behavior and (5) a *description of the learner*. Integrating these five elements, Wilson, Robeck, and Michael (1974) listed these five requirements of well-formulated behavioral objectives:

1. Statement of *conditions* or *stipulations,* in essence describing the learning task and its constraints (*content*).

2. Designation of the *learner* (such as a fourth-grade pupil or a ninth grade mathematics student).

3. Use of *action verbs* (such as to construct, to define, to order) that indicate observable activities, although sometimes more complex objectives stated as inferred processes (such as to solve, to analyze, or synthesize, or to apply) may be used.

4. Specification of an outcome (product).

5. Specification of the *standard* or *criterion* of an expected or acceptable level of performance with a possible time limitation.

Illustration:

Objective: Given 20 addition problems consisting of 5 two-digit numbers arranged vertically (condition or content), a pupil in the fourth grade (learner) can write (action verb-observable process) the answer (the written answer being the product) to 18 out of 20 problems in not more than 5 minutes (standard or criterion, quantity, and time specified).

When a standard or criterion is specified for a test item that parallels an objective, for example that 80 percent of the students will answer a given item correctly, it is said to be *criterion-referenced*. Tests which consist of several criterion-referenced items are called criterion-referenced tests. Scores on such tests indicate not only the level of student performance, but also the degree to which teachers are considered accountable for having their students meet a standard of performance that may have been set either by the teacher or by administrators. *Domain-referenced* tests refer not only to tests that are criterion referenced but also to the objectives that are organized into broad categories called *domains,* each of which reflects what its underlying sets of objectives share in common. For example, in the area of reading, a domain would be reading comprehension. The particular sets of objectives which define the elements comprising reading comprehension are each spelled out in their respective individual objectives and associated test items.

A practical problem faced by anyone setting out to write behavioral objectives based on goal statements is to know when one has completed the task. Specifically, how many objectives are necessary before the goal has been circumscribed? Mager (1962) suggested reading through the list of objectives and asking oneself: Is there anything else I expect of individuals who have attained this goal? Goal attainment also may be defined as meeting the standard of a certain proportion of the associated objectives, e.g. 80 percent.

CONTRIBUTION OF BEHAVIORAL OBJECTIVES

Although it is possible to find objections, both practical and theoretical, to behavioral objectives, education has been lax about making its objectives specific and measurable. Between the subjectivity of values and the objectivity of facts, a balance is needed that behavioral objectives facilitate. In helping educators pinpoint their intentions, behavioral objectives will encourage better educational management, more effective classroom procedures, superior feedback to the learner, and a more satisfactory accounting to the public.

SOME LIMITATIONS OF BEHAVIORAL OBJECTIVES

1. Complex behaviors involving inferred processes (to comprehend, to analyze, to synthesize, to perceive) are difficult, if not impossible, to define in any precise, observable way. They also omit any reference to the student himself: his attitudes, motivations, feelings, and thought processes. Unless these aspects of the learner enter into the teaching/learning experience, the learning situation can become mechanical and artificial. Wilson, Robeck, and Michael (1974) proposed the use of *inferred process objectives* as a means of keeping them in perspective with the outcome and product objectives.

2. Behavioral objectives are painstaking and tedious to write. As a consequence many educators never get around to preparing them. Moreover, once written, they are of little value unless they have matching test items, observation checklists, or scoring criteria and procedures.

3. Michael Polanyi (1966) defended the notion of "tacit knowing"—those unmeasurables which underlie an individual's skill or competence in real world problem-solving situations and show up in the impressions formed by his associates. This orientation is supported by the inability of a computer program to simulate some aspects of human intelligence because it cannot evaluate what it cannot count, as human beings obviously do.

1.   Mager, R. F. *Preparing instructional objectives.* Palo Alto, Calif.: Fearon, 1962.
2.   Kibler, R. J., Barker, L. L., and Miles, D. T. *Behavioral objectives and instruction.* Boston: Allyn and Bacon, 1970.
3.   Wilson, J. A. R., Robeck, M. C., and Michael, W. B. *Psychological foundations of learning and teaching* (2nd ed.). New York: McGraw-Hill, 1974.
4.   Polanyi, M. *Tacit dimension.* New York: Doubleday, 1966.

SUMMARY OF THE TAXONOMY OF EDUCATIONAL OBJECTIVES—
COGNITIVE DOMAIN[1]

1.00   *Knowledge*   Remembering something previously encountered.
   1.10   *Knowledge of specifics*   Recall of information bits with concrete referents.
      1.11   Knowledge of terminology
      1.12   Knowledge of specific facts
   1.20   *Knowledge of ways and means of dealing with specifics*   Includes methods of inquiry, chronological sequences, standards of judgment, patterns of organization within a field.
      1.21   Knowledge of conventions: characteristic ways of testing ideas and phenomena (usage, style, etc.)
      1.22   Knowledge of trends and sequences
      1.23   Knowledge of classifications and categories
      1.24   Knowledge of criteria
      1.25   Knowledge of methodology, methods of inquiry, and problem-solving approaches.
   1.30   *Knowledge of the universals and abstractions in a field*
      1.31   Knowledge of principles and generalizations
      1.32   Knowledge of theories and structures
2.00   *Comprehension*   Understanding of material being communicated, without necessarily relating it to other material.
   2.10   *Translation* from one language or form of communication to another
   2.20   *Interpretation*   The explanation or summarization of a communication
   2.30   *Extrapolation*   Extension of trends beyond the given data
3.00   *Application*   The use of abstractions in particular and concrete situations
4.00   *Analysis*   Breaking down communication into its parts so that organization of ideas is clear
   4.10   *Analysis of elements*   Recognizing assumptions and distinguishing facts from hypotheses
   4.20   *Analysis of relationships*
   4.30   *Analysis of organizational principles* of structure and arrangement
5.00   *Synthesis*   Putting elements into a whole
   5.10   *Production of a unique communication*
   5.20   *Production of a plan for operations*
   5.30   *Derivation of a set of abstract relations*
6.00   *Evaluation*   Judging the value of material and methods for a given purpose
   6.10   *Judgments in terms of internal evidence*   Logical accuracy and consistency
   6.20   *Judgments in terms of external evidence*   Consistency with established standards or models

---

1.   After Bloom, B. S., Engelhart, M. D., Furst, E. J., Hill, W. H., and Krathwohl, D. R., *Taxonomy of Educational Objectives, Handbook I: Cognitive Domain,* New York: David McKay Co., 1956. By permission.

**SUMMARY OF THE TAXONOMY OF EDUCATIONAL OBJECTIVES—
AFFECTIVE DOMAIN**[1]

1.0 *Receiving (attending)*   The willingness to attend to or receive certain stimuli.

   1.1   Awareness—to be conscious of stimulus events.
   1.2   Willingness to receive—to attend willingly, without avoidance.
   1.3   Controlled or selected attention—to differentiate figure and ground.

2.0 *Responding*   Active involvement and participation.

   2.1   Acquiescence in responding.
   2.2   Willingness to respond.
   2.3   Satisfaction in response.

3.0 *Valuing*   The worth of a thing, phenomenon, or behavior.

   3.1   Acceptance of a value.
   3.2   Preference for a value.
   3.3   Commitment.

4.0 *Organization*   The organization, interrelationship, and ordering of values.

   4.1   Conceptualization of a value.
   4.2   Organization of a value system.

5.0 *Characterization by a value or value complex*   The generalization and integration of a total world view or philosophy.

   5.1   Generalized set—one's basic orientation or point of view.
   5.2   Characterization—the peak of the internalization process.

1.   After Krathwohl, D. R., Bloom, B. S., and Masia, B. B., *Taxonomy of Educational Objectives, Handbook II: Affective Domain,* New York: David McKay Co., 1956. By permission.

NEWTON S. METFESSEL, WILLIAM B. MICHAEL, AND DONALD A. KIRSNER

INSTRUMENTATION OF THE TAXONOMY OF EDUCATIONAL OBJECTIVES: COGNITIVE DOMAIN[1]

Taxonomy Classification	KEY WORDS	
	Examples of Infinitives	Examples of Direct Objects
1.00 Knowledge		
1.10 Knowledge of Specifics		
1.11 Knowledge of Terminology	to define, to distinguish to acquire, to identify, to recall, to recognize	vocabulary, terms, terminology, meaning(s), definitions, referents, elements
1.12 Knowledge of Specific Facts	to recall, to recognize, to acquire, to identify	facts, factual information, (sources), (names), (dates), (events), (persons), (places), (time periods), properties, examples, phenomena
1.20 Knowledge of Ways and Means of Dealing with Specifics		
1.21 Knowledge of Conventions	to recall, to identify to recognize, to acquire	form(s), conventions, uses, usage, rules, ways, devices, symbols, representations, style(s), format(s)
1.22 Knowledge of Trends, Sequences	to recall, to recognize, to acquire, to identify	action(s), processes, movement(s), continuity, development(s), trend(s), sequence(s), causes, relationship(s), forces, influences
1.23 Knowledge of Classifications and Categories	to recall, to recognize, to acquire, to identify	area(s), type(s), feature(s), class(es), set(s), division(s), arrangement(s), classification(s), category/ categories
1.24 Knowledge of Criteria	to recall, to recognize, to acquire, to identify	criteria, basics, elements
1.25 Knowledge of Methodology	to recall, to recognize, to acquire, to identify	methods, techniques, approaches, uses, procedures, treatments
1.30 Knowledge of the Universals and Abstractions in a Field		
1.31 Knowledge of Principles, Generalizations	to recall, to recognize, to acquire, to identify	principle(s), generalization(s), proposition(s), fundamentals, laws, principal elements, implication(s)
1.32 Knowledge of Theories and Structures	to recall, to recognize, to acquire, to identify	theories, bases, interrelations, structure(s), organization(s), formulation(s)

1. Metfessel, Newton S., Michael, William B., and Kirsner, Donald A., "Instrumentation of Bloom's and Krathwohl's Taxonomies for the Writing of Educational Objectives." Reprinted from *Psychology in the schools,* Vol. VI, No. 3, pp. 227–231, July 1969. By permission.

INSTRUMENTATION OF BLOOM'S AND KRATHWOHL'S TAXONOMIES

TABLE I. (Con't).

Taxonomy Classification	KEY WORDS Examples of Infinitives	Examples of Direct Objects
2.00 Comprehension		
2.10 Translation	to translate, to transform, to give in own words, to illustrate, to prepare, to read, to represent, to change, to rephrase, to restate	meaning(s), sample(s), definitions, abstractions, representations, words, phrases
2.20 Interpretation	to interpret, to reorder, to rearrange, to differentiate, to distinguish, to make, to draw to explain, to demonstrate	relevancies, relationships, essentials, aspects, new view(s), qualifications, conclusions, methods, theories, abstractions
2.30 Extrapolation	to estimate, to infer, to conclude, to predict, to differentiate, to determine, to extend, to interpolate, to extrapolate, to fill in, to draw	consequences, implications, conclusions, factors, ramifications, meanings, corollaries, effects, probabilities
3.00 Application	to apply, to generalize, to relate, to choose, to develop, to organize, to use, to employ, to transfer, to restructure, to classify	principles, laws, conclusions, effects, methods, theories, abstractions, situations, generalizations, processes, phenomena, procedures
4.00 Analysis		
4.10 Analysis of Elements	to distinguish, to detect, to identify, to classify, to discriminate, to recognize, to categorize, to deduce	elements, hypothesis/ hypotheses, conclusions, assumptions, statements (of fact), statements (of intent), arguments, particulars
4.20 Analysis of Relationships	to analyze, to contrast, to compare, to distinguish, to deduce	relationships, interrelations, relevance, relevancies, themes, evidence, fallacies, arguments, cause-effect(s), consistency/consistencies, parts, ideas, assumptions
4.30 Analysis of Organizational Principles	to analyze, to distinguish, to detect, to deduce	form(s), pattern(s), purpose(s), point(s) of view(s), techniques, bias(es), structure(s), theme(s), arrangement(s), organization(s)

INSTRUMENTATION OF THE TAXONOMY OF EDUCATIONAL OBJECTIVES: AFFECTIVE DOMAIN[1]

Taxonomy Classification	KEY WORDS	
	Examples of Infinitives	Examples of Direct Objects
5.00 Synthesis		
5.10 Production of a Unique Communication	to write, to tell, to relate, to produce, to constitute, to transmit, to originate, to modify, to document	structure(s), pattern(s), product(s), performance(s), design(s), work(s), communications, effort(s), specifics, composition(s)
5.20 Production of a Plan, or Proposed Set of Operations	to propose, to plan, to produce, to design, to modify, to specify	plan(s), objectives, specification(s), schematic(s), operations, way(s), solution(s), means
5.30 Derivation of a Set of Abstract Relations	to produce, to derive, to develop, to combine, to organize, to synthesize, to classify, to deduce, to develop, to formulate, to modify	phenomena, taxonomies, concept(s), scheme(s), theories, relationships, abstractions, generalizations, hypothesis/hypotheses, perceptions, ways, discoveries
6.00 Evaluation		
6.10 Judgments in Terms of Internal Evidence	to judge, to argue, to validate, to assess, to decide	accuracy/accuracies, consistency/consistencies, fallacies, reliability, flaws, errors, precision, exactness
6.20 Judgments in Terms of External Criteria	to judge, to argue, to consider, to compare, to contrast, to standardize, to appraise	ends, means, efficiency, economy/economies, utility, alternatives, courses of action, standards, theories, generalizations
1.0 Receiving		
1.1 Awareness	to differentiate, to separate, to set apart, to share	sights, sounds, events, designs, arrangements
1.2 Willingness to Receive	to accumulate, to select, to combine, to accept	models, examples, shapes, sizes, meters, cadences
1.3 Controlled or Selected Attention	to select, to posturally respond to, to listen (for), to control	alternatives, answers, rhythms, nuances
2.0 Responding		
2.1 Acquiescence in Responding	to comply (with), to follow, to commend, to approve	directions, instructions, laws, policies, demonstrations
2.2 Willingness to Respond	to volunteer, to discuss, to practice, to play	instruments, games, dramatic works, charades, burlesques
2.3 Satisfaction in Response	to applaud, to acclaim, to spend leisure time in, to augment	speeches, plays, presentations, writings

1. Metfessel, Newton S., Michael, William B., and Kirsner, Donald A., "Instrumentation of Bloom's and Krathwhohl's Taxonomies for the writing of educational objectives." Reprinted from *Psychology in the schools,* Vol. VI, No. 3, pp. 227–231, July 1969. By permission.

INSTRUMENTATION OF THE TAXONOMY OF EDUCATIONAL OBJECTIVES: AFFECTIVE DOMAIN

Taxonomy Classification	KEY WORDS	
	Examples of Infinitives	Examples of Direct Objects
3.0 Valuing		
3.1 Acceptance of a Value	to increase measured proficiency in, to increase numbers of, to relinquish, to specify	group membership(s), artistic production(s), musical productions, personal friendships
3.2 Preference for a Value	to assist, to subsidize, to help, to support	artists, projects, viewpoints, arguments
3.3 Commitment	to deny, to protest, to debate, to argue	deceptions, irrelevancies, abdications, irrationalities
4.0 Organization		
4.1 Conceptualization of a Value	to discuss, to theorize (on), to abstract, to compare,	parameters, codes, standards, goals
4.2 Organization of a Value System	to balance, to organize, to define, to formulate	systems, approaches, criteria, limits
5.0 Characterization by Value or Value Complex		
5.1 Generalized Set	to revise, to change, to complete, to require,	plans, behavior, methods, effort(s)
5.2 Characterization	to be rated high, by peers in, to be rated high by superiors in, to be rated high by subordinates in, and	humanitarianism, ethics, integrity, maturity
	to avoid, to manage, to resolve, to resist	extravagance(s), excesses, conflicts, exorbitancy/ exorbitancies

SOME LIMITATIONS IN ASSESSING OBJECTIVES IN THE AFFECTIVE DOMAIN

1. The state of the art in devising reliable and valid measurements of objectives associated with such constructs as attitudes, self-concepts, motivation, emotion, and feelings is often marginal. For example, two individuals on a so-called self-concept test may mark the same response position on a rating scale. If it is low, one person actually may feel inferior to others on this item, whereas the second person is self-confident but self-critical on that particular item (the capacity for self-criticism is not the same as having a poor self-concept). If, on the other hand, the two individuals rate themselves high, one could be covering up a feeling of inferiority, whereas the other really feels on top of things. Altogether, these examples bring into question both the reliability and validity of such instruments portraying a sampling of affective objectives.

2. Attitudes and feelings, like the weather, tend to be changeable, unpredictable, and sensitive to many factors, both inside and outside the learning situation. Hence, writing widely applicable and stable affective objectives is correspondingly difficult.

3. The cause-and-effect relationships between attitudes and feelings, on the one hand, and performance and achievement, on the other, are little understood and seldom straightforward. For example, there is no broad, consistent body of evidence that children who exhibit positive attitudes toward school or self, necessarily tend to work harder or to achieve at a higher level than do those children who show corresponding negative attitudes. Perhaps some children who feel good about things are more secure, relaxed, and less motivated to extend themselves. A recent study on effective teaching, in fact, revealed a tendency for "competent" teachers to have students with higher cognitive achievement indicators but lower affective indicators, whereas the reverse tendency was true for the "incompetent" teachers.*

4. There is likely to be a negative relationship at certain stages of development between age and measured attitudes. Young children (age 5-6), for instance, respond very positively to most experiences, but begin to differentiate along a broader range of feelings as they grow older and become more discerning, critical, or analytical. The result is a shift from more positive to less positive responses as time passes. Although this observation suggests a negative shift in attitude resulting from the learning experience itself, especially in longitudinal studies, it is probably a developmental shift in the child's maturity level.

5. Attitudes are sensitive to such factors as newness, novelty, and the "upbeat" nature of a beginning enterprise or fresh start. A shift in a less positive direction is probable as the experience becomes routine and familiar. In a pretest-posttest design, such as the beginning and end of a school year, this measured shift to a lower position on an attitude scale for reasons of adaptation to novelty becomes confounded with the possibility of an actual downturn in attitudes for reasons related to shortcomings in the program or setting. These confounding factors could compromise the validity of attitudinal measures reflecting affective objectives.

---

* Coker, H., Medley, D. M., and Soar, R. S. How Valid Are Expert Opinions about Effective Teaching? *Phi Delta Kappan*, 1980, 62, (2), 131–134, 149.

6. Wherever attitudes are involved, individuals in general tend to have predispositions that are more often positive than negative. The predisposition resembles what has been characterized as the "80–20" phenomenon.* Other things being equal, something like 80% of the population are prone to be positive and 20% are negative. Data collected in group settings also are influenced by the "bandwagon" or "contagion" effect, or the impact of a dominant personality. The bipolar predisposition just described would make difficult the universal application of measures of selected affective objectives.

7. Last but not least is the *invasion of privacy* question (Family Rights and Privacy Act). Many affective instruments may violate this statute unless carefully screened for objectionable content. Either prior written consent from the participants or their parents/guardians, if the participants are underage, or anonymity may be possible alternatives. As a general rule, the objectives and instrumentation should be restricted to the educational setting, avoiding attitudes and behaviors outside the school environment.

In spite of the foregoing cautions, measurement in the affective domain can provide useful information. Gallup polls, public acceptance or resistance, the act of casting ballots in an election, and an entire gamut of so-called unobtrusive evidence, all reflect this important dimension. In relation to affective objectives in learning the purpose of this section is precautionary, not disclamatory.

---

* First observed in research on suggestability by Clark Hull in the 1920's. Subjects were attached to sensitive indicators which would register any body movement forward or backward. They were then instructed to stand perfectly still while the investigator repeatedly suggested that they were falling forward. No one stood perfectly still. Eighty percent moved forward and twenty percent actually moved backward.

"A question well-stated is a question half-answered."

Anonymous

CHAPTER SEVEN

CRITERIA AND GUIDELINES FOR PLANNING, PREPARING, WRITING, AND EVALUATING THE RESEARCH PROPOSAL, REPORT, THESIS, OR ARTICLE.

The final, most important question asked of a research or evaluation study is, *What does it mean?* Each previous section has contributed to the foundation on which conclusions must rest. Careful planning, designing, instrumentation, and statistical analysis form a composite prerequisite to reaching sound conclusions.

This chapter is concerned with how one presents the results of an investigation. Criteria and guidelines are included to assist the researcher in planning, preparing, writing, and evaluating the research proposal, report, thesis (dissertation), or professional journal article.

FORM FOR THE EVALUATION OF AN ARTICLE[1,2]

Characteristic	Completely Incompetent (1)	Poor (2)	Mediocre (3)	Good (4)	Excellent (5)
1. Problem is clearly stated					
2. Hypotheses are clearly stated					
3. Problem is significant					
4. Assumptions are clearly stated					
5. Limitations of the study are stated					
6. Important terms are defined					
7. Relationship of the problem to previous research is made clear					
8. Research design is described fully					
9. Research design is appropriate for the solution of the problem					
10. Research design is free of specific weaknesses					
11. Population and sample are described					
12. Method of sampling is appropriate					
13. Data-gathering methods or procedures are described					
14. Data-gathering methods or procedures are appropriate to the solution of the problem					
15. Data-gathering methods or procedures are utilized correctly					
16. Validity and reliability of the evidence gathered are established					
17. Appropriate methods are selected to analyze the data					
18. Methods utilized in analyzing the data are applied correctly					
19. Results of the analysis are presented clearly					
20. Conclusions are clearly stated					
21. Conclusions are substantiated by the evidence presented					
22. Generalizations are confined to the population from which the sample was drawn					
23. Report is clearly written					
24. Report is logically organized					
25. Tone of the report displays an unbiased, impartial scientific attitude					

1. Wandt, Edwin, California State College, Los Angeles.
2. Not all of these twenty-five criteria or characteristics are appropriate in the evaluation of a given article.

A RESEARCH PROPOSAL: A CHECKLIST OF ITEMS FOR POSSIBLE INCLUSION[1]

The following is a checklist of items which are typically included in a research dissertation or report. Not all of the suggested categories are necessary or appropriate for all studies, and the order of items within chapters may vary somewhat. These items are intended to serve as a guide:

CHAPTER I: THE PROBLEM
_____ Introduction
_____ Background of the problem (e.g., educational trends related to the problem, unresolved issues, social concerns)
_____ Statement of the problem situation (basic difficulty — area of concern, felt need)
_____ Purpose of the study (goal oriented) — emphasizing practical outcomes or products
_____ Questions to be answered or objectives to be investigated
_____ Conceptual or substantive assumptions (postulates)
_____ Rationale and theoretical framework (when appropriate)
_____ Delineation of the research problem (explication of relationships among variables or comparisons to be considered)
_____ Statement of hypotheses (conceptual rendition subsequently followed by operational statements in Chapter I or in Methodology Chapter)
_____ Importance of the study — may overlap with statement of problem situation
_____ Definition of terms (largely conceptual here; operational definitions may follow in Methodology Chapter)
_____ Scope and delimitations of the study (narrowing of focus)
_____ Outline of the remainder of the thesis or proposal

CHAPTER II: REVIEW OF RELATED LITERATURE
_____ Organization of the present chapter — overview
_____ Historical background (if necessary)

Purposes to be Served by Review of Research Literature
_____ Acquaint reader with existing studies relative to what has been found, who has done work, when and where latest research studies were completed, and what approaches involving research methodology, instrumentation, and statistical analyses were followed (literature review of methodology sometimes saved for chapter on methodology)
_____ Establish possible need for study and likelihood for obtaining meaningful, relevant, and significant results
_____ Furnish from delineation of various theoretical positions a conceptual framework affording bases for generation of hypotheses and statement of their rationale (when appropriate)
Note: In some highly theoretical studies the chapter "Review of Literature" may need to precede "The Problem" chapter so that the theoretical framework is established for a succinct statement of the research problem and hypotheses. In such a case, an advance organizer in the form of a brief general statement of the purpose of the entire investigation should come right at the beginning of the "Review of Literature" chapter.

----

1.   Joan J. Michael, California State College, Long Beach, and William B. Michael, University of Southern California.

Sources for Literature Review

_____ General integrative reviews cited that relate to the problem situation or research problem such as those found in *Review of Educational Research, Encyclopedia of Educational Research,* or *Psychological Bulletin.*

_____ Specific books, monographs, bulletins, reports, and research articles – preference shown in most instances for literature of the last ten years

_____ Unpublished materials (e.g., dissertations, theses, papers presented at recent professional meetings not yet in published form, but possibly available through ERIC)

_____ Selection and arrangement of literature review often in terms of questions to be considered, hypotheses set forth, or objectives or specific purposes delineated in problem chapter

_____ Summary of literature reviewed (very brief)

CHAPTER III: METHODOLOGY OR PROCEDURES

_____ Overview (optional)

_____ Description of research methodology or approach (e.g., experimental, quasi-experimental, correlational, causal-comparative, or survey)

_____ Research design (Spell out independent, dependent and classificatory variables and sometimes formulate an operational statement of the research hypotheses in null form so as to set the stage for an appropriate research design permitting statistical inferences.)

_____ Pilot studies (as they apply to the research design, development of instruments, data collection techniques, and characteristics of the sample)

_____ Selection of subjects (This is concerned with sample and population.)

_____ Instrumentation (tests, measures, observations, scales, and questionnaires)

_____ Field, classroom or laboratory procedures (e.g., instructions to subjects or distribution of materials)

_____ Data collection and recording

_____ Data processing and analysis (statistical analysis)

_____ Methodological assumptions

_____ Limitations (weaknesses)

_____ Possible restatement of conceptual hypotheses from problem chapter in operational form relative to instrumentation and experimental procedure or design followed (operationally stated hypotheses can also be put in null form to furnish an optional third set of hypotheses amenable to statistical testing) – if not done elsewhere.

_____ Summary (optional)

CHAPTER IV: FINDINGS (ANALYSIS AND EVALUATION)

_____ Findings are presented in tables or charts when appropriate

_____ Findings reported with respect to furnishing evidence for each question asked or each hypothesis posed in problem statement

_____ Appropriate headings are established to correspond to each main question or hypothesis considered

_____ Factual information kept separate from interpretation, inference, and evaluation (one section for findings and one section for interpretation or discussion)

Note: In certain historical, case-study and anthropological investigations, factual and interpretive material may need to be interwoven to sustain interest level, although the text should clearly reveal what is fact and what is interpretation.

_____ Separate section often entitled "Discussion," "Interpretation," or "Evaluation" ties together findings in relation to theory, review of literature, or rationale

_____ Summary of chapter

CHAPTER V: SUMMARY, CONCLUSIONS, RECOMMENDATIONS
_____ Brief summary of everything covered in first three chapters and in findings
portion of Chapter IV
_____ Conclusions ("so what" of findings; often the hypotheses restated as inferences with some degree of definitive commitment and generalizability)
_____ Recommendations (practical suggestions for implementation of findings or
for additional research)

CRITERIA FOR EVALUATION OF A RESEARCH REPORT, ARTICLE, OR THESIS[1]

I. Title of article or report

    A. Precise identification of problem area, often including specification of independent
        and dependent variables and identification of target population.

    B. Sufficient clarity and conciseness for indexing of title

    C. Effective arrangement of words in title

II. The problem

    A. Description and statement of problem

        1. Statement of basic (felt) difficulty or problem situation—significance and im-
           portance of the problem area in either basic or applied research.

        2. Careful analysis of known and suspected facts and explanation of existing
           information and knowledge that may have some bearing on problem—the
           spelling out of specific factors giving rise to the basic difficulty, of their inter-
           relationships, and of their relevance to the problem area.

        3. Soundness of the logic underlying selection of variables or factors to be studied
           and expression of their relationship to the problem area.

        4. Systematic and orderly presentation of the interrelationships of relevant facts
           and concepts underlying the problem.

        5. Clear identification of the problem statement through use of an appropriate
           heading or paragraph caption (the same requirement holding for other major
           categories of the research).

        6. Succinct, precise, and unambiguous statement of the research problem (includ-
           ing the delineation of independent, dependent, and classificatory variables),
           of the major questions to be resolved, or of the objectives to be investigated.

        7. Distinction (if required) between problems or questions that are either factually
           oriented or value oriented.

        8. Distinction in the instance of theoretically oriented research or of basic research
           between the purpose, which is often goal-oriented or instrumental in relation to
           certain pragmatic objectives, and the research problem which is primarily
           directed toward the finding of relationships, the making of comparisons, or
           the noting of changes (possible cause and effect relationships) relative to
           operationally formulated research hypotheses.

---

1. Michael, William B., University of Southern California, 1967.

    B. Sufficient delimitation of the problem area—narrowing of the scope without becoming concerned with a trivial problem.

    C. Review and evaluation of the literature pertinent to problem areas.

        1. Adequacy and relevance of the previous investigation cited with reference to the basic difficulty posed, design of the current investigation, procedures followed, and projected analysis of data.

        2. Appropriate development of a rationale or theoretical framework from the research studies cited with reference to the current problem under investigation.

    D. Clear-cut statement of the conceptions, assumptions, or postulates underlying the problem being investigated.

    E. Precise statement of (1) hypotheses or (2) deduced consequences of theories or (3) the objectives of a study (objectives being most common in survey and descriptive research).

        1. Hypotheses involving relationships and comparisons.

        2. Presentation of deducible consequences or predictions (if any) that are logically consistent with an hypothesis (i.e., antecedent—consequent statement: If A exists, then B follows).

    F. Definitions of terms

        1. Clarity in the definitions of key terms and variables (especially constructs).

        2. Use of operational definitions whenever possible.

III. Design and methodology (procedures)

    A. Logic, structure, and strategy of study carefully delineated.

        1. Distinction made between whether the research involves variables manipulated and controlled by the investigator (usually found in experimental research) or whether an *ex post facto* situation exists involving the analysis of data already available or collected as in most field studies and correlational investigations.

        2. Appropriate use of paradigms, flow charts, or schematic models.

        3. Specification of threats to external and internal validity of the design employed.

    B. Clear description of samples studied.

        1. Mode of selection of subject cited (e.g., random assignment, matching, voluntary participation, or convenience by being available).

        2. Data regarding how representative a sample is relative to a population.

        3. Information concerning the possible operation of selective drop-out and survival of the fittest.

    C. Adequate information pertaining to the reliability, validity, and standardization properties of instrumentation: psychometric characteristic of scales or tests used.

    D. Sufficient description of operational or field procedures followed in the collection of data—where, when, and how data were obtained.

    E. Coordination of the specification of the relationship between the null (statistical) hypotheses and the research (problem) hypotheses.

    F. Appropriateness of the statistical treatment and data processing procedures.

G. Evidence of a preparatory pilot study having been conducted.

H. Procedure clearly enough described so that other investigators can replicate (repeat) the study performed under essentially comparable conditions in the future.

I. Statement of methodological assumption such as adequacy of reliability and validity of measures, representativeness of samples, fulfillment of appropriate requirements for carrying out statistical tests.

IV. Presentation and analysis of data

A. Logical and orderly exposition in terms of the framework of the hypotheses, deductions, objectives, or questions asked in conjunction with the statement of the problem.

1. Objective rather than subjective or speculative presentation.
2. Analysis consistent with and supported by the facts obtained.
3. Absence of overgeneralizations or sweeping statements that go beyond the data.
4. Relationships of the findings to previously cited research explicitly shown.
5. Negative findings relative to the hypotheses as well as positive findings presented with minimal distortion or bias.
6. Uncontrolled factors influencing data outcomes appropriately cited and discussed.
7. Weaknesses in the data honestly conceded and discussed with appropriate emphasis.
8. Lack of confusion between facts and inferences clearly shown—separation of analysis of findings from interpretation and discussion of findings.
9. Resolution of contradictions, inconsistencies, or misleading elements in the findings.

B. Appropriate and clear use of charts, tables, figures, and graphs.

V. Summary and conclusion

A. Precise and accurate statement of (1) the problem, (2) the methodology followed, and (3) the findings without the introduction of new or irrelevant information.

B. Conclusions at a scope and level of generality justified by the data presented.

C. Appropriate caution exercised and necessary qualifications made in drawing conclusions.

D. Conclusions in a form that other investigators can understand and subsequently verify.

E. Conclusions coordinated with the tentative acceptance or rejection of the research hypotheses presented or with the objectives or questions posed.

F. New questions set forth for possible investigation—recommendations for additional research in the problem area study.

G. Recommendations concerning implementation of the research findings when appropriate relative to the objectives stated in the purpose of the investigation (most frequently encountered in survey studies and action research).

RESEARCH METHODOLOGY—A DISSENTING VIEW

The prerequisite of originality is the art of forgetting, at the proper moment, what we know.

Arthur Koestler

The dominant theme of this Handbook is to be planful and systematic—ideally, to deduce hypotheses from theory and put them to the test or to set objectives, arrange procedures, and intentionally achieve a planned mission.

B. F. Skinner, the psychologist, whose impact on education is only beginning to be felt through such innovations as the modern teaching machine, operant conditioning, and behavior modification, vigorously dissents from any formal view of "the scientific method." In remarks from his book *Cumulative Record*, he discusses what he calls his "unformalized principles of scientific practice." [1]

1. "When you run onto something interesting, drop everything else and study it."

2. "Some ways of doing research are easier than others." [And in searching for an easier way to do something, one may develop more efficient techniques and also discover unforeseen phenomena.]

3. "Some people are lucky." [New ideas and discoveries often are accidental.]

4. "Apparatuses sometimes break down." [And one stumbles upon unexcepted and fruitful consequences.]

Skinner summarizes his point of view in these words:

This account of my scientific behavior . . . is as exact in letter and spirit as I can now make it. The notes, data, and publications which I have examined do not show that I ever behaved in the manner of Man Thinking as described by John Stuart Mill or John Dewey or in reconstructions of scientific behavior by other philosophers of science. I never faced a Problem which was more than the eternal problem of finding order. I never attacked a problem by constructing a Hypothesis. I never deduced Theorems or submitted them to Experimental Check. So far as I can see, I had no preconceived Model of behavior—certainly not a physiological or mentalistic one and, I believe, not a conceptual one. [2]

Another strong argument for the value of an informal approach to scientific research is presented by Arthur Koestler in his scholarly work *The Act of Creation*[3]—a comprehensive documentation of the thesis that discovery, invention, and originality whether in science, technology, or the arts is remarkably unsystematic, unforeseeable, and "accidental."

All of this is reminiscent of the Persian fairy tale of the Three Princes of the Isle of Serendip (Ceylon) who periodically would sally forth on to the mainland in search of one thing or another. While they never fulfilled any of their intended missions, they always returned with *other* discoveries or experiences even more marvelous. Hence, the term *serendipity*—the finding of valuable or agreeable things not sought for.

1. Skinner, B. F. *Cumulative Record*. New York: Appleton-Century-Crofts, Inc., 1959, pp. 76–100.
2. Ibid, p. 88. Also cited in Gage, N. L. *Handbook of Research on Education*. Chicago: Rand McNally, 1963, p. 101.
3. Koestler, Arthur. *The Act of Creation*. New York: MacMillan, 1964.

APPENDIX

TABLE A[1]

Percent of Total Area under the Normal Curve between Mean Ordinate and
Ordinate at Any Given Sigma-Distance from the Mean

$\dfrac{\bar{x}}{\sigma}$	.00	.01	.02	.03	.04	.05	.06	.07	.08	.09
0.0	00.00	00.40	00.80	01.20	01.60	01.99	02.39	02.79	03.19	03.59
0.1	03.98	04.38	04.78	05.17	05.57	05.96	06.36	06.75	07.14	07.53
0.2	07.93	08.32	08.71	09.10	09.48	09.87	10.26	10.64	11.03	11.41
0.3	11.79	12.17	12.55	12.93	13.31	13.68	14.06	14.43	14.80	15.17
0.4	15.54	15.91	16.28	16.64	17.00	17.36	17.72	18.08	18.44	18.79
0.5	19.15	19.50	19.85	20.19	20.54	20.88	21.23	21.57	21.90	22.24
0.6	22.57	22.91	23.24	23.57	23.89	24.22	24.54	24.86	25.17	25.49
0.7	25.80	26.11	26.42	26.73	27.04	27.34	27.64	27.94	28.23	28.52
0.8	28.81	29.10	29.39	29.67	29.95	30.23	30.51	30.78	31.06	31·33
0.9	31.59	31.86	32.12	32.38	32.64	32.90	33.15	33.40	33.65	33.89
1.0	34.13	34.38	34.61	34.85	35.08	35.31	35.54	35.77	35.99	36.21
1.1	36.43	36.65	36.86	37.08	37.29	37.49	37.70	37.90	38.10	38.30
1.2	38.49	38.69	38.88	39.07	39.25	39.44	39.62	39.80	39.97	40.15
1.3	40.32	40.49	40.66	40.82	40.99	41.15	41.31	41.47	41.62	41.77
1.4	41.92	42.07	42.22	42.36	42.51	42.65	42.79	42.92	43.06	43.19
1.5	43.32	43.45	43.57	43.70	43.83	43.94	44.06	44.18	44.29	44.41
1.6	44.52	44.63	44.74	44.84	44.95	45.05	45.15	45.25	45.35	45.45
1.7	45.54	45.64	45.73	45.82	45.91	45.99	46.08	46.16	46.25	46.33
1.8	46.41	46.49	46.56	46.64	46.71	46.78	46.86	46.93	46.99	47.06
1.9	47.13	47.19	47.26	47.32	47.38	47.44	47.50	47.56	47.61	47.67
2.0	47.72	47.78	47.83	47.88	47.93	47.98	48.03	48.08	48.12	48.17
2.1	48.21	48.26	48.30	48.34	48.38	48.42	48.46	48.50	48.54	48.57
2.2	48.61	48.64	48.68	48.71	48.75	48.78	48.81	48.84	48.87	48.90
2.3	48.93	48.96	48.98	49.01	49.04	49.06	49.09	49.11	49.13	49.16
2.4	49.18	49.20	49.22	49.25	49.27	49.29	49.31	49.32	49.34	49.36
2.5	49.38	49.40	49.41	49.43	49.45	49.46	49.48	49.49	49.51	49.52
2.6	49.53	49.55	49.56	49.57	49.59	49.60	49.61	49.62	49.63	49.64
2.7	49.65	49.66	49.67	49.68	49.69	49.70	49.71	49.72	49.73	49.74
2.8	49.74	49.75	49.76	49.77	49.77	49.78	49.79	49.79	49.80	49.81
2.9	49.81	49.82	49.82	49.83	49.84	49.84	49.85	49.85	49.86	49.86
3.0	49.87	49.87	49.87	49.88	49.88	49.89	49.89	49.89	49.90	49.90
3.1	49.90	49.91	49.91	49.91	49.92	49.92	49.92	49.92	49.93	49.93
3.2	49.93	49.93	49.94							
3.3	49.95									
3.4	49.97									
3.5	49.98									
3.7	49.99									

1. From Spence, J. T., et al., *Elementary Statistics*, Appleton-Century-Crofts, Inc., New York, 1968. In turn, adapted from Lindquist, E. L., *First Course in Statistics*, Revised, Houghton Mifflin; original source: Table B, Tables for Statisticians and Biometricians, edited by Karl Pearson and published by Cambridge University Press.

TABLE B[1]

Values of *t* for One-tailed and Two-tailed Tests
at Specified Significance Levels

Degrees of Freedom (*df*)	Test	Significance Level			
	One-tailed:	.050	.025	.010	.005
	Two-tailed:	(.100)	.050	.020	.010
1		6.314	12.706	31.821	63.657
2		2.920	4.303	6.965	9.925
3		2.353	3.182	4.541	5.841
4		2.132	2.776	3.747	4.604
5		2.015	2.571	3.365	4.032
6		1.943	2.447	3.134	3.707
7		1.895	2.365	2.998	3.499
8		1.860	2.306	2.896	3.355
9		1.833	2.262	2.831	3.250
10		1.812	2.228	2.764	3.169
11		1.796	2.201	2.718	3.106
12		1.782	2.179	2.681	3.055
13		1.771	2.160	2.650	3.012
14		1.761	2.145	2.624	2.977
15		1.753	2.131	2.602	2.947
16		1.746	2.120	2.583	2.921
17		1.740	2.110	2.567	2.898
18		1.734	2.101	2.552	2.878
19		1.729	2.093	2.539	2.861
20		1.725	2.086	2.528	2.845
21		1.721	2.080	2.518	2.831
22		1.717	2.074	2.508	2.819
23		1.714	2.069	2.500	2.807
24		1.711	2.064	2.492	2.797
25		1.708	2.060	2.485	2.787
26		1.706	2.056	2.479	2.779
27		1.703	2.052	2.473	2.771
28		1.701	2.048	2.467	2.763
29		1.699	2.045	2.462	2.756
30		1.697	2.042	2.457	2.750

1. Adapted from Spence, J. T., et al., *Elementary Statistics*, Appleton-Century-Crofts, Inc., New York, 1968. In turn, abridged from Table III of Fisher and Yates: *Statistical Tables for Biological, Agricultural and Medical Research*, 4th Ed., 1953, Oliver and Boyd, Ltd., Edinburgh.

TABLE C[1]

Values of Chi-square (χ^2) for Two-tailed Test
at Specified Significance Levels[2]

Degrees Freedom (*df*) Test:	Significance Level		
	.050	.020	.010
1	3.84	5.41	6.64
2	5.99	7.82	9.21
3	7.82	9.84	11.34
4	9.49	11.67	13.28
5	11.07	13.39	15.09
6	12.59	15.03	16.81
7	14.07	16.62	18.48
8	15.51	18.17	20.09
9	16.92	19.68	21.67
10	18.31	21.16	23.21
11	19.68	22.62	24.72
12	21.03	24.05	26.22
13	22.36	25.47	27.69
14	23.68	26.87	29.14
15	25.00	28.26	30.58
16	26.30	29.63	32.00
17	27.59	31.00	33.41
18	28.87	32.35	34.80
19	30.14	33.69	36.19
20	31.41	35.02	37.57
21	32.67	36.34	38.93
22	33.92	37.66	40.29
23	35.17	38.97	41.64
24	36.42	40.27	42.98
25	37.65	41.57	44.31
26	38.88	42.86	45.64
27	40.11	44.14	46.96
28	41.34	45.42	48.28
29	42.56	46.69	49.59
30	43.77	47.96	50.89

1.   Adapted from Spence, J. T., et al., *Elementary Statistics*, Appleton-Century-Crofts, Inc., New York, 1968. In turn, abridged from Table IV of Fisher and Yates: *Statistical Tables for Biological, Agricultural, and Medical Research*, 4th Ed., 1953, Oliver and Boyd, Ltd., Edinburgh.

2.   When $df = 1$, the significance level for a *one-tailed test* can be stated as $\frac{1}{2}p$ of a two-tailed test. In that event, the .05 level of significance is 2.71; $\frac{1}{2}$(.050), or .025, $=$ 3.84; $\frac{1}{2}$(.020), or .010, $=$ 5.41; and $\frac{1}{2}$(.010), or .005 $=$ 6.64.

TABLE D[1]

Values of r at the 5% and 1%
Levels of Significance

Degrees of Freedom (df)[2]	Significance .050	Level .010	Degrees of Freedom (df)	Significance .050	Level .010
1	.997	1.000	24	.388	.496
2	.950	.990	25	.381	.487
3	.878	.959	26	.374	.478
4	.811	.917	27	.367	.470
5	.754	.874	28	.361	.463
6	.707	.834	29	.355	.456
7	.666	.798	30	.349	.449
8	.632	.765	35	.325	.418
9	.602	.735	40	.304	.393
10	.576	.708	45	.288	.372
11	.553	.684	50	.273	.354
12	.532	.661	60	.250	.325
13	.514	.641	70	.232	.302
14	.497	.623	80	.217	.283
15	.482	.606	90	.205	.267
16	.468	.590	100	.195	.254
17	.456	.575	125	.174	.228
18	.444	.561	150	.159	.208
19	.433	.549	200	.138	.181
20	.423	.537	300	.113	.148
21	.413	.526	400	.098	.128
22	.404	.515	500	.088	.115
23	.396	.505	1000	.062	.081

1.   Spence, Janet T., et al., *Elementary Statistics, Second Edition.* New York: Appleton-Century-Crofts, Inc., 1968, p. 236. In turn, a portion of Table D is abridged from Table VI of Fisher and Yates: *Statistical Tables for Biological, Agricultural, and Medical Research,* 4th edition 1953, published by Oliver and Boyd, Limited, Edinburgh, by permission. The remainder of the table is from *Statistical Methods,* by George W. Snedecor, © 1946 by the Iowa State College Press, Ames, Iowa, by permission.
2. $df = N - 2$, where N is the number of pairs of scores.

TABLE E[1]

Values of ρ (rank-order correlation coefficient)
at the 5% and 1% Levels of Significance

N (No. of pairs)	.050	.010
5	1.000	—
6	.886	1.000
7	.786	.929
8	.738	.881
9	.683	.833
10	.648	.794
12	.591	.777
14	.544	.714
16	.506	.665
18	.475	.625
20	.450	.591
22	.428	.562
24	.409	.537
26	.392	.515
28	.377	.496
30	.364	.478

1.   Spence, Janet T., et al., *Elementary Statistics, Second Edition.* New York: Appleton-Century-Crofts, Inc., 1968, p. 237. In turn, computed from Olds, E. G., Distribution of the sum of squares of rank differences for small numbers of individuals, *Ann. Math. Statist.*, 1949, 20, 117–118, the Institute of Mathematical Statistics, by permission.

AUTHOR INDEX

Alkin, M. C., 5, 9
Anderson, S. B., 29
Apple, M. W., 27
Bailey, J. P., 204
Baker, R. L., 87, 111
Barker, L. L., 208-209
Beck, I. H., v
Bellack, A. A., 27
Bent, D. H., 204
Bentler, P. M., 204
Bernstein, A. L., 169
Best, J. H., 204
Bloom, B. S., 7, 15, 27, 210-215
Bock, R. D., 204
Borg, W. R., 35, 36-39, 56-58, 132-135,
   137-139, 168, 190
Borich, G. D., 29
Bounds, W. G., Jr., 169
Brigham, C. C., 150
Bruning, J. L., 169
Buros, O.K., 117
Campbell, A. A., 132
Campbell, D. T., 7, 54, 59-60, 62-73, 75, 77,
   79, 83-84, 88-94, 99, 118, 113, 185, 196,
   203
Cantril, H., 90
Carroll, L., 219
Cohen, J., 204
Cohen, P., 204
Coker, H., 216
Cook, T. D., 203
Cooley, W. W., 7, 27, 204
Cormier, W. H., 169
Cotton, J. W., 180
Cox, J., 20-21
Cronbach, L. J., 29, 84-85, 89, 92, 95, 102,
   119, 124, 164, 167, 170, 172, 174
Cyphert, F. R., 115
Davis, F. B., 118, 125
DeCecco, J. P., 17
Demaline, R., 114
Dinham, S.M., 169, 202
Dixon, W. J., 202
Dressel, P. L., 27
Duncan, C. P., 180
Ebel, R. L., 109-110
Edwards, A. L., 90, 99, 144, 203
Einstein, A., 31
Englehart, M. D., 210
Erlebacher, A., 93
Ezekiel, M., 204
Ferguson, G. A., 202
Festinger, L., 132
Fisher and Yates, 229-230
Fitz-Gibbon, C. T., 7, 28
Foley, W. J., 6-7, 27
Fox, K. A., 204
French, J. W., 118, 120, 125
Fruchter, B., 120, 124, 127, 203
Furby, L., 89
Furst, E. J., 210
Gage, N. L., 188, 226
Galileo, 157
Gall, M. D., 34, 132
Gallo, P. S., Jr., 169
Gant, W. L., 115
Gephart, W. J., 6-7, 27
Glaser, R., 17
Glass, G. V., 203

Gold, R. Z., 204
Gorsuch, R. L., 204
Guba, E. G., 6-7, 27
Guertin, W. H., 204
Guilford, J. P., 120, 124, 127, 159, 163, 186,
   197, 203
Guttentag, M., 29
Guttman, 142-144
Haber, A., 203
Hagen, E., 106, 117, 195
Hammond, R. L., 6-8, 27
Hanson, R. A., 111
Harmon, H. H., 204
Harsh, J. R., v
Hastings, J. T., 7, 27
Hays, W. L., 203
Hellmuth, J., 93
Helmer, O., 115
Hill, W. H., 210
Hinkle, D. E., 203
Hopkins, K. D., 203
House, E. R., 7
Huck, S. W., 169
Hull, C., 217
Hull, C. H., 204
Huxley, T. H., 41
Infeld, L., 31
Isaac, S., 3
Jenkins, J. G., 204
Jenkins, J. J., 147
Joreskog, K. G., 204
Jurs, S. G., 203
Katona, G., 132
Katz, D., 132
Kerlinger, F. N., 52, 80-81, 140-141, 146, 163,
   204
Kibler, R. J., 208-209
Kintz, B. L., 169
Kirk, R. E., 203
Kirsner, D. A., 212, 214
Kliebard, H. M., 27
Koestler, A., 226
Krathwohl, D. R., 15, 211-215
Krejcie, R. V., 192-193
Kuder-Richardson, 124
Lefever, D. W., 33
Lehmann, I. J., 27
Lenke, J. M., 114
Lev, J., 203
Levine, M., 7
Likert, 142
Lincoln, Y.S., 27
Lindeman, R. H., 204
Lindheim, E., 110
Lindquist, E. L., 227
Linton, M., 169
Logan, C. A., 169
Lohnes, P. R., 7, 27, 204
Lord, F. M., 89
Lufler, H. S., Jr., 27
Madaus, G. F., 7, 27
Mager, R. F., 207-209
Masia, B. B., 211
Massey, F. J., 202
McCall, R. B., 169, 203
McNemar, Q., 203
Medley, D. M., 216
Mehrens, W. A., 27, 109-110
Merenda, P. F., 204
Merrifield, P. R., 204

Merriman, H. O., 6-7, 27
Metfessel, N. S., 6, 9, 15, 17, 151-155, 212, 214
Meyer, W. J., 53
Michael, J. J., 221
Michael, W. B., v, 6, 9, 11-12, 15, 17, 118, 120, 125, 151-155, 169, 184, 187, 198, 204, 208-209, 212, 214, 221
Miles, D. T., 208-209
Millman, J., 110
Minium, E. W., 203
Mitzel, H. F., 204
Morgan, D. W., 192-193
Morris, L. L., 7, 28
Munsinger, H., 96
Nie, N. H., 204
Nunnally, J. C., 120, 127, 146-147, 204
Olds, E. G., 231
Oppenheim, A. N., 118, 133
Osgood, C. E., 144-147
Owens, T. R., 7
Patton, M. Q., 27
Payne, D. A., 27
Pearson, K., 227
Pedhazur, E. J., 204
Polanyi, M., 209
Popham, W. J., 7, 27, 110
Provus, M. M., 6-8, 27
Rabinowitz, W., 204
Rasp, A., Jr., 115
Rentz, C. C., 114
Rentz, R. R., 114
Resta, P. E., 87
Rippey, R. M., 7
Robeck, M. C., 2, 169, 184, 187, 208-209
Roscoe, J. T., 203
Rummel, R. J., 204
Runyon, R. P., 203
Russell, W. A., 147
Rutman, L., 29
Sanders, J. R., 3, 8, 13, 27, 133
Sax, G., 27
Schumaker, J. A., 203
Schwartz, R. D., 88, 90-92, 118, 133
Scriven, M., 7-8, 150
Sechrest, L., 88, 90-92, 118, 133
Shavelson, R. T., 203
Shaw, M. E., 118, 144
Siegel, S. S., 148, 169, 177-179, 203
Skinner, B. F., 226
Snedecor, G. W., 230
Snider, J. G., 146-147
Soar, R. S., 216
Soloman, 68, 74-75
Sorbom, D., 204
Spearman, 172
Spearman-Brown, 174
Spence, J. T., 180, 227-231
Stake, R. E., 7-8
Stanley, J. C., 54, 59-60, 62-73, 75, 77, 79, 83-84, 89, 91, 93-94, 99, 123, 127, 185, 196, 203
Steinbrenner, K., 204
Struening, E. L., 29
Stufflebeam, D. I., 1-3, 6-7, 9, 14, 19, 21, 27
Subkoviak, M. J., 27
Suci, G. J., 145-146
Tannenbaum, P. H., 145-146
Tatsuoka, M. M., 204
Thompson, M., 29
Thorndike, E. L., 101

Thorndike, R. L., 106, 117, 123-124, 127, 195
Thorndike, R. M., 204
Thurstone, 142
Timm, N. H., 205
Tyler, R., 9
Underwood, B. J., 180
Van de Geer, J. P., 205
Van Dalen, D. B., 32, 46, 50, 60, 62-73, 76-77, 99
Walberg, H. J., 29
Walker, H. M., 203
Webb, E. J., 88, 90-92, 118, 133
Weinberg, G. H., 203
Weiss, C. H., 133
Weiss, D. J., 205
Wiersma, W., 203
Wiley, D. E., 27
Wilson, J. A. R., 11-12, 169, 184, 187, 208-209
Winer, B. J., 203
Wittrock, M. C., 27
Worthen, B. R., 3, 8, 13, 27, 133
Wright, J. M., 118, 144

SUBJECT INDEX

Accountability, educational, 10-14
Affective domain, 211, 214-217
Analysis of covariance, 183
Analysis of variance, 158, 182-183
Article, evaluation of, 220
Attitude scaling, 142-148
Bar graph, 161
Behavioral objectives, 207-209
Binomial test, 148
Cancellation of effects, 81-82
Canonical analysis, 201
Central tendency, measures of, 158-159
Chi square, 158, 177-181
CIPP, evaluation model, 6, 10-14
Class interval, 160
Coefficient of determination, 194
Cognitive domain, 210, 212-213
Computer analysis, 40
Confounding, experimental, 81-82
Control, experimental, 80-81, 88
Correlation
    Accuracy in prediction, 195, 198-199
    Coefficients of, 158
    Graphic representation, 162-163
    Interpreting coefficients of, 194-197
    Method of, 3
    Techniques of, 168
Criterion-referenced tests, 108-111, 208
Critical ratio, 174-175
Crossbreaks, analysis of, 163
Cumulative frequency, 161
Delphi technique, 114-115
Discriminant function analysis, 200-201
Domain-referenced measurement, 111, 208
Evaluation, models of, 6-18
Evaluation, types of
    Adversary, 7
    Context, 10-14
    Decision-oriented, 3, 6-7
    Formative, 3, 5
    Goal-free, 7, 150
    Goal-oriented, 7
    Implementation, 5
    Input, 10-14
    Models of, 6-18

Outcome, 5
Planning of, 1, 5
Process, 3, 5, 10-14
Product, 3, 5, 10-14
Program, 4-6
Progress, 5
Summative, 3, 5
Transactional, 7
Experimental design, models of, 64-79
Experimental method, 3
Experimenter bias, 85
Factor analysis, 158, 201-202
Factorial designs, 76-79
False positives and negatives, in prediction, 195
F-ratio, 182
Frequency distribution, 160
Frequency polygon, 161
Generalizability of research findings, 82-83
Goal-free evaluation, 7, 150
Grade level scores, 106
Guttman scale, 142-144
Guinea pig effect, 90
Halo effect, 85
Hawthorne effect, 85
Histogram, 161
Hypothesis testing, 3, 184-189
Interaction between variables, 81-82, 84-85
Interviews, 39, 131-132, 138-141
Item analysis, 116-117, 173
"John Henry" effect, 85
Kuder-Richardson formulas, 124
Likert scale, 142
Matching, disadvantages of, 99
Mean, 158-159, 166-167
Measurements, kinds of, 90, 149, 151-155
Median, 158-159
Median test, 179
Mode, 158-159
Multivariate statistical analysis, 183, 200-205
Needs assessment, 5, 19-26
Norm groups, 107
Norm-referenced tests, 108-111
Null hypothesis, 184-185
Objectives, 4, 17, 207-209
One-tailed test of significance, 185
Pearson r, 168, 170-171
Percentile equivalents, determined graphically, 164-165
Percentile ranks, 104, 112
Pilot study, 34
Placebo effect, 86-87
Point-biserial correlation coefficient, 173
Population, in sampling, 189
Post hoc error, 86
Preamble effect, 90
Product-moment correlation coefficient, 170-171
Program evaluation, 4-6
Questionnaires, 58, 130, 133-137
Range, 158-159
Rank-difference correlation coefficient, 172
Rasch scaling, 112-114
Rating errors, 85
Raw scores, 104
Reactive and nonreactive measures, 90
Regression, statistical, 93
Regression analysis, multiple, 200-202
Reliability, 123-127, 174
Research, kinds of
 Action, 42, 55-58
 Case, 42, 48-49

Causal-comparative, 42, 50-51
Correlational, 42, 49
Descriptive, 42, 46
Developmental, 42, 47
Field, 42, 48-49
Historical, 38, 42, 44-45
Quasi-experimental, 42, 54
True experimental, 42, 52-53
Research methodology, a dissenting view, 226
Research proposal check list, 221-223
Research report, article, thesis, 223-225
Role selection, 90
Sample size, 96, 190-193
Sampling, general, 132, 189-193
Sampling error, 189
Scattergrams, 162-163
Scores, kinds of
 Gain, 89
 Grade level, 106-107
 Percentile ranks, 103-105
 Raw, 104
 Stanine, 103, 105
 Standard, 103, 105-106
 T- 103, 106
 z- 103, 105-106
Self-fulfilling prophecy, 85
Semantic differential, 144-148
Semi-interquartile range, 158
Spearman-Brown formula, 124, 126, 174
Spearman rho, 172
Standard deviation, 158-159, 166-167
Standard scores, 105, 112
Stanines, 105
Statistical methods, overview, 158
Statistical power, 186
Statistical significance, 184-189
Surveys, 128-133
Systems approach, 2
Taxonomy, of educational objectives, 210-217
Tests, form for evaluating, 102
Tests, kinds of, 149
Thurstone scale, 142
t-ratio, 158
Triangulation, in measurement, 92
t-test, 176
Type I and Type II errors, 185
Two-tailed tests of significance, 185
Validity, 119-123
Validity, kinds of
 Concurrent (see criterion-related), 121, 122
 Construct, 121-122
 Content, 119, 121-122
 Criterion-related, 119, 121-123
 Experimental, 76
 External, 59, 62-63, 76
 Face Validity, 119
 Internal, 59-61, 76
 Predictive (see criterion-related), 123, 198-199
Variables, kinds of
 Background, 44
 Classificatory, 44
 Control, 44
 Dependent, 44, 95
 Independent, 44, 84, 95
 Intervening, 44
 Organismic, 44
Variability, measures of, 158-159
Variance, control of, 3, 80-81
z-ratio, 158
z-scores, 105
z-test, 174-175